SEEING
EYE GIRL

*A Memoir of Madness,
Resilience, and Hope*

BEVERLY J. ARMENTO

SHE WRITES PRESS

Published 2022
Printed in the United States of America
Print ISBN: 978-1-64742-391-9
E-ISBN: 978-1-64742-392-6
Library of Congress Control Number: 2021925333

For information, address:
She Writes Press
1569 Solano Ave #546
Berkeley, CA 94707

Interior design by Tabitha Lahr

She Writes Press is a division of SparkPoint Studio, LLC.

Names and identifying characteristics have been changed to protect the privacy of certain individuals.

Dedicated to my:

Fourth Grade Class, Spring Valley Elementary School
Paramus, New Jersey
1963–1964

and

Sixth Grade Class, McIntosh Middle School
Sarasota, Florida
1964–1965

Chapter 1

CHINCHILLAS AND COMMUNISTS

February 1956
Passaic, New Jersey

"Chinchillas," Momma whispers. "They're raising chinchillas in our basement. Come over here and listen."

Momma presses her ear against the exposed iron pipe in our tiny kitchen. The black protrusion comes out of the floor near the sink and rises to the ceiling. It goes up to Sammy Lamont's apartment on top of us and then all the way to the fourth floor.

Momma's wearing one of her many cocktail dresses—this one pink, strapless, with a tightly fitting bodice and a full chiffon skirt of many layers that falls to the middle of her calf and swishes when she walks. Her hair, combed straight forward from her dark-brown, two-inch-radius cowlick, forms a frizzy, golden halo around her pale face. She's been awake all night while Ron Radzai, my stepfather, has worked the eleven-to-seven assembly-line shift at the United States Rubber factory, just two blocks away on Passaic and Market. It's in the long quiet of dark nights that Momma plans her next move against our enemies: the Guineas and the communists.

"Get over here and listen, Beverly," Momma says. She jerks me against the pipe. I fit right below her head. "Those bastards, those communist sons of bitches, are breeding chinchillas right under our noses," Momma spits in my ear, her voice scratchy, her breath all Lucky Strikes and coffee. "Can you hear them?"

"Yes," I lie.

Momma grips and twists my arm. There are no chinchillas down there and none of my Italian relatives are there, either. She's waiting for me to argue with her so she'll have a reason to beat me.

It's seven in the morning, and I'm running late for school. I'm fifteen and in ninth grade; I'm the editor of the school newspaper and president of the Latin Club and the Library Pages. Mrs. Peterson, the newspaper faculty advisor, meets with the staff early on Tuesday mornings. I have to be there. *The Wilsonian*, our paper, is to receive a Stephen Crane Memorial Certificate in recognition of the high-quality journalism demonstrated in our series on tuberculosis prevention. I'll accept the award on behalf of our school.

Strong Beverly lives at school. Weak Beverly lives here at home.

• • •

One Saturday after Momma first heard the chinchillas, I saw two workers unlock the basement door. I followed them into the damp darkness, full of pipes, machinery, and electrical wires. Crouching down, I inched my way along the dirt floor, peering to see signs of cages or chinchillas. One of the men spun around, shined his flashlight in my face, and shouted, "What are you doing here, girl?"

"I'm looking to see if there are any animals in here—like chinchillas," I said.

"Are you crazy? Why would chinchillas be here? Now you get out." He aimed his light on the door.

"Might be a few rats down here," the second worker said, laughing.

I didn't dare tell Momma about my trip to the basement.

•   •   •

"What do you hear? What are they saying?" Momma asks as we lean into the pipe, our heads touching but our minds miles apart.

"I can't tell; I just hear sounds," I lie again.

"How many people do you hear?" she demands. "Listen hard, you son of a bitch."

The front door opens and closes with a thud. Ron Radzai is home from work. Just in time.

But not soon enough.

Momma slaps me across my face, grabs my skinny arm, and locks her teeth on an already bruised place. My knees buckle. I pee a little in my pants. I wince and blink a few times to keep the tears away. But I don't make a sound.

Momma and I are face-to-face. I look into her once-clear blue-green eyes, now clouded over. For the first nine years of my life, Momma was blind. But then her sight was restored. Now, only six years after her two successful corneal transplants, Momma's eye disease has reinfected both corneas. A deep sadness fills me.

Momma's going blind again.

•   •   •

We're at war.

It's Momma and us kids against the Italians and the communists, characters who inhabit her mind and soul and our daily lives.

Ever since my Italian father abandoned my sister and me and left Momma with no child support, they've been after us. Countless, nameless other Italians, all somehow related to Dad, lurk behind corners and wait for opportunities to kidnap us girls.

It's been ten years since I last saw Dad, and my memories are fading. I keep the image of him in my mind. He's tall, like a movie star, with twinkling black eyes, a square jaw, bushy eyebrows, jet black hair, and a huge smile. Every once in a while, he pops up in a dream, but he's really ancient history to me. I wonder what he did to Momma to make her so angry with him, even after all this time. There's a lot more to this story than I'll ever know.

Momma's an expert on the communists, the Soviet Union, Nikita Khrushchev, J. Edgar Hoover, and Senator Joseph McCarthy. She listens to radio programs, and when her eyes were good, she read every newspaper and magazine article on the Red Scare and the Iron Curtain. The communists have infiltrated our country, and now even our own home. They have the nuclear bomb and use radiation to alter your body and your mind. Many people are spies and they're in cahoots with the Italians. Most of the actors and actresses in Hollywood are communists, as are most people in government. All my teachers are lefty communists. They're all around us.

This is the world according to Momma.

• • •

Late that night—after homework and a mashed potato and hamburger dinner, after Ron Radzai and Momma silently play gin rummy until he leaves for the night shift—something frightens me awake.

"Beverly," Momma whispers. "Get up. Bring your sister and come to my room."

This isn't the first time Momma has gotten me out of bed, and it won't be the last. Sharon and I moan but obey and walk down the short hallway. Ronnie and Mikey, my half-brothers, huddle in the middle of the bed, swaddled in blankets and surrounded by stacks of newspapers. Ronnie rubs his sore, red eyes with his fist. I pull a tissue out of my pocket and dab at his tears.

The doctors at the Manhattan Eye and Ear Institute told us that both my brothers have Momma's eye disease and they, too, will eventually lose their vision. I don't know how the disease skipped over Sharon and me and afflicted these little boys, but this knowledge leaves me devastated and guilty over my own good sight.

"Get up here and cover up," Momma orders. She crouches on the mattress, her head on her knees, her chiffon skirt blousing out around her. "Cover your chest. Cover your crotch. The communists are upstairs. They're shooting radiation down." Momma lifts her head and points to the ceiling. "They're going to sterilize all of us," she whispers. "Hurry up." She crosses her arms in front of her breasts, her private parts well hidden in the multiple layers of her skirt.

Momma's notions about communists are integral parts of our lives, but this is the first time she's woven a tale of danger. I know how to be polite and just shut up when she goes on and on about things that aren't true. Talking back and trying to correct Momma are not good ideas. When she's agitated, there's hell to pay, and hell most always involves me. So I act like I believe her and don't give her a reason to smack me.

All this acting makes me nervous and anxious. The radiation story, though, makes me afraid.

"The most important thing in 'Duck and Cover' is to stay calm," I remember Mrs. Aber, my fourth grade Little River Elementary teacher, saying when the air raid siren blared and all of us kids squatted under our desks, one arm covering our eyes, the other the back of our necks. Even though World War II was over, the bad guys—the Soviets—were still out there, and they wanted Americans dead. A bomb could drop at any time and you'd have to protect yourself from the flames, flying glass, and radiation.

"You never know where you'll be or if an adult will be nearby to help you—so you have to be able to take care of yourself,"

Mrs. Aber told us. "Go to a shelter or hide under furniture. Be sure to cover your head. Be alert at all times."

"Maybe we should go to the closet," I suggest to Momma.

"Cover us with the newspapers and blankets," Momma says.

I remember Mrs. Aber saying that even newspapers can help you. Maybe Momma is right. I grab a stack of papers.

"Is a bomb going to blow us up?" I ask. I haven't heard a siren and wonder if other people are ready for the radiation. "Do the neighbors know to hide?"

"Cover us," Momma hisses, a high whistle escaping through her teeth.

I pull the newspapers and blankets over the mound of flesh in the center of the bed. We wait. For the communists to get us. For the radiation to strike through the ceiling like lightning or to burst through the walls like an uncapped water hydrant.

All I hear are five humans breathing—terror in, panic out.

Ronnie whimpers. I reach over, pat his back. Sharon's chest heaves against my back. The heat from our fear-filled bodies is suffocating. My heart hammers up my arms and pounds in my ears.

How have the communists gotten into Sammy Lamont's apartment? He's in Sharon's fifth grade class. We play kickball and hide-and-seek with him most days after school. Surely his mother wouldn't let some strange communist into her bedroom to shoot radiation down at us. What if they are up there? Why would anyone want to sterilize us? I have so many questions I want to ask Momma. But I remain silent.

"We have to get out of here. We have to go somewhere safe." Momma's words tumble from her lips, barely audible, almost lost in our makeshift bomb shelter. "Go get your shoes on. Take your blankets with you."

I rush Ronnie and Mikey into their bedroom and cram their bare feet into their shoes. Sharon meets us in the dark hallway with my shoes. My heart pumps faster. I have to think of some way to convince Momma to stay here, make her think that going out into the radiation is not a good idea, that we'll be safer hiding under the bed. But I'm mute.

Momma paces around the living room. A long blanket drapes over her shoulders and trails onto the floor, all but covering her strapless party dress but not the clear plastic, open-toed, sling-back heels on her feet. All four of us kids wear long pants and long-sleeved shirts—our winter sleeping clothes, gifts from the local church.

"Put your blankets around you," Momma says. "It's cold outside."

Sharon and I grab the boys' hands. We follow Momma out of the apartment door, through the dark hallway, past the stairs, and out of Building 221 into the bitter night air. A single street light guides Momma onto Sixth Street, where on weekends we play hopscotch and hang around the ice cream man's truck. She turns left. We follow the asphalt to its dead end, right into the heavily overgrown lot where Sharon and I like to catch fireflies. We never go far into this field because it's full of broken glass, tall weeds, and snakes—or so we've been told by other neighborhood kids.

Momma doesn't stop at the edge of the field tonight.

The grasses part for her as she silently strides into the abyss. We follow blindly, like four little ghosts; it's as though we have no choice, that we've lost our free will and any good sense we might otherwise have had. The wet, sharp grasses lash our legs, the cold air burns our faces. We cling to our blankets—blue, cream, white—all dragging on the ground. We cling to our bewilderment, our fear, and the illusion of hope—hope that this blackness, this night, might end and that we will find our mother at the far side of this field, our mother as only one of us ever knew her—as a loving and intelligent woman.

· · ·

We walk for a long time. The boys cry. I'm afraid of Momma's ideas and the way her confused mind draws us into the raw unknown. She doesn't need me, her seeing eye girl. She walks confidently, alone.

A dim light shines ahead. A red-brick, two-story church emerges from the dark grasses. A bell tower points to heaven. There's a strange, two-dimensional feel to the visage before us, like we've walked onto a movie set placed here for the next scene, the one we're about to enact.

"The Most Holy Name of Jesus Slovak National Catholic Cathedral," I read out loud from the sign.

"Go see if the doors are open," Momma says.

I run up a dozen shallow stone steps and pull hard on the black metal handles on the tall, arched wooden doors. "They're locked."

"What's this building?" Momma points to a cream-colored, two-story brick building next door to the church. A large, golden cross protects the front door. A porch light illuminates a half-dozen steps and small entryway.

"It's probably the rectory," I say.

Momma turns and heads toward the building. We follow.

Momma rings the doorbell. I shiver and pull my blanket closer. She rings the bell again.

A warm glow illuminates the glass upper half of the door. One of the slats on the Venetian blind moves. The door opens. A tall man in a long, black bathrobe stands before us. My eyes fix on his blond hair.

Thank you, God. He's not Italian.

The priest looks at us, his blue eyes wide, his round mouth open as he waits for God to send him the right words. "Bless you, my children," he says, making the sign of the cross with a bold sweep across his body.

I bawl. Loud, deep sobs of relief and disbelief. I stand in front of a priest in the middle of the night, in my bedclothes, completely disoriented, embarrassed, and unsure if I'm more afraid of communists or my mother, who has just led us to a Catholic church. After all, this is where she promised to raise us girls, a promise she never intended to keep. A bargain-swap for our baptisms, *acatholic* recorded in the formal church records alongside Momma's name. "I saved you from Catholicism," she's told me all these years.

The priest ushers us inside to a reception area with several upholstered chairs and a sofa; he disappears and returns with a pile of blankets.

"Please find a comfortable place for the children to rest," he says to me.

Momma tosses her blanket on a chair and stands in the middle of the room, resplendent in her strapless dress, her breasts bursting forth creamy and full. The priest guides Momma into another room. Will she tell him about the communists, the radiation, the Italians? What will he tell her? I feel strange—like my body is floating, like it all may really be a dream, a wild drama that might end as suddenly as it began. But I'm awake—wide awake, lying on the floor of the rectory of a National Catholic Cathedral. It's not a dream. Momma's led us to this place and I, her oldest child, was unable to stop her, unable to protect my sister and brothers.

Please, can you help me, God? I silently plead. *Help me know what to do, what to say. Can you show me a sign? Please God. Please.*

• • •

Early in the morning, before first light, the priest feeds the five of us cereal and milk. Then he drives us home.

I dress for school.

Just like any other day.

• • •

Chapter 2

MY BEDROOM

My life wasn't always like this. Ten years before, when I was five, I thought of my life as a fairy tale. I had all the wondrous things a girl could want: A two-story dollhouse, the handsome furnishings mirroring those in our home. Many dolls, each with beautiful clothes, just like the scores of pretty outfits hanging in my own closet. An easel for the finger-paint worlds I created most afternoons. A round bucket of dark-chocolate wooden Lincoln Logs. And enough miniature cups and saucers for all the tea parties I could ever hope to have. I kept all the treasures in my very special bedroom, the one painted eggshell blue and lit with candles, or so it seemed, for the three lamps gave off warm, amber light that soothed me and my almost-one-year-old sister, Sharon, who slept in a crib in my bedroom.

Best of all, I had a momma who painted with me and a dad who tossed me up in the air and always caught me.

There are two other things I recall about my life before it changed. One is having the mumps. I'd jump up on the living room sofa to see my big fat cheeks and laugh out loud into the gold-framed mirror. The other is the fight that bled over into my beloved bedroom. This was the first time I heard anyone use curse words, the first time I witnessed violence. It was the first time I thought there might be something seriously wrong with my parents' marriage.

This fight was the first big clue that my life was really not a fairy tale.

February 1946
Yonkers, New York

"Dad, can you take me to the park tomorrow?" I ask when he's ready to tuck Anna and me into bed. Anna is my new favorite doll, her dark brown plastic face molded into a permanent smile, her tiny cloth body the perfect size for clutching close to mine.

My parents gave Anna to me for my fifth birthday the last day of January. It was Christmas time when I first saw her in the department store window and pointed her out to Dad.

"Well, maybe now that the war's over," Dad said.

She wasn't under the Christmas tree, so I thought he'd forgotten. I should have known I could count on him. On my birthday, there she was, in a big box next to my cake.

"I have to work tonight, but after I rest up, we'll all go to the park tomorrow. Now let's read until you fall asleep," Dad says, checking his watch. I wish he could stay and tell me stories all night. But I know he has to leave for work soon.

I also know that after he leaves, the Blond Man will come to see Momma. I don't like when the Blond Man hugs and kisses Momma, and I don't like the way he looks at me, all stern and cross-eyed. When he comes to visit, I run to my bedroom and play with my dolls.

Long after Dad kisses me goodnight, I hear the Blond Man's voice and Momma's laughter. Everyone in my family has dark hair, but this man's long, thick, yellow curls cascade onto his forehead and his skin is a pale, creamy white.

The Blond Man has been visiting Momma since Sharon was just a baby, when Dad was away in the navy, stationed in South Carolina. Now that the war's over, Dad is home. But the Blond Man still comes to visit.

In a few minutes, Momma comes into my bedroom to make sure Sharon and I are asleep. Momma's been blind for so long she knows where everything is, especially me. I close my eyes and breathe heavily. This is enough to trick Momma, who kisses me on the cheek and whispers, "I love you," before she closes the door without a sound.

Pretty soon, I'm asleep.

• • •

A thunderous noise jolts me awake. It's dark in my bedroom and I think I'm dreaming. But then I hear my father's angry voice.

"Get out of here," Dad roars. "Get out of my house, you bastard. Stay away from my wife." Glass shatters. Loud noises sound like a truck has bashed into the living room wall.

"Get your filthy hands off me," Blond Man hollers.

A wailing cry pierces the walls and invades my room. It's Momma. I pull my legs up to my chest and clasp Anna closer to me. The bedroom door bursts open and three bodies tower above my bed. The hallway light illuminates Momma, Dad, and the Blond Man.

I grab Anna and jump out of bed just as the Blond Man, who wears only his underpants, falls onto my white coverlet. Dad grabs a hunk of the man's curls, yanks him up off the bed, and punches him in the face. "I'll teach you to come over here, you son of a bitch."

Momma raises her arm and slams Dad on his back. "Stop it, Tony," she screams, her voice hoarse and strained. "Stop it. You'll kill him!"

I gasp. Why isn't Momma hitting the Blond Man?

"Stop, Momma. Stop, Dad. Stop fighting," I plead from my hiding place behind the dollhouse.

No one listens to me. The Blond Man grabs Dad's shirt and smashes him in the jaw with his fist. Dad falls to the floor. The pain flies across the room and onto my face. The Blond Man pulls Dad to his feet and hits him again. And again. Momma pummels Dad's back.

I can't bear to see my dad beaten like this. He's helpless, lifeless. Dad needs me. The Blond Man is going to kill him. I'm frantic. Dad moans. Sharon stands in her crib, slamming her body back and forth into the bars. Her screams fill the bedroom. Momma's wails ring in my ears.

My heart races, about to explode. I have to do something. I have to help Dad. Get up. Be brave. Stop the fight. There's no one else who can help. *Get up. Go. Do something.* What can I do? I drop Anna, run from my hiding place, raise my arm, and smack Momma on her back.

"Stop. Stop. Stop. Don't hit Dad."

Deafening noises close in on me. I cower behind my dollhouse, curl into a tight ball around Anna. Hide from the violence, from my shock, from my sadness, from the people who love me. I hate the Blond Man. This is all his fault.

•   •   •

"Police. Open up."
Finally. Silence.

•   •   •

I shiver, look up, and see slats of wood a few feet above my head. Where am I? I'm lying all cramped up in a ball on the floor under my tea table. My chest and arms ache like I've fallen off the swings. But I didn't fall. Why am I on the floor? I'm supposed to be on my bed. What happened?

Slowly, last night's trauma comes into my mind. I see Dad, the Blond Man, Momma—their clenched fists. Why were they all so angry? I've never seen my parents fight and scream. I've never seen them hit one another.

"Oh, no, oh, no," I sob into Anna's soft body. It's all there in my mind, running in slow motion: angry hands smashing bone, the harsh voices, my terrified sister, my fear. I see me: I raise my arm. I hit Momma.

"Oooooh." I curl around Anna, and we cry, cry for the longest time.

Finally, I sit up. Look around. My beloved bedroom is wrecked. My dollhouse is on its side, all the furniture clumped in the corners. My dolls are sprawled across the floor. Crimson blood soils my bed covers. Lincoln Logs are scattered around the room.

The wreckage. It's all there. The fight reruns like a movie in my mind.

I stand up, remember my sister's frightened sobs. She's sleeping now. Her butt sticks up in the air, legs tucked under her like a frog; her curly, dark brown hair falls onto the mattress and hides her face. Splotches of dried blood dot the blanket wadded up under her head.

I stroke her back and whisper, "I love you, Sharon."

She doesn't stir.

I open my bedroom door and peek out into the hall. Broken glass covers the carpet. I turn back, find a pair of socks in my dresser, and slip on my saddle shoes. I tiptoe into the kitchen.

Momma is at the table, a coffee cup in her hand. Her yellow nightgown hangs cock-eyed off her shoulder. An eerie silence fills the kitchen, like smoke enveloping a burning house.

Usually Momma would be frying an egg and bacon for my special Saturday breakfast. She'd say, "How are you this lovely morning, darling?" But today Momma doesn't say anything. There's no food cooking. Nothing moves. Not even Momma. There's nothing usual about today.

Momma doesn't know I'm here. She doesn't hear my saddle shoes crunch the broken glass as I walk into the room. And she's never, ever seen me. She only knows me by the sounds I make or the way I feel when she touches my body, like when she moves her fingers over my face to know what I look like. She's blind, but she knows how to do everything and she knows where everything is because she has figured it all out.

Momma's rare eye disease was diagnosed when she was only three months old. She gradually lost sight until she was eighteen, when she became totally blind. When she was a child, her parents and five older brothers taught her how to work in the vegetable garden, clean the house, cook, find her way around town, and even iron clothes.

Momma is an artist. When she was in high school, she drew Norman Rockwell pictures on the chalkboards and signed them with a big swirl starting at the tail of the R and encircling her initials: AER. Alett Evelyn Robinson.

• • •

I stand in the kitchen for a long time and stare, in a trance, at the scene in our home. I'm dizzy, like I just got off a merry-go-round. Broken dishes litter the floor, the countertop. Thick, red spaghetti gravy stares at me from the floor. It's the bowl of pasta cousin Margaret brought for our dinner—her special meatballs are scattered around Momma's chair.

Cousin Margaret comes over to visit a lot. She helps Momma with the baby and takes us all to the park. When Dad was away in the war, Margaret was Momma's seeing eye helper, teaching her how to find her way around Yonkers and how to cook Italian food. She and Momma are about the same age and the same size. They swap clothes, and they're great friends now.

Momma told me she was lonely when she and Dad first moved to Yonkers.

"This was the first time I was away from my family and I had no friends," she explained. "Everything in my new city was strange to me, including all my new relatives, who often spoke Italian when I was in the room and did things that were unusual to me, like cooking huge meals and talking loudly at the dinner table. I didn't know how to get around the city and I didn't know any of the Italian ways—how to cook the traditional foods, how to keep our home the way my husband expected. I was so happy when Margaret and I became friends." Momma smiled. "She's taught me so much."

• • •

Momma looks smaller than usual today. Her bare feet dangle in the air between her chair and the floor. I have to clean this mess up. Momma's going to slip, cut her feet. I have to protect her, make sure she doesn't have an accident. I've learned to pick up my toys, put everything away in its proper place, and never, ever leave a glass sitting on a countertop where it could be knocked to the floor. The mess in our apartment deeply saddens me, but I can't take time to be sad. I know how dangerous the mess is to Momma's safety. I'm the big sister, the oldest child, Momma's special helper. It's my job to take care of this problem and I know how to do it.

Momma sits frozen. I've never seen her like this. I want to run to her, hug her, kiss her, tell her I love her. But the lead in my saddle shoes keeps me in this spot. I stand and stare. I'm frozen like Momma. After a while I think maybe I should go see what else needs to be cleaned up. I turn slowly and walk into the living room where we gather each evening to snuggle on the plush beige sofa and plan for the adventures that we'll have the next day.

One of my favorite pictures is on the floor. I pick it up. Glass shards fall away from the gold frame. A handsome woman in a dressy suit, hat, and gloves stares out at me, offering her brochures: *Fastest Trains, Ships, Airplanes.*

"My mother was suspicious of Italian immigrants so she really didn't like it when I showed up with an Italian boyfriend," Momma told me when she hung this picture. "I had to keep secrets from her. So, on my eighteenth birthday, in January of 1940, I ran away from home. Your dad and I got married by the justice of the peace in my hometown, Warsaw, New York. We took the train to Yonkers. I drew this picture at Christmastime, but my mother didn't understand the clues I gave her about what I was going to do."

• • •

I walk back into the kitchen and gaze at Momma through the fog in my brain. She always looks like the beautiful woman in her drawing, but today she looks strange. I'm frightened. Where's my mother? Where's my father?

"Where's Dad? What happened last night? Why was everyone screaming and fighting?" I blurt out.

Momma's silent. She stares into the emptiness of the kitchen, her nightgown moving up and down her thin body with her every breath. Finally, she lifts her hand. Touches the package of Lucky Strikes. Picks it up. Takes out a cigarette. Taps it on the table. Sticks it in her mouth. Feels around on the table. Finds the matchbook. Snaps off a match. Strikes it. Holds the flame close to her face, searches for the end of her cigarette.

I know this routine. But today Momma's every movement is exaggerated, painful to watch. Everything is in slow motion. Momma's hand and arm are rigid, like they're not attached to her body. I'm mesmerized as I watch the Momma I love turn into a robot. The fire lights up Momma's face. The shiny black and blue marks under her right eye glisten.

My arms are heavy at my side. My body sinks to the floor. I sob into my fists. "What's happening?" I wail. "What's happening?"

Momma is silent.

Nothing moves. At long last I stand, look at Momma. All I can say is, "I'll get Sharon out of bed."

"Yes," Momma says, her voice faraway and low. "Then you can have some cereal and go out to play."

I don't want to go out to play. It's not a normal day. Everything is different today. Something terrible happened last night in my bedroom. Something has changed in my life.

At this moment, I don't know just how much.

But I do know that Dad will not be taking me to the park this afternoon.

• • •

I pick up the broken glass, scoop up the spilled spaghetti, and clean my bedroom. I manage to hoist my dollhouse onto my tea table, and then I arrange all the furniture in the right rooms and display my dolls and toys in their regular places. But my room isn't so grand anymore.

I change Sharon's diaper, wash her up, feed her, put her in the buggy, and wheel her around and around the neighborhood for hours, until we're both tired and dizzy. I bump into curbs and ignore my friends who want me to play. I'm in a daze, going through the motions of acting normal while the horror movie keeps playing in my mind. I can't turn it off.

• • •

It's Monday. Dad hasn't been home all weekend. Momma's spent most of the time in her bedroom. I'm ready to go to kindergarten with Anna. She's clean and wears a pink outfit to match my pink sweater.

Most days, Momma puts Sharon in the stroller and we walk around the corner onto Ashburton Avenue. We go past St. Joseph's Roman Catholic Church, where the priest baptized Sharon a few months ago, and on to my elementary school. But today Momma says I have to walk by myself.

"Don't talk to your father if you see him," she says. "He's a bad person. And do you have Anna in your arms? You can't take her to school today."

So I walk out of our first-floor apartment at 59 Mulford Gardens and down the three steps of the concrete stoop without Anna. This is where my family takes photos—of Dad with me on my tricycle, of Momma and me pushing my baby buggy, the fancy one with a sun shade. Our four-story, red-brick building towers over me today and casts a cold shadow as I walk the half-block out to the street.

I remember sunnier days when I ran to the intersection to trade with the junk man—a big silver ball for a few pennies. During the war, my special project was to make the balls from the silver lining in cigarette packages I collected from neighbors and Momma and Dad. I soaked the inner linings in a bowl of warm water until I could rub off the paper. What was left was a thin silver sheet. Once I had a pile of silver, I wadded the sheets into a big ball. I wasn't sure what the junk man did with all the silver, but Momma said I was helping America win the war. Now that the war was over, the junk man didn't come any more. But the pony man did.

Momma took Sharon and me out to have our photographs taken on a handsome black and white palomino just a few weeks ago. It was cold, and Momma dressed my sister in the special white cap cousin Margaret had knitted, the one with a funny peak that makes Sharon look like she has a horn coming out of her head. I wore my jodhpurs and my favorite saddle shoes. Once Sharon was secure in the saddle, I stood beside the pony and held on to her so she didn't fall off. Then the man boosted me up for my own photo.

• • •

I turn onto Ashburton Avenue and walk toward my three-story, red-brick school. Dad waits for me near the entrance. He has a strange look on his face.

I cry, making loud sobbing noises, as I run toward him. A bulging black and blue bump sits squarely in the middle of his forehead, and his right eye is swollen closed. He looks scary. My hand flies to my right eye. I touch it, soothing Dad's pain. Momma said I shouldn't talk to him. But I want to. I love Dad. I want to grab on to him and tell him how much I love him and want him to come home.

Dad bends down and looks into my eyes. I want to climb on his knee, put my arm around his shoulder, and wait for him to tell me everything is going to be all right. Instead he puts his hands on my arms and pulls me close to him.

"This is for you and your sister." He presses two quarters into my hand and closes my fingers over them. "I want you to know that I love you, Beverly. I love Sharon. I will always love both of you."

I sob. Loud. Hard.

Dad stands. Turns. He walks away.

I run home, screaming. Where is Dad going? Why did he walk away? What is happening?

I can't stop crying.

Momma puts me to bed and closes my bedroom door.

Chapter 3

MIAMI

I'm on the train for a long time. Days, it seems. I rest, my face plastered against the cold window, staring at golden fields, dirty cities, and children taking a break from hopscotch to wave at the conductor.

When the train finally stops, everything in my life is different. Everything is gone.

My dollhouse. Gone. Dolls. Baby buggy. Lincoln Logs. My clothes. Gone. All gone. Where is all my stuff? All our furniture is gone. All my Italian relatives are gone. Cousin Margaret. Gone. The worst thing is that my dad is gone.

And the strangest thing of all is that the Blond Man is now my stepfather. He has a name, Ron Radzai. But Momma calls him "Tony." That's crazy. My dad's name is Tony.

"Where's my dad?" I ask Momma. She ignores me.

"Tony is a war hero—he jumped out of airplanes," Momma tells me. "He was injured and has a Purple Heart. He's worked hard all his life. Had to drop out of school to work in the Pennsylvania coal mines to help support his family. He's going to be your new daddy."

I don't want a new daddy. I want my dad. I don't know why she tells me this. The Blond Man never even talks to me. I'm not going to call him daddy. None of this makes me forget the fight or want to call him Tony. That's my father's name. The Blond Man is Ron Radzai to me.

I miss my dad every day. I miss him at the park, where he should be pushing me on the swings. I miss him telling me he loves me. I make motion pictures in my mind of the happy times I remember with my father, like the last bedtime story he told me.

"Please tell me the story of when you fell in love with Momma," I begged him.

"You've heard this story so many times you could tell it to me," Dad said, laughing.

"Yes, but I love when *you* tell it."

"Remember that before the war, there was a time when lots of businesses closed and many people were out of work," Dad said. "Your grandfather, Pasquale, said to me, 'Tony, you have to quit school and go to work to help your mother and me.' So I joined the Civilian Conservation Corps, one of President Roosevelt's work projects, and was assigned to Letchworth State Park in western New York. There I worked with the other men to plant trees, build stone walls and bridges, and construct cabins. The CCC sent buses out to the neighboring towns to pick up girls and bring them to the Friday night dances.

"One evening, here comes this tiny girl with curly brown hair and thick glasses. 'Would you like to dance with me?' I asked her. 'Oh, yes,' she said.

"I twirled her across the dance floor. We laughed really hard. She couldn't stop talking about her six brothers, her sister, and her mother. She said she was going to be a great artist. I was surprised. She told me she was diagnosed with a rare eye disease when she was a baby and she was almost totally blind now.

"'How are you going to be an artist?' I asked her.

"She pressed a tiny notepad into my hand. I turned the pages and saw detailed drawings of stylish women, some in bathing suits and others in party dresses. I thought to myself, *I want to know this cute girl.* 'How'd you do these?' I asked your mother."

"But she wasn't my mother yet," I said.

"You're right," Dad said. "Not yet. But hold on. The best part's about to happen."

I was ready for the best part. I placed my hand on Dad's face, anticipating what was coming next.

"Close your eyes now, Beverly. Your momma-to-be came close to me and ran her fingertips along my jaw bone and up the sides of my face." Dad guided my hand along the outline of his angular face, across his square chin, over the rough hairs that covered most of his cheeks. Then Dad moved my hand to my face. Together, we traced my jaw.

"I have a chin like yours," I said softly. "But no beard."

Dad laughed. He placed my hand back on his face, and we traced his deep eye crevices, his thick eyebrows, his broad nose, his high cheek bones, his hair line, and his ears.

Dad guided my fingers across my eyes, through my thick eyebrows, along my nose, my high cheekbones, and my dark brown hair line, and around my ears.

"Dad, my face feels like yours," I said, opening my eyes.

"Yes, you look a lot like me," Dad said. "And back then, when your mother-to-be first did that to my face, do you know what she did next?"

"She drew your face," I said with a triumphant smile.

"She did. It was at that moment that I fell in love with your mother," Dad said, a big smile on his face. "Her drawing looked just like me."

• • •

This is a much better movie of my dad than the other one that plays in my mind: the movie of the fight. Now when I think of Dad and become sad, I play my happy movie and run my fingertips along my jaw to remember what he looks like.

I don't need a movie to remember my mother, because she's right here with me. She looks pretty much the same but she acts different from the mother in my memory. Then again, some of this is because she's five months pregnant and her tummy's getting big. She doesn't smile and laugh out loud like she did back in Yonkers. She doesn't hug and kiss me anymore. Instead, she pinches me when she gets mad and calls me names like "you Guinea bastard."

This is all very confusing to me. I can't figure out why Momma has changed, why she's upset so much of the time. I try to please her by doing all the jobs she gives me and by staying out of her way. This works most of the time. But not always. Sometimes she gets so mad at me, she smacks me across my face.

I was shocked the first time Momma hit me. This was new. It doesn't shock me anymore, but it does make me sad every time. Now I duck to get out of her way whenever she comes near me. No one ever hit me when we lived in Yonkers.

Now even Yonkers is gone. I'm in a strange city where it's always hot and exotic flowers grow along the roadside, where storms called hurricanes scatter coconuts onto the grass so children can grab them up, and where my new home is about as large as my old bedroom in Yonkers. It's a tiny trailer. No toilet. No sink. No water. Everyone in the trailer-park housing project walks along a tamped-down path to a bathhouse to pee, shower, and wash dishes. The place smells like poop and rotten eggs, the floor's wet and slippery, and the lines for the shower and the toilet are always long. Once inside, I scrunch down real small so the girls in line can't see me through the thin white curtain that shrouds each stall.

I don't even have a bedroom now. Sharon and I sleep on a hard sofa in the living room, near the two-burner gas stove, next to the tiny closet where we keep the poop-pot. I miss my dollhouse, my bicycle, and my dolls. I miss my fancy dresses and black patent leather shoes. I miss all my Italian relatives, especially my cousin Margaret and my godfather, Michael, who threw me up in the air like Dad did. Back then. When we lived in Yonkers.

All I have now is Anna, who's still my best friend. I pester Momma, asking her, "Where are all my toys?" But she acts like she doesn't hear my questions and says nothing.

• • •

In those first months in Miami, my life in Yonkers seemed like a distant memory. Now that I was off the train, my mind was foggy. I was weak and confused. Nothing made sense. I would be well into adulthood before I'd learn that the journey from Yonkers to Miami was longer than I ever could have imagined.

A year and a half had passed from the time of the Yonkers fight to our arrival in Miami. Many things happened in those eighteen months: Momma took Sharon and me on the train to western New York to stay with her family; someone disposed of all of our Yonkers possessions; a jury trial found Ron Radzai guilty of third-degree assault; he was sentenced to a year in prison; the sentence was suspended because of his WWII service and with the stipulation that he stay away from Tony Armento's wife; Dad left town and assumed an alias; Momma couldn't locate Dad and thus couldn't force him to pay child support; Momma became pregnant with Ron Radzai's child; and something strange happened to Momma's mind.

In August of 1947, Momma took the train to Warsaw to get Sharon and me, and we rode the train to Yonkers to pick up Ron Radzai. We all then boarded a train for Miami. It was only late in life that I discovered evidence of these things from family stories, photographs, letters, and newspaper articles. What happened to Sharon and me in Warsaw? I know we were separated. Sharon lived with Momma's sister, and I stayed with Momma's best friend, Bernice. Did I go to school? Was I loved and nurtured? I don't know. I have no memory of those eighteen months. None. Eighteen months of my life are lost in my mind somewhere and I have yet to locate them.

October 1947
Miami, Florida

"Be sure to dump the pot before you go to school," Momma says. She points to the big green poop-pot that sits in our tiny closet. The closet has just enough room so I can close the door, pull down my pants, squat, and pee late at night when it's too dark and scary to walk over to the bathhouse. Momma can't close the door anymore because her stomach's getting big with our new baby.

Ron Radzai, Momma, and I use the pot. Sharon still wears diapers at night. The pot's like the one we use to cook spaghetti, with a handle on each side and a wide-open top. By morning, it's full of pee and poop. One of my jobs is to get the pot cleaned up and ready to use the next night.

I like my household tasks. They're matter-of-fact parts of my daily ritual. Life with a blind mother teaches me to pay attention to details, to see the jobs that need to be done, to anticipate when something, like dishes left in the sink, is going to be a problem. I feel like a grown-up when I see something that needs cleaning or moving and I just get up and do it. Most times, no one notices, but that's okay. I'm still the big sister, the oldest child, and Momma's special helper.

I grab the pot by its handles and hoist the heavy, smelly mess up to my chest, push open the door, and step onto the four rickety wooden steps that lead down to the muddy path everyone uses to go to the bathhouse. I peer over the pot to see my way down the steps. The stench burns my eyes, and they water. I have to go slowly or else I'll fall and really have a mess to clean up. I gag and think I might throw up. I vow every morning when I dump the pot that I won't vomit.

Once I'm down the steps, I could close my eyes and follow my nose to my destination, but I keep them wide open to see everything and everybody.

I tag along behind a lady who's on the same mission and follow her through the open door on the side of the bathhouse marked "Women." Along the far wall are ten showers and ten toilet stalls. On the opposite wall are a dozen sinks, including some deep ones for washing dishes and clothes.

Everyone in the trailer park uses the bathhouse, and sometimes all the stalls are full and the line snakes out the door. This morning, there's no wait. I hurry toward a toilet just as my pot gets so heavy, I can't hold it any longer. I set the edge of the green pot against the white porcelain lip of the toilet and slant it so all the stuff inside slides into the toilet. Some of it splashes back on my face and some poop goes on the floor beside the toilet. I wipe my face with the back of my hand but leave the poop on the floor. I hate it when other folks don't clean up their mess, but I've been late for school once already and the school year's just starting. I look away and hurry outside with my empty pot.

I set my pot under a spigot on the outside of the building, turn on the water, swirl it around, and dump it out. Then I race back to our trailer and set the pot outside in the sunshine so it'll dry by evening, when we'll use it again. I grab my books and lunch bag, tell Momma I'm leaving for school, and start my walk.

There are no trees in the trailer park, but once I get outside the chain-link fence and onto the main street, lots of peculiar-looking palm trees, their long branches swaying in the breeze, accompany me to school. Coconuts cluster at their tops like wads of giant figs. I search the ground to see if one has fallen so that Ron Radzai can cut it open for me to drink its sweet milk.

Lots of coconuts fell a few weeks ago when Hurricane George came through and Ron Radzai, Momma, Sharon, and I walked up and down the streets and collected a bunch of them. Ron Radzai knows how to cut them open with a screw driver and hammer. Then Momma, Sharon, and I take turns drinking milk from the hole. After the milk's gone, he hits the nut again and we each grab a chunk. This is one good thing Ron Radzai does that my father never did. That's because we didn't live in Miami. You just can't go around and pick up coconuts in Yonkers. But I don't find any coconuts today. I guess they're all gone now.

• • •

School is my favorite part of the day, but I have a difficult time adjusting to school in Miami. I'm so confused by all the changes in my life, I spend a lot of time daydreaming and worrying about where my father is, why Momma's always mad, and where my toys are. Mrs. Leak notices and writes a note to Momma and Ron Radzai on my report card:

> *Beverly is reading quite nicely. She does her work well but seems afraid of something. If you can help me figure out what it is, I would appreciate it.*
> *—Louise Leak, First Grade Teacher, Shenandoah Elementary, Miami, February, 1948*

June 1948

"When will your moving truck get here?" Mattie Lou Kinnard, a tall, stately woman, asks Momma. She's the manager of Victory Homes Housing Project for WWII veterans.

We're standing in the empty living room of our new, two-bedroom, white cinder block home, surrounded by hundreds of houses that look just like ours, filled with families with fathers who fought in the War. I think it'll be easy to get lost in the project. Each long, rectangular, one-story building has a porch on both ends. That's how you can tell two families share a building. We moved up on the waiting list because Ron Radzai had a Purple Heart, Momma's blind, and our trailer park was condemned by the Dade County Health Department after the sewer pipes burst and awful-smelling slop ran all over the bathhouse and out onto the paths. They told us we had thirty days to get out. Momma says we're lucky we were accepted at Victory Homes.

"There's no moving truck; this is all we have," Momma says, pointing to our few bags and six-month-old baby Ronnie's folding crib. We loaded all our possessions in the taxi that drove us across town. Clothes and a few pots, including the poop-pot, hang out of the open paper grocery bags propped against the wall. Here, we'll be able to make our spaghetti in the green pot again. The first thing I checked as soon as we walked in here was the bathroom. It has a toilet, a sink, and even a bathtub.

"Oh, heavens," Mrs. Kinnard says. "Let me see what I can get for you." She hurries out the screen door.

We'll sleep on flattened cardboard boxes Mrs. Kinnard has brought over tonight.

I don't care. Sharon and I have our own bedroom again.

And tonight, I can pee in a toilet.

Chapter 4

THE SEEING EYE GIRL

September 1948
Victory Homes Housing Project, Miami, Florida

I'm the man.

Momma says the man should walk on the sidewalk closest to the road so he can protect anyone walking with him, especially if there's an accident. Now that I'm seven, I'm old enough to guide Momma across town. So, when we go shopping, I slip my arm in hers and take up my position nearest the traffic.

The blazing Miami sun barges through the open windows of our apartment this Saturday and the sweetness of honeysuckle fills the air. Everything in our kitchen is white. The sun's glow bounces off the refrigerator door and lights up the Formica table top like jewels in a pirate's treasure chest. It casts Momma in the spotlight; her shoulder-length brown hair glows as she bends over the stroller to run her hands over baby Ronnie's face, as she has done with Sharon and me for years.

Momma wears her white high heels, blue short shorts, and a new ivory knit shirt that's neatly tucked in at her narrow waist and cinched with a wide brown belt. I've dressed eight-month-old Ronnie in a blue and white sailor outfit with a matching hat. The navy blue embroidered anchors reflect the color of his eyes. Silky white hairs peek out from under his hat. He was nodding off in his stroller but is roused now by Momma's touch.

Sharon and I often dress like twins, even though I'm four years older. Today we wear our matching bloomer and triangle halter sets that Momma's made, white background with big red and yellow polka dots.

Momma's very talented and knows how to make patterns that fit us girls. With her special sense of touch, she attaches the pattern to the material with straight pins. Then she moves her left hand along the pattern, guiding her scissor-wielding right hand. She lays the pieces on the table to form the shape of the final product and says, "Beverly, come and check out these bloomers."

She counts on me to be her eyes. I'm Momma's special helper and I know exactly how to line up the material so the patterns match. Once I tell her everything's in place, she stitches the seams with our Goodwill-Singer sewing machine. Then I attach elastic to a safety pin and thread it through the waist and leg seams.

Momma makes many of our clothes; the rest come from a neighborhood church. Two women bring us bags of clothes every few months, chosen for our sizes. And it's all free.

We're finally ready to go. I usher everyone outside, pick up the stroller, and place it on the sidewalk. Then I turn back to lock up the house.

Ron Radzai's inside sleeping. He drives a truck at night, delivering food to area grocery stores, so he sleeps all day. I seldom see him when he's awake and he doesn't use many words so I don't really know much about him yet, even though he's been with us ever since we moved to Miami over a year ago. I miss my dad and all the fun times we used to have. Ron Radzai never plays games with us kids the way Dad did. Every once in a while, though, he takes us to the beach, and on special occasions he makes crunchy potato pancakes for dinner. He lets me take a turn grating potatoes and flipping the golden-brown pancakes in the hot, bubbling oil. These are the times I think it's okay to have a stepfather.

Today, I get to be Momma's seeing eye girl. That means I'm in charge of our family. I sing the opening lines of "It's a Lovely Day" and wave my arms like I'm a chorus conductor. Even though no one sings along with me, I know they'll all follow my directions until we get back here with our groceries.

"Step down one," I say to Momma when we come to the edge of the concrete porch. I stand at her side, my left arm nestled into the crook of her right arm. Momma's dark sunglasses hide her cloudy eyes but not the big blotches of orange rouge she's rubbed onto her cheeks or the bright red lipstick that bleeds out over the skin beyond her mouth. I don't dare tell Momma she's missed her lips. Sometimes people stare at her, then at me, and I'm sure they want to ask a few questions, but they never do.

Folks in our neighborhood think Momma's snooty. She never looks at them and doesn't say things like, "Hello, Pauline"—mainly because she just can't see Pauline. I'm always with Momma whenever she goes outside. She doesn't know her way around yet, seeing as we recently moved here.

I position Sharon behind the stroller and place her little hands next to Momma's. Even though she's just three, it's her job to keep going straight and not run into anything. She loves to talk and move fast, so I remind her to slow down. Her thick dark brown hair is already wet and her arms glisten with sweat. I touch my forehead. I'm wet too. I wipe my hand on my bloomers, and we get started. I keep my right hand free in case I need to grab the baby buggy or do anything else to keep our family safe as we go on our journey.

"We'll walk straight for a block and then we'll cross the street," I tell Sharon and Momma so they know what's ahead, what the plan is. We walk out of the project, past the Victory Homes playground with its swings, slide, and see-saws. Occasionally I find coins near the monkey bars and hide them under the mattress Mrs. Kinnard brought over for Sharon and me. We pass Little River Elementary, my new school. As we approach the corner, I push my left arm in toward Momma's body to let her know we're slowing down. No one taught me how to do this, I just made it up and it seems to work. Momma knows my arm signals, but I keep talking to make extra sure she and Sharon understand what to do.

I like being in charge. It reminds me of being in school, where I always wave my hand in the air. I like to be the first one to know the answer. I sit in the front row and usually the teacher picks me to be the captain of the kickball team. That's when I feel like singing. Actually, I don't have a very good voice, but I like to sing anyway. Last year at Shenandoah Elementary, the music teacher asked me to sing out a line of a song we were practicing. When I did, she said, "Now, honey, you just move your lips but don't sing out loud when we go on the stage." I understood right then and there that I wasn't much good at singing. But I don't care. I still do it every chance I get.

"Stop now. Let's wait for the light." I look both ways to check out the traffic. I judge how fast the cars are coming. I glance at the sleeping baby and straighten his hat. My arm is dark brown against his chalk-white skin. My dad has dark brown hair and chocolate-milk skin like Sharon and I have. Ron Radzai has real pale beige skin and blond hair, just like our new baby. Sharon and I don't look anything like baby Ronnie, but we all have the same momma. I think that's real funny. How we all came out so different.

"Okay, we're ready to go now," I say, tugging on Momma's arm, leading her in the right direction. "The road has two lanes. It's safe to go." When we get across the street, I say, "Step up—curb." I grab the front rung of the stroller and pop it up onto the sidewalk. "We'll step back and wait here for the bus."

I read the signs across the front of each bus to make sure we take the right one. I raise my arm to let the driver know we're waiting for him. He gets out and lifts the baby stroller onto the bus and then Sharon, Momma, and I get on board. I'm always the last one, so I can make sure we haven't dropped anything.

"Thank you," I say to the bus driver. "Please let me know when we get to the Food Fair stop." I like talking to the driver like that. It lets him know I'm the one in charge.

We sit at the front of the bus near the driver. A few stops later, a Negro lady and her children get on the bus. She also has a baby in a stroller. This time the driver looks straight ahead and doesn't get off to help her. That's rude. She struggles to lift the buggy up the stairs. Then she walks all the way to the back of the bus before she turns to sit down.

"Here's a seat," I shout.

Momma jabs me in the side with her elbow. "Mind your own business," she says.

Momma's told me that all the poor folks live here in the northwestern part of Miami—the white folks in Victory Homes and the colored folks in Liberty City. She said the rich businesspeople don't want us poor people, especially the Negroes, living downtown. That's why they put lots of buses out here, so we can get to the shops and the Negro ladies can get to work in town cleaning houses. At the grocery store, there will be signs on the bathrooms and water fountains: COLORED ONLY. WHITE ONLY. My school has only white kids. The colored kids have their own school in Liberty City. I asked my teacher why we don't all go to the same school.

"That's just the way it is," she says.

That's what Momma says too. But none of this makes any sense to me. The water is the same in both fountains.

• • •

Momma's been blind for as long as I can remember. Soon after she was born, she had sore eyes and the doctors told her parents she had corneal dystrophy and that she'd go blind one day. She even had to stay out of school for two years because her eyes hurt so much. That was when she started drawing pictures of beautiful women. She has them in a big folder she brings out now and then. We sit around and look at the drawings, and I say, "You're a great artist, Momma."

When Momma was well enough to return to school, the principal held her back two years. That meant she was in her sister Lena's class. Momma hated that. Lena was two years younger than Momma and they fought all the time. Being in her class just about turned Momma off of school altogether. But she liked to learn. The teachers asked her to draw illustrations on the board with colored chalk. Then everyone in school knew what a good artist she was.

Dad used to be Momma's seeing eye guide. He always hooked his arm through Momma's like I do now and told her where to step and when to stop. I held Momma's hand back then, but I never guided her until we moved to Miami. Now there's no Dad and no Italian cousins to help out, and Ron Radzai's always at work or sleeping—so that means it's all up to me.

I'm the seeing eye girl now.

Once we get to the store, Momma and I push the grocery cart and Sharon steers the stroller. We block the entire aisle as we make our way through produce, picking up things that are on the list Momma and I made up before we left home. She shows me how to touch the fruit and vegetables to make sure they're fresh. We buy a few apples and oranges. I select the best-looking, ripest ones, but always get green bananas because they last longer. I turn the fruit over and over to make sure there are no bruises or worms.

We load up our cart and head to the checkout line. Whew. We're almost finished. We may get out of the store without an incident. Momma usually finds all sorts of reasons to get mad at me, even when we're out in public. I'm always on my toes, trying to please her, trying to say the right things. Sometimes I know why she's mad. But most of the time I have no idea what has set her off.

Just when I feel a sense of relief, it happens. "You god damned son of a bitch," Momma hisses in my ear, then grabs my arm and pinches it.

Momma's an expert pincher. She knows right where to find a little meat.

She holds my flesh between her fingers and twists it for the longest time before she finally lets go. I wince but don't make a sound. I put the bread and milk on the counter and act like nothing's the matter. I'm an expert actress. I've had lots of practice this last year. I scurry past the cart, away from Momma.

The cashier stops punching in numbers and stares straight at Momma. Sharon hollers, "You stepped on my foot." Ronnie poops in his diaper and the smell fills the tiny space. I bump into the lady in front of me and she says, "Oops."

"I'm sorry," I mumble, keeping my head down.

Momma moves past the cart and pinches me again. This time, I piddle a little in my pants.

The cashier gives Momma a funny look and starts with our order: "milk, 43 cents; bread, 14 cents; ground beef, 55 cents; jam, 35 cents; soup, three cans for 25 cents; cereal, 35 cents; apples, 25 cents; bananas, 11 cents, gelatin, three packs, 25 cents; cabbage, 10 cents; oranges, 10 cents. You owe two dollars and eighty-eight cents."

"Momma, we need three dollars," I say. Momma gives me the money and the cashier hands me a dime and two pennies. I put the twelve cents in Momma's hand. Then it's all over.

Nobody talks on the trip home.

• • •

Momma knows her way around our apartment really well because everything's in its special place. All the dishes and food have their own locations on the shelves so she can open a certain cabinet, reach in to the right, and grab the peanut butter just where she knows it'll be. There's a plan for all the food and supplies for Ronnie. In the baby cabinet, jars of meat go one behind the other along the left wall. The next row is for vegetables, and the last is for fruit. When a jar is taken out, we move the rest up toward the front so Momma knows how much we have left. It's my job to make sure everything is in its place, or else Momma will get the honey instead of the peanut butter, and that'll make her mad—mad at me since it's my responsibility to make sure we all follow the household rules.

"Put the groceries away, Beverly, and make up some sandwiches for you and Sharon," she tells me as soon as I get the bags out of the stroller. "And Ronnie needs his diaper changed."

Momma is back in charge.

My job as Seeing Eye Girl is over for today.

Chapter 5

JUST MOMMA AND ME

October 1948

The first beating
comes when I am
seven.

"Go wait for me in the living room," Momma says as I help her get the baby ready for bed. Her tone of voice tells me I'm in trouble. I replay in my mind everything I've said this evening, everything I've done, trying to see what's aggravated Momma. I can't find anything. Sometimes I do nothing wrong but Momma is mad anyway. Seems like she's always mad now that we live in Miami. I have to get ready for what's going to happen next.

I have a hundred gallons of urine in me. My legs dangle in mid-air over the floor, my pink pajamas soaked with sweat, my arms numb and tingly. I peer into the toilet to see how much I've peed, but I can't tell. I have this awful feeling in the pit of my stomach. I have to be empty, totally empty.

"Go, go, go," I urge my body.

Once I know I'm ready, I walk into the living room and sit on a crate to wait for Momma. We have a few mismatched chairs and a sofa in the living room, things Mrs. Kinnard got for us from local charities. Several wooden grocery crates that Ron Radzai brought home from work are scattered about. The one I'm sitting on says "Florida Oranges" down its sides.

There are no pictures or mirrors on the white walls like we used to have in Mulford Gardens in Yonkers. I remember the huge gold-framed mirror above our beige sofa. I'd laugh and jump on the cushions so I could see my fat cheeks when I had the mumps, just two years ago. I remember my toy box, overflowing, all my dolls sitting up straight on my bed. I remember my fancy clothes, each outfit with matching shoes, hat, and purse. I remember it all, including the last day I saw my father.

The window in the living room is open and I peer through the screen into the foggy night. I imagine that the hundreds of white concrete homes that look just like ours have vanished in the heavy night air. There is no one to help me, to save me from my mother and from the whipping I'm about to get.

The house is stale from all the Lucky Strikes Momma and Ron Radzai smoke one right after another. Sharon and Ronnie are in bed. Ron Radzai's at work. It's just Momma and me.

And the radio.

"Heartaches." I usually like to whistle along. I don't feel like whistling or singing tonight, even though I know all the words to the popular songs.

Your Hit Parade's top 15 countdown plays every Saturday evening, and Momma and I always sing along. My absolute favorite show, though, is on Sunday evening: *The Shadow*. I sit in front of our brown RCA Victor radio and stare at the mesh speaker. "Who knows what evil lurks in the minds of men? The Shadow knows. Ha, ha, ha," the radio says in unison with me as I make the creepy laugh deep in my throat. Then I wait for the ending. "The weed of crime bears bitter fruit. Crime does not pay." I say the words out loud. Once *The Shadow* is over, it's time for bed. I keep the refrain going in my head until I fall asleep, ". . . only the Shadow knows, only the Shadow knows."

My crate is as close to the front door as I can get. I imagine opening the door and walking into the mist, walking back to Yonkers. Instead, I scoot up, rest my back against the living room wall, and wait.

Waiting for Momma is almost as bad as what's going to happen when she arrives in the living room. I stare down the short hallway where baby Ronnie sleeps in a bassinette in Momma and Ron Radzai's bedroom. Sharon and I sleep on a mattress in the other bedroom. Even though she kicks me, I wish I were on the mattress right now instead of sitting on this crate that's giving me splinters in my legs.

I turn my thoughts to school.

"What happened to your eye?" the principal asked on my first day at Little River Elementary just a month ago. I had bruises up and down my arms and a black eye.

"I walked into a door," I said.

"Oh," she said, then turned and left the office.

It's so easy to fool people. Momma has never told me to lie about my bruises, but I know I have to find excuses for my blacks and blues. I made up all sorts of stories at first and people acted like they believed me, and I've just gotten better and better at lying. What would happen if I told the principal my mother bites and smacks me? Would she do anything? I don't think so. But what if the principal came to visit Momma? She would be furious and beat me even more. I'm not willing to take that chance.

I gave the secretary the big brown envelope Momma put together for me with all my records from kindergarten in Yonkers, first grade at Shenandoah Elementary, and copies of all my shots.

"Why don't you roam around a bit while I process your papers?" the secretary said. "Our school was built in the Spanish style and I think you'll enjoy the courtyard. I'll come find you when I'm ready to take you to your new class."

The corridor enveloped me in a flood of sunlight and warm Florida air. On my left, doors opened to each classroom. To my right, tall, rounded arches cut out of the thick concrete walls softened the lines between nature and learning. Best of all was that the one-story stucco school wrapped completely around a large, open, grassy courtyard. I'd never seen anything so beautiful. This was my school.

My heart beat hard as I stepped into the rectangular courtyard. I breathed in the fresh, earthy smell of the newly cut lawn and smiled. The semicircular concrete stage drew me toward it. I climbed the steps, sat on the top one, admired my new school, and wondered which classroom would be mine. Perhaps I'd play tag here during recess. Or I'd be on the stage, acting in a play or singing with the chorus. This was my new home. I was in love with Little River, the most magical school I'd ever seen.

Within the hour, I was in Miss Virginia Curl's second grade class. She gave me a desk at the front of the classroom, where I had a clear view of the courtyard.

I'm happy in school. Safe, secure, free to be myself. School is where I'm spontaneous, outgoing, gregarious, funny. I'm talkative, not afraid of measuring my words or saying something wrong. My teachers love me, encourage me, want me to do well. They'd never hit me or curse at me. In school, I am Strong Beverly. At home, I am Weak Beverly, afraid to say too much, frightened of Momma's reactions to me, afraid of my own shadow.

Maybe tomorrow I'll see James Lashe on the way to school. We'll laugh and walk on the logs that surround the parking area. Maybe I'll lose my balance and fall off. He'll grab my hand and we'll laugh some more. Maybe he'll bring me a glistening white gardenia from his mother's garden. I'll bring it to my face, drink in its sweet fragrance, and smile at him. James has a chicken breast and his ribs stick out funny under his shirt. The other kids make fun of him, but I like him and he likes me. Sometimes I think he sees my bruises but he never says anything about them.

Click-click. Momma's high heels are coming. She's only five feet tall, but she towers over me. Tonight, she wears pink shorts with a tight white T-shirt. Momma dresses like a model now that we live in Miami.

Momma wastes no time once she's near me. She always knows where I am. Even though she's blind, she can see silhouettes. I sometimes think she's not really blind because she can always find the silhouette that is me.

"You're just like your father," she screams.
"No good. Taking, taking."
Her voice is shrill. She snatches me by my arm.
Yanks me off the crate.
Flings me onto the floor.
Kicks me in my side.
I curl into a ball and cry.
Whoosh! A flood escapes from between my legs.
I piddle all over the floor.
She kicks me again and
grabs my hair as she
pulls me through
the wet mess.
Wiping the floor
with me,
a mop.

"No, no, Momma, no, no, no," I gasp, unable to catch my breath.

My pink pajamas are soaked. Somehow, I keep piddling. I have an endless supply of urine. I can't control it. The more I pee, the more she shouts and kicks. Then she pulls me up from the floor and sinks her teeth into my arm. She must taste my water. I taste it. I smell it.

I hear Nat King Cole's voice coming through a long, dark tunnel.

"You goddamned Guinea, you. You're hurting my eyes. Clean up this mess."

Momma's high heels click-clack into her bedroom. I lie on the floor a long time and sob. But I force myself to stop, afraid I'll lose control like I did the last time I saw Dad. My body aches, but I tell myself it doesn't hurt that bad. I hate it when Momma hits me. I'm not a bad girl.

Dear Jesus, can you help me? I don't want to hurt Momma's eyes. I don't want to eat too much. I need my father. I need you to help me, Jesus.

Finally, I get up. The radio's still on.

"Peg o' My Heart . . ."

I snap off the radio knob. Get a rag. Clean up the floor. I strip my pink pants and top off and wash them in the bathroom sink. I look at my body.

Momma's teeth marks are etched into my arm.

Bruises well up on my sides, legs, and arms.

Tomorrow I'll wear long pants and a long-sleeved shirt to school.

Chapter 6

ANGELS WATCHING OVER ME

November 1949

As soon as our next baby, Michael Robert, is born on August 30, 1949, the doctors say he is seriously ill with hydrocephalus. Everyone in the family is sad. He stays in the hospital for a month. When we finally bring him home, I learn how hard it is to take care of a sick baby. I've dressed Ronnie and Sharon, changed their diapers, washed them up, and fed them. But with Mickey, I have to be careful to hold his large head and to rock him just so when he's irritable and crying. Ron Radzai and Momma take him back to the hospital for another surgery to drain some of the fluid off his brain.

Even though everyone is busy worrying about our baby, Momma still comes up with all sorts of creative ways to punish me. This time it's for lying about something, like how many raisins I picked out of the cereal box or how much marshmallow I spooned from the jar. There's no sense in denying any of it. Once Momma gets onto something, she's not going to let it—or me—go.

She catches me by my arm, pinches me hard. Strips off my clothes. I'm standing stark naked, right in the middle of the kitchen. She throws me on the floor, grabs one of Ronnie's cloth diapers, unfolds it, stretches it around my buttocks, and jams a safety pin into my side. *Don't scream.* She picks up a bar of white soap and pulls off the wrapper, then drags me out to the low concrete stoop in front of our house.

Our front porch is at the center of my universe. Right across the street is the big Victory Homes playground, where all the kids in the housing project swing, hang from the monkey bars, skip rope, kick balls, and see-saw. The park is the cut-through we use to get to Little River Elementary, just a few blocks away on Seventy-seventh Street. It's the place where, if you're high on the monkey bars, you can see my house and me, sitting alone, bare-chested and diapered, clutching a bar of soap.

"Sit here and eat this soap until you learn to stop being a liar, you son of a bitch," Momma says. "I'll show you to talk back, to make up stories, you bastard."

It's another hot and humid Saturday in Miami. My biggest fear is that James Lashe, my boyfriend, will come by and see me sitting here, sucking on a bar of soap, naked except for the tight white diaper. I do pray, though, that if James comes by, he'll run home and return with a freshly cut gardenia for me. For the rest of my life, gardenias will elicit memories of the unspoken bond we shared, of the innocent tenderness and pain reflected in his eyes, of our childhood friendship, sealed by reasons we are now, as eight-year old kids, unable to articulate.

I scoot into the white cinder block wall, pull my legs up, and make myself invisible. I stick my head into my knees. If I can't see anyone, maybe no one can see me.

The soap's bitter. I gag. The foam slobbers out of my mouth and creates bubbly trails down my chest. I cup my hand, force a glob of suds out of the corner of my mouth, into my palm, and swipe it on the diaper. If I do this fast enough, I can catch the suds before they escape down my throat. I smile. This is the way out of my dilemma.

There's nothing else left to do but to talk to Jesus.

"Momma tells me I'm a liar. I did eat a few raisins, but not that many. I hope you'll forgive me. I'm sorry to be so bad. I want to be good. Please help me and help Momma too." A verse I know from Sunday school—Psalms 51:2 (King James Version)—comes into my head. I tag it onto my prayer: "'Wash me thoroughly from mine iniquity and cleanse me from my sin.' Thank You, Jesus, for all my blessings."

I pray for a long time that day and try to strike a bargain with Jesus. I promise Him I'll become a missionary and travel the world spreading the Gospel if He will make this soap disappear.

• • •

Ever since we moved to Victory Homes, I've gone to Little River Baptist Church. Momma wants me to go to a Methodist Church but there's not one close by, so the Baptist Church has to do. Momma says I'm supposed to be Catholic but she "saved me from the Catholic Church and that awful name, Madalena." Madalena, an immigrant from San Mauro Forte, Italy, was Dad's mother. She died from pneumonia when he was only seven and he wanted to honor her by naming his first daughter after her, as was the Italian tradition. But Momma wouldn't have it. She won the name battle but promised to raise me as a Catholic in order to have me baptized.

So much for promises.

It's all a little confusing, but when anyone asks, I say I'm Baptist.

The church is right across the street from my school. Early each Sunday morning, I get Sharon and myself dressed and we go off for our walk through the park, past the monkey bars and swings, and across the street to church.

If Sharon and I are lucky, Momma gives us five pennies for

the collection plate. That's when we take the long way to church and stop at MacSweeney's, where the curved glass front of the penny-candy display case is taller than I and wider than both my arms stretched straight out. Mr. MacSweeney slides open the back door of the candy case, squats down, and stares at us over the rows of candy as we labor over our selection. There are so many choices our heads swoon: Tootsie Rolls, black and red licorice sticks, candy cigarettes, Sugar Daddy pops, Bazooka Joe bubble gum, Bit O Honey, Kits, and Necco Wafers. We hope Jesus doesn't mind if we use a few pennies for us. We stuff the candy into our pockets and run the rest of the way to church.

When it's time for communion, the minister says, "Take and eat. This is My body." Sharon looks up at me. I nod my head and we each pop a Necco Wafer in our mouth. We let it slowly melt before we crunch it into a thousand pieces. I prayerfully confess all my sins to Jesus and thank Him for all He has done for me, especially sharing His money.

The Baptist minister is so full of God's love he wants the entire congregation to confess their sins and accept Jesus Christ as their Lord and Savior. Every Sunday, he asks those who want to be saved to come down to the front of the church and kneel at the altar. After his invitation, the entire congregation sings:

Just as I am, without one plea,
But that Thy blood was shed for me . . .

There must be a thousand verses. Everyone sings softly, their heads bowed. I sway to the music as all the sinners walk to the altar. I want to get out of my seat, walk straight down the aisle, and confess my sins right there in front of everyone. Each week, I just about get up my nerve to be saved. But by that time, the hymn always ends. Then the minister prays over the kneeling parishioners, and my opportunity for that week is over.

I want more than anything to wear a long, white robe, get dunked in the big tank on the altar, be cleansed and saved, and hear the minister say in his loud, booming voice, "I baptize you in the name of the Father, the Son, and the Holy Spirit." I plead with Momma to let me get baptized, but she says I've been baptized and I can't do it again.

Finally, a brilliant thought comes to me. If I've been baptized, I must be saved. If I'm saved, then all my sins are forgiven and washed away. Jesus is standing beside me to shield me from harm. For a long while I thought Dad would return, but now I doubt that's going to happen. I like the idea that Jesus is looking out for me, that He will protect me. This new notion will drive my religious zeal for many years and give me comfort and confidence that all will be well, that I'll be safe.

I tell my friends at school that Jesus is my Lord and Savior. If they believe in Him, they'll go to heaven. At recess, kids gather around me in the grassy courtyard and listen as I preach. "Jesus saves you from sin," I say, making my voice rise and fall just like my Baptist minister. I motion toward heaven and hell, make big flourishes with my arms, and close my eyes as I turn my head to the sky.

I'm practicing for the day I'll be a missionary.

●　●　●

My soap is now rounded on all the edges. I thank Jesus that a crowd hasn't gathered to watch my shaming. My diaper is soaked and sticky from all the suds I've wiped on it. I wait for Momma to come out to the porch, to tell me I can come in, that I've eaten enough soap, that I've had long enough to straighten up. But no such luck. Momma's in no hurry. I duck my head back between my legs and suck on the soap again.

Jesus is in no hurry to change things for me either.

I'm going to have to solve this problem by myself.

Chapter 7

MOMMA CAN SEE

My Mother

My mother, my mother,
My mother is she,
With two beautiful eyes
That could not see.
One day from school I came,
I heard someone call my name.
With bandages off,
My mother could see.
A thrill I'll remember
Until eternity.

February 17, 1950

"Beverly, Beverly." Momma's voice comes through the screen door. She's been in Jackson Memorial Hospital for the last thirteen days. I've waited for this day—imagined how she'll change, how our lives will be different now that she can see. I wonder if she'll love me again like she used to.

She can see me! My heart thumps in my throat, tears flow down my cheeks. I have so many mixed thoughts about my mother and this day. I'm excited and happy that Momma's corneal transplant has been successful, and optimistic that this miracle will bring back the mother I love, the one still in my Yonkers memories. But I'm also apprehensive and afraid she'll always be angry with me, perhaps even more now that she can see how much I look like Dad. I can only hope for the best. I pull the screen door open.

"Momma, Momma!"

She gets up from her chair. We stand there in the living room, frozen for a moment, staring at each other. Then I run into her open arms and sob. I'm so relieved. My Yonkers Momma *is* back. She holds me for the longest time, our bodies pressed tightly together, my face lost in her bosom. Her heart throbs in my ear. "Oh, Momma, I am so happy," I say.

Momma's distracted by the blaring radio on the table beside her chair. She turns and snaps it off, but not before I hear the broadcaster talking about the big speech Senator Joseph McCarthy gave a few days ago in West Virginia. That's when he said lots of folks working at the State Department were communists. Momma is an expert on the communists and likes to keep up with all the news.

"Stand over here and let me see how pretty you are," she says. She sits down in her favorite upholstered chair and pulls me close. She puts her hands on my face, touches my hair, my wet cheeks, my nose, mouth. Her fingertips trace my square jaw. She's done this before—only this time she can see the brown of my hair, the flush on my cheeks, my almond skin. She can see the four bands of lace down the front of my sleeveless white blouse and the white flowers on my black, loosely gathered cotton skirt—a skirt she made for me.

I realize that in all of my nine years and seventeen days of life, this is the first time Momma has actually seen me.

Momma has bathed, nursed, diapered, caressed, and burped me. She has hit, pinched, kicked, and bitten me. She has encouraged, nurtured, protected, intimidated, and terrified me. But today, Momma is finally seeing me, her firstborn. She can see my smile, my tears, my face—the face that looks just like Dad's. Square chin, deeply set dark eyes, broad nose, high cheekbones.

• • •

One day about two weeks before, our neighbor Mrs. Knight received a telegram while I was in school: "Please read the telegram Mrs. Radzai just received." She ran to our front door just as a telegram was delivered to Momma. Mrs. Knight read it out loud: "Call me immediately. I have a cornea for you. Dr. Palmer." Mrs. Knight grabbed Momma's hand and they ran from house to house in Victory Homes, trying to find someone who had a telephone.

Today, corneal transplants are done as outpatient surgery, but in 1950 the surgery was not at all common. It took an hour and a half of surgery and Momma lying in bed with sand bags around her head for two weeks to keep the stitches from breaking.

Dr. Bascom H. Palmer, Momma's doctor, was no common ophthalmologist. Today, the Bascom Palmer Eye Institute at the University of Miami's Miller School of Medicine is the number one research, teaching, and medical eye facility in the country, dedicated to Palmer's vision that everyone, regardless of wealth, is entitled to quality eye care. Momma's surgery was paid for by the Florida Lighthouse for the Blind, and Dr. Palmer himself did the surgery.

• • •

I look at Momma with new eyes too. She's so pretty, but today she looks funny. I realize she has no eyebrows or eyelashes. Dr. Palmer had to shave them off for the surgery. She looks small, too. She lost weight in the hospital. Her blue shirtwaist dress hangs loosely around her body. Her face is white, pale, tired. Her brown hair is messy, and she's not wearing any makeup. But her face is full of happiness, and her eyes twinkle.

At least, her right eye twinkles. It's sparkling, blue-green, and clear as a gem. But her left eye is cloudy and opaque, like a layer of wax paper is covering her eyeball.

I realize I'm staring into Momma's eyes. She senses this also. We both laugh out loud and hug each other again.

"I'm looking for the stitches," I say.

"They're so tiny, you probably can't see them," she says. She pulls open the eyelids on her right eye so I can see the curvature of her eyeball, but I can't see any stitches. "Dr. Palmer cut off my old cornea and sewed on one from Mrs. Oser. She had to lose her eye because she had a tumor pressing on her optic nerve, but her cornea was good."

"Am I looking at Mrs. Oser's cornea?" I ask.

"Yes, you sure are. It's a miracle," Momma says. "I'm so lucky. I hope I can meet Mrs. Oser one day and thank her for this wonderful gift she's given me."

"Does she only have one eye now?" I ask.

"Dr. Palmer had to take her eye out after he removed her cornea," she says, "but he put a glass eye into her socket. He told me it looks just like her real eye. She's going to be healthy now that the tumor's gone."

• • •

It is highly unusual for a living donor to contribute a cornea. Dr. Palmer had examined Momma two years ago. He said she was the perfect candidate for a transplant, but he had to have just the right conditions before he could perform the surgery—that she and the donor had to be in the right place at the right time. (This was long before Eye Banks, where corneas can be preserved for longer periods of time, were established.) By the time he had the right conditions, Momma had been blind for ten years, had four children, and was plagued by poverty and strange ideas in her mind.

. . .

Momma and I explore each other's faces as though she's a momma bear and I her stray cub and we've reunited after a long absence. It feels so good, like the old days, back when we lived in Yonkers, when she would take me out to ride on my tricycle. We'd go to the park, climb on the big rocks, pose so Dad could take a picture. Then we'd enjoy a picnic lunch. We'd laugh, play with my dolls, and stroll along the paths with my baby buggy. Momma would kiss me, hold me, and love on me. For a moment, I think I'm five years old again and Dad will come out of the bedroom, pick me up, toss me in the air, and tickle me.

But it is just Momma and me. I'm the very first family member she's seen since her transplant, and I get to see her alone for this private moment. Dr. Palmer didn't let anyone in her hospital room when he changed her bandages, so she hasn't even seen Ron Radzai yet. For me, this is a quiet and precious time, like all those moments so long ago when Momma and I touched each other in loving ways, talked with gentle voices, and laughed with gusto. It is a moment I will long cherish, a moment in space where time stands still and we say to each other, in so many unspoken words, *I love you. I still love you.*

But our love fest doesn't last long.

I jump away from Momma's embrace. "I have to get Sharon and Ronnie before their school closes," I tell her before running out the door and down the street toward the Victory Homes Day Care.

Sharon and Ronnie scamper back to the house with me, squealing, "Momma can see, Momma can see," all the way. At two, Ronnie's not quite sure what's happening, but he's always eager to follow the lead of his older sisters. Sharon is five and doesn't miss a beat. Our baby brother, Mickey, is in the hospital, too sick to be at home.

There's quite a commotion at the house now, as we three kids and our momma do the first visual family inspection. She touches Ronnie's towhead hair and runs her fingers over his pale skin. Sharon and I, with our darker, olive-toned skin and dark brown hair and eyes, pose a sharp contrast to Ronnie's coloring. Momma is intrigued. She touches everything: our clothes, our bodies, and especially our faces. She runs her hands over Sharon's face, over Ronnie's, and describes every detail—our colors, our smells, our shapes. It's almost like Momma has new ears and hands and a new nose as well as a new eye. She puts Ronnie on her lap, and Sharon and I sit on the floor, hanging our arms and our heads on Momma's chair, on Momma's legs. There hasn't been this much touching, talking, and loving going on in our house for many years. It's all so wonderful I fear it may be a dream. But for now, it is all real, and I'm so very happy.

Momma is back, and everything is going to be okay.

• • •

"What should we fix for dinner?" Momma finally asks.

"Spanish rice," Sharon and I say at once. Ronnie chimes in, "Anish ice."

"Beverly, go see if we have everything we need. But first, you kids get out of your school clothes."

We laugh, jump up and down, and holler, "Momma can see, Momma can see!"

I change Ronnie's diaper, dress him in his pajamas, put on a pair of shorts and a shirt, take Ronnie into the kitchen, place him in his high chair, tie on his bib, and pour a bunch of Cheerios on his tray. We're still chanting, "Momma can see, Momma can see."

"Sharon, get the frying pan out," I say in between our gleeful squeals. I gather up two cans of diced tomatoes, a large onion, and a box of white rice. I get a very large red and an equally large yellow bell pepper, as well as a package of hot dogs, from the refrigerator. Since it's a special occasion, we'll have our absolute favorite: sliced hot dogs in our Spanish rice.

Momma comes into the kitchen to survey the dinner preparations. She has combed her hair and put on lipstick. I've moved the radio to the kitchen, and we're all laughing and singing along with the Andrew Sisters' "I Can Dream, Can't I?" There's a lot of noise and frivolity in our little apartment.

"Guess what's in my hands," I say to Momma, my hands behind my back.

"Peppers," she guesses.

I feel bold, like a new person—one who can joke with her mother. For a moment, I recapture the innocence and confidence of my early days, before the fight, when I was spontaneous and strong, verbal, and outgoing. That's how I still am at school. But for so long I've had two personalities: the school me and the home me. The home me has been mute—afraid to make the wrong move, to say something that triggers Momma's wrath. But here, this day, all that changes. I'm free and playful. I give my school personality, Strong Beverly, permission to appear at home.

"Close your eyes and hold out your hands," I say.

Momma obeys and squeezes her eyes shut.

I place the red bell pepper in her open palms. She smiles the biggest smile I've seen in a long time. Of course Momma knows immediately that this is a bell pepper, and she also knows that it's red. She learned to tell the difference years ago, when she was a teenager, as her sight was fast fading and she was preparing meals for her mother and siblings back in Warsaw, New York. She learned to differentiate the smell, the taste, and the size of the bitter green pepper from the sweeter and usually larger red pepper in the same way she found her way around the objects in her bedroom, bathroom, kitchen, and garden by using her senses of touch and smell and by storing all this information in pictures she created in her mind.

Momma plays along with me. She keeps her eyes closed as she gently cups the huge, five-inch-long pepper with her small hands. She rubs her fingertips up and down the ridges of the pepper, outlining each section, going from the bottom up to the stem each time, from the most-narrow to the widest part of the pepper. By the time Momma gets to the top of each section, it takes all of her fingers to grasp and cover the top lobe where the fleshy fruit blends into its firm stem. She moves her hands around the pepper in a methodical manner, in the same way she's touched our faces all these years.

When Momma's fingertips come to a little scar, she stops, outlines it, and pauses to gauge how long and deep it is. She uses her pinkie to trace the base of the stem, then brings the pepper up to her nose, inhaling its earthy essence. There's a big, satisfied grin on her face.

Sharon and I watch, intrigued. Ronnie's busy, playing with his Cheerios.

"I will guess that this is a big red pepper." Momma laughs, her eyes still closed.

Sharon and I whoop and holler. We clap our approval. Ronnie jumps up and down in his high chair and squeals. Cheerios dance through the air and bounce to the floor.

Momma opens her eyes to confirm her guess. But when she looks at the pepper, her hands tremble.

"Oh, my, it's *so* red! Oh, my." Momma's voice cracks. Her eyes are wide. She cries. We all quiet down.

"It's *so* red. It is *so* beautiful. Look at this, there's a little orange in the crease. And the stem is so green. Wow, it's so beautiful, it is so red," Momma says between her deep sobs. She holds the pepper up to see how the light shines off its vibrant skin.

Momma shows the pepper to Sharon and me as though she thinks we've never seen a red pepper before.

I look at the pepper. She's right. It *is* so red—a beautiful, vivid, deep red. And it has three major sections that I've never noticed before. The stem's brilliant green base is a five-pointed star that grabs on to the pepper's three sections. I, too, feel as if I'm seeing a red bell pepper for the first time.

We're so busy with the pepper that we don't see Ron Radzai sneaking up behind Momma. He grabs her around the waist and twirls her around into his arms. In an instant, I'm holding the red bell pepper. Momma and Ron Radzai kiss, dance around the kitchen, *inspect* each other, and laugh from deep in their bellies.

"Now that you've seen me, you'll probably run off with some handsome millionaire," Ron Radzai says.

Everyone laughs so hard we all cry. Sharon and I fall on the floor, double over in our crying-laughing spells. My joy collides with my pain, hidden deep within. I am so relieved that my real momma has returned, at last. I have a haunting feeling I'm being too optimistic. But I refuse to let my doubt dampen our jubilation, this moment of pure happiness with the mother of my dreams.

After a whole lot of carrying-on, we get back to fixing dinner. Momma doesn't want to, but she eventually cuts the beautiful red bell pepper in half. She has trouble lining up the knife right where she wants it. She has cut peppers all her life, but now that she can see the knife and the pepper, she has trouble coordinating her hands with her eyes. Over the coming weeks, she'll reach for various things and find that they're a few inches away from where she thought they were.

"Now I have to make my hands work with my new eye," Momma says, laughing. She keeps asking me, "Beverly, is this the way these peppers usually look? Is this the way the hotdogs should look?"

I'm still Momma's Seeing Eye Girl.

I'm so happy.

Momma cuts the peppers into strips. She sets our kitchen stool in front of the stove, and Sharon and Ronnie hop up and take turns tossing the pepper into the rice. Ron Radzai twists the can opener onto the first can of tomatoes, turning and turning until the lid pops free. He dumps the tomatoes into the rice, then opens the second can. He chops the onion, and I cut up the three hot dogs we'll add to the Spanish rice, making real thin slices so everyone will get several pieces.

Pretty soon, we have the most colorful dinner we've ever had: a pan of Spanish rice. As we eat, Momma talks non-stop about all the bright colors around us. She hasn't seen her own food, her clothes, her family, for over a decade now. And for a decade before that, much of what she saw was fuzzy and out of focus.

Momma is like a kid with a new toy. She stands in front of the mirror, staring at herself, at her hair, her face. She practices putting on lipstick and rouge. She smells and touches every-thing, like she used to, but now that she can use her eyes, at least her right eye, Momma narrates her new world, giving me a different perspective on the little things I've taken for granted.

Momma's a new person. I pray this Momma is here to stay.

• • •

Three weeks later, someone pounds on our door in the middle of the night, waking me up. Momma and I arrive in the living room about the same time. Red blinking lights bounce off our white walls.

Ron Radzai is at work. It's just Momma and us kids at home. She snaps on the wall light switch and opens the door.

Two police officers stand in the doorway.

"Are you Mrs. Alett Radzai?" one of the police officers asks.

Momma nods yes.

"We just received a call to take you to Jackson Memorial Hospital."

"Oh, no," Momma cries. "My baby is dead."

Mickey has been in the hospital for over a month now. He was there all the time Momma was in for her corneal transplant and has been so sick that the doctors have kept him there ever since.

"We don't know why," one of the officers says. "We were just asked to take you immediately to the hospital."

"I can't leave my kids here alone," Momma says.

"I can do it," I say.

The officer looks at me. "How old are you, young lady?"

"I'm nine."

"Okay," the officer says. "Mrs. Radzai, go change your clothes, get your purse, any medications you need, and let's go. Your daughter can take care of things here."

Momma does as she is told. After the police take her away, I lock up the house and check on Sharon and Ronnie. They're sleeping soundly. I get up early in the morning and write a note for Ron Radzai, who's not home from work yet. Then I fix cereal for the kids, get them dressed, and walk them over to daycare. I run to get to school on time.

All morning I wonder if Mickey died.

It's not until much later that day that Ron Radzai tells me what happened.

• • •

Dr. Palmer was waiting for Momma when the police officers delivered her to Jackson Memorial Hospital that evening.

"I'm going to operate on your left eye tonight," Dr. Palmer said.

"I can't do it," Momma said. "My kids are home alone."

"They'll get along without you for a while. You'd better take advantage of this chance. I don't know when another cornea will come along."

Mrs. Elsie Wagner had just died at Jackson Memorial. An Austrian refugee, and the only one in her family to survive the horrors of Nazi Germany, she'd been in the United States since the mid 1940s and was a volunteer nurse with the Red Cross. She had a brother who was blind, and she wanted to "repay" her new country for the good life she'd enjoyed here by donating her eyes to others.

Within hours of Mrs. Wagner's death, two corneal transplants were performed using her healthy corneas. Both recipients were rushed to Jackson Memorial in police squad cars. Dr. Palmer transplanted one of Mrs. Wagner's corneas onto Momma's left eye.

After her recovery from the second surgery, Dr. Palmer measured Momma's vision and said it was 20/20. She didn't even need to wear glasses.

• • •

"I'm going to return to my art work," Momma announces at dinner her first night home after the second surgery.

I'm excited about this plan. Momma will be happy once again, doing something she loves. It will be like the old days, when she and I laughed out loud as we smeared finger paints onto large sheets of art paper clipped to my easel.

Momma brings out her portfolio and spreads out the many drawings she did as a teenager before she totally lost her eyesight—mainly charcoal pencil drawings of beautiful women, dressed in a wide array of fashionable clothes. We each decide on our favorites. The girl in a party dress is my choice. Momma places Sharon's, Ronnie's, and my selections in gold-colored frames and hangs them in the living room.

"Will you draw me?" I ask.

"You will be my first model. I'll draw you sitting at the kitchen table."

• • •

Soon Momma is able to bring Mickey home from the hospital. She spends many hours cradling our ten-month-old baby in her arms and singing to him.

One day, Momma calls to me. She's in the living room, the baby in her arms, his spindly legs hanging limp on her chest, his oversize head cradled on her shoulder. "Look at the sky," she says. It's a clear, beautiful day. The sky is a deep, brilliant blue, the clouds puffy, glistening white as magnolia petals. The sun's rays splay out behind a billowing cloud, outlining it in shimmering gold and silver. The cloud is so bright I can hardly look at it.

"God is sending me a message," Momma says.

I place my hand on our baby's back. I know what the message is, and I am sad.

Momma has known the pain of death before. When she was only twelve, her beloved father, Levi, had a sudden cerebral hemorrhage and died, devastating his eight children and his wife, Flora, and changing the family dynamic forever. It was soon after her father's death that Momma's sore eyes became so sensitive to light that she confined herself to her darkened bedroom for two years, leaving school and her friends aside. Her father was the one who'd loved her most. She knew that soon she'd also lose her precious sight.

Now Momma has to face losing her own beloved baby boy. The doctors say there is nothing more they can do. All we can do is love on him. Sharon, Ronnie, and I sit on the floor near Momma, touch Mickey gently, and sing lullabies to him.

"You are a beautiful baby, Mickey," Momma repeats over and over, stroking his back.

Mickey dies in Momma's arms the next day, six weeks after her second surgery.

Chapter 8

THE PINK SKIRT

February 1951

"I pledge my head to clearer thinking, my heart to greater loyalty . . ." I say, my hand on my chest, at my after-school 4-H meeting. There are fifteen fourth-, fifth-, and sixth-grade girls in my group. Most of us would rather be in Girl Scouts, but 4-H is the only club available at Little River Elementary. So far, we've planted vegetable seeds in a boxed garden and plotted their growth on chart paper, made bread from scratch, and practiced setting the table for a formal dinner party.

"For our next big project, we're each going to make a skirt," the 4-H leader announces. "It's going to be completely handmade. We'll start at our next meeting in two weeks. I've placed the patterns for three different skirts on the table. Choose the one you'd like to make. For each skirt, there's a list of the materials you'll need to buy."

The pattern for the circle skirt consumes the most room on the table, and it also takes the most material of all three patterns. I don't like these poodle skirts that some of the older girls wear, and it is way too much cloth for a short girl like me. So I move along and look at the second pattern. It's for a loosely gathered skirt with a wide cloth waistband and a pocket on each side. This one might work. I like the way it looks, and the pockets are handy for tissues and erasers. I choose the third pattern, though. It's for a loosely gathered skirt with three bands of elastic at the waist. I don't have a skirt like this, but all my bloomers have elastic at the waist and I like the way the rubber holds everything in place.

Now that I've selected my pattern, the next trick is to get Momma to buy my supplies without reminding me that Dad doesn't support me and that I cost too much already. I need two yards of cloth, a matching spool of thread, a needle, and enough ¼-inch elastic to go around my waist three times.

After Sharon and I wash and put away the dinner dishes that evening, I whisper, "Let's do Red Riding Hood tonight."

"Oh, good," Sharon says. "I'll get our props ready."

Our repertoire includes a half-dozen fairy tales I've adapted for three actors. We perform most nights for an audience of two. Momma and Ron Radzai play gin rummy at the table while our enactments swirl around them in the kitchen. I'm the screenwriter, narrator, and director, Sharon is the stage manager and creative designer, and Ronnie is in charge of maintenance and sound effects. The door frame between the kitchen and living room defines our stage, and the adjoining wall provides ample cover to hide props, costumes, and actors. Sometimes we practice only a time or two in the bedroom before a new production, but we've done this one many times and even Ronnie knows his parts.

Sharon and Ronnie place a big, empty cardboard box on its side in a corner of the kitchen so that the opening faces away from the audience. Then they spread out a sheet on the floor near Ron Radzai's feet. The three of us disappear from the kitchen to get into our costumes and gather the rest of our props. It's now time to get into place for our evening show.

"Tonight, our feature performance is *Little Red Riding Hood*," I announce in a loud voice from my position in the center of the doorway.

"Ronnie plays Grandmother and the Hunter." Ronnie enters, takes a bow, lies down on the sheet and wraps it up around his body.

"Sharon is the Wolf." Sharon peeks her head into the kitchen.

At last, I say, "Beverly is Little Red Riding Hood."

Momma and Ron Radzai clap and continue playing cards.

"One day, Little Red Riding Hood goes off through the woods to bring a treat to her grandmother," I say. My long-sleeved red shirt, tied around my neck, drapes across my back like a cape. I hold up my lunch bag in my left hand so the audience can see that I'm carrying Grandmother's treat.

"She stops to pick some flowers for her grandmother." I bend over, picking invisible blossoms. "Who does she meet? It's Mr. Wolf." I point to the doorway.

From stage right, the Wolf ambles in on all fours. Sharon wears a brown towel safety-pinned around her neck. The towel covers her back and hangs down over her legs and arms. She stops and looks up at Little Red Riding Hood.

"Where are you going?" the Wolf asks.

"To see my grandmother in that cottage." Red Riding Hood points toward the sleeping grandmother. The Wolf moves off stage but slinks back in the door, low to the floor, trying to be invisible, as she moves toward the cottage. Red Riding Hood turns her back and continues picking flowers. Before you know it, the Wolf is inside the house. She grabs Grandmother.

"No, no," hollers Grandmother.

The Wolf drags Grandmother across the floor and into the cardboard box. Then the Wolf climbs into bed and draws the sheet up to her neck.

Little Red Riding Hood completes her flower-picking and walks to the cottage. She opens the door and stands at her grandmother's bedside. "Oh, Grandmother, you look strange," she says. "What big eyes you have."

"The better to *see* you with," the Wolf says.

"What a big mouth you have."

"The better to *eat* you with," the Wolf shouts, jumps out of bed, and lunges at Little Red Riding Hood, who raises her arms, backs up, and screams.

All of a sudden, the Hunter (Ronnie) appears, center stage, holding a weapon (my baton) up in the air. The Hunter raises the baton and pretends to strike the Wolf. The Wolf drops over dead, all four legs up in the air. Ron Radzai and Momma laugh.

"Little Red Riding Hood, Grandmother, and the Hunter lived happily ever after. The end," I say.

Sharon jumps up and grabs Ronnie's hand, and I grab his other hand. We stand in the doorway and bow deeply.

Momma and Ron Radzai laugh, put their cards down, and clap. The actors grab the props and run off stage, squealing all the way to the bedroom.

"Good job," I say to Ronnie and Sharon, giving each of them a big hug. I grab the list of supplies for my new skirt and race back to the kitchen, my red cape bobbing across my back.

"I'm going to make a skirt in 4-H," I say, out of breath. I hand the list to Momma. "Here's what I need."

"Can you get this stuff for her?" Momma passes the list over to Ron Radzai.

"What color do you want?" he asks, not looking up from his cards.

"I don't care," I say. "Choose a color you like."

They return to their card game.

I exhale and hurry back to the bedroom to congratulate my actors on a job well done. Attending a play always puts people in a good mood. I lay back on my mattress and smile. Being an actress is good for your soul.

. . .

The next day after school, a flat paper bag is atop my pillow. I sit on the mattress and stare at the green label on the bag, the big flourish of an R announcing the Richards name. Some of the older girls talk about this large department store downtown where the rich people shop. I rub my hand across the label and pick up the bag. I clutch it to my chest for the longest time. Finally, I open the bag and slide out a bundle of soft pink fabric, a spool of pink thread, a package of three needles, and a wad of pink elastic, enough to go around my waist three times. I run my hands over the rubbery polka-dots, each about the size of a Boston Baked Bean, that playfully adorn the pink cotton. I finger the dots—first the blues, then the greens, finally the reds. I lie back on my bed and drape the material over my chest. Then I bring it up to my face. I smell it. I hug it.

Then, I sob.

This is the first nice thing Ron Radzai has done for me since he became my stepfather some three years ago. Images of the fight linger in my mind. The Blond Man. The blood. The screaming.

But the Blond Man bought all my supplies as soon as I asked. He selected a lovely piece of fabric and took care to match the thread, and even the elastic. I imagine him in the fabrics section of the department store. Perhaps he saw flowered material but thought, *She already has a flowered skirt.* Then he fingered a striped bolt of cloth and said, "That wouldn't look good on her." Finally, he picked up this gorgeous pink material and perhaps he said, "That's perfect. It's just the right color and the polka dots are unusual, just like she is."

He found a girly pink, not just an ordinary color. A pink with character—the polka dots, raised off the cotton, scattered about in a playful, spontaneous way. He picked this out just for me, his stepchild. I wonder if Ron Radzai cares for me, if he thinks of me as his child.

What color would my real dad have selected for me? My memory of him blurs more each year. It's hard for me to remember the details of his face. I run my fingers across my eyebrows and over my chin, but it's difficult to imagine how a tall, dark, Italian man would look with my chin. Momma has hidden all the photos of our Yonkers family, so I depend on the fading pictures in my mind to know if I actually do see him in the crowds on the street.

Swinging at the park, walking hand in hand, reading stories at bedtime, and feeling his tender hand on my shoulder—these memories of Dad comfort me. Ron Radzai never does any of these things with Ronnie. I've never seen him dress Ronnie or play with him. He seldom talks at all. I wonder if he'd like to read a story to his son at bedtime or toss him up in the air, tickle him, and make him laugh out loud. He never looks directly at Sharon or me. I wonder if he's sorry he beat up Dad.

I guess I can forgive him, especially now that he's given me this beautiful pink gift.

He'll be proud of the skirt I make.

Chapter 9

THE SPELLING BEE

April 1951

"Get up, Beverly," Momma says. "We need to do the laundry today." She kneels beside my mattress, rocking my arm back and forth.

We usually do the wash on Saturdays, but today is Friday. It's time for me to get up to go to school, not do the laundry. This is the first time in all my years at school I have had perfect attendance. I plead with Momma to let me go to school—not just for my attendance record, but because today is the big spelling bee.

"Momma, I'm the spelling champion at school and today's the county spelling bee. I have to go to school. My teachers depend on me."

"I depend on you too," she insists. "We need to do the wash today."

I know not to argue with her; that will make matters worse. Trouble is, I don't know what else to say that will convince Momma I have to go to school. I tell her I'll do the wash right after school. I tell her that I beat everyone at Little River in the spelling bee and I'm the one going on to the county contest. But she isn't going to hear of it. She's determined the wash is going to happen today, and that's that. I try to use logic to negotiate with her, but she's not going to change her plan. There's no good reason why the clothes have to be cleaned today. But that doesn't matter. She wants them clean. That's all there is to it.

I suppose I could defy her—dress and just leave for school. I'll not do that. It's not in me to disobey Momma. I never have. I won't start now. Plus, by now, I'm afraid of her. I know the consequences. They're worse than staying home from school.

I know I have to do the wash, but I don't have to be happy about missing school and the spelling bee. For the rest of the morning, I do what I am told. But I don't say a word to Momma.

I've gotten used to the silence in our home. In some ways, I find it comforting. The silence is a huge void that allows me to retreat to the worlds of my books and my daydreams.

There's a fragile tipping point between silence and Momma's rage, triggered by the wrong look, the wrong word, the wrong tone of voice. Sometimes, though, it's nothing that Sharon or Ron Radzai or I do or say, just something that happens in Momma's mind. Those are the most frightening times because I don't anticipate the chaos, the screaming, and the beatings that have come to fill our lives. Anticipation doesn't help much, but it does allow me a moment to steel myself against what happens next. It is never good, so I've learned how to placate Momma, tiptoe around, do what needs to be done, and stay out of the way. I've learned how to lie, how to tell her what she wants to hear. Most days even I believe the half-truths that easily come out of my mouth.

When Momma had her sight restored, I had this fantasy that my Yonkers Momma had returned. That notion was short-lived. Soon after Mickey's death, the pinching, biting, and cursing once again filled our Victory Homes apartment. Today, I know I am one word away from a beating, so after a quick shredded wheat breakfast, I get started on the wash.

I know my teachers will be upset that I'm not in school. Everyone at Little River is excited about the spelling bee, and I intended to be the county winner. I prepared for this day and now I feel like I've been pushed off a cliff. But I don't know what else I can do. So I do what Momma wants me to do.

First, I separate the white clothes from the dark ones and make two big mounds on the floor near the washer. I get up on a stool, put the dirty white clothes in the Maytag tub, and add the soap. That's the easy part. While the clothes wash, I sit on the floor, my back against the vibrating tub, and read *The Three Musketeers* by Alexandre Dumas, my recent selection from the school library. I'm about twenty pages in and I've lost track of the plot even though I can pronounce all the words. Being the spelling champ has gone to my head.

After the clothes slog around, I get back up on my stool, hang my body over the side of the washer, and grab a corner of a sheet. I pull it up out of the tub, wring it out by hand, squeezing out the suds and water. I drop the sheet into the tub of clear water I've put on the floor, then squat over the shiny, silver metal tub, pushing the sheet through the hot water. The clean white cloth billows up. The soapy bubbles turn into rainbows, the cloth a parachute I'll use to fly far away.

Water drips everywhere, down my chest and all over the floor. I thread the sheet through the wringer at the top of the washer and it does the rest of the work. The gray, cloudy water runs back into the washer. The sheet becomes a long, flat board that I fold into a white plastic basket. Once it's full, I lug the basket to the side yard, bumping it up and down against my belly with each step. We have four long clotheslines that stretch from the house to the six-foot-tall chain-link fence that separates us from the railroad tracks.

• • •

There are no trains to keep me company today but I can make them appear in my mind. Their mournful sounds in the distance lull me to sleep at night, and their clanging bells jolt me awake each morning. I wait every year for the long, slow circus trains to arrive. That's when the fence makes tic-tac-toe games on my body as I catch the smells of the elephants and horses that precede the stock cars and hang in the air long after the caboose passes. Performers wave to me from their ornate orange, red, and yellow coaches that announce the Ringling Bros. and Barnum & Bailey Circus.

Children jump up and down in their seats and holler, "Come, come with us!"

I'm so close to the train I can look into their eyes. I shout back, "What's your name? Where are you going?"

It would be easy to climb over the fence. I could grab one of the children's hands, swing onto the slow-moving train, and join the circus. I could be a trapeze artist and turn somersaults high above everyone's head. I'd soar from one high wire to another. Or I'd ride one of the handsome horses in my bright crimson and gold costume, my long brown hair flying in the wind. All the people would stand up and cheer. I'd bow deeply and wave to the crowd. Then I'd help the other kids pack up the train, and we'd be off to the next city.

When the long train passes, I lean back into the fence, savoring the last sights and sounds. I never actually go to a circus, but that's all right. I have my own private performance right here at Victory Homes.

• • •

I'm on a stool, pinning a sheet to the clothesline, when two women come to the front screen door. I recognize them; they are the teachers who supervise the school spelling bee. My heart pounds so fast, I think I'm going to suffocate. I'm in trouble. I run into the house just as Momma invites them into the living room. They look around for a place to sit.

The younger teacher is short and thin, with curly, long blonde hair, heart-shaped red lips, and a small button nose. She's crisp in a white blouse with puckered, capped sleeves, a full blue skirt, and sandals. She sits on the Florida Oranges crate and her lacy white crinoline pops up into her lap. The sunbeam coming through the front window lights up her face.

The older teacher is tall, with shoulder-length brown hair that rests on the white collar of her tan, blue, and rust-colored striped dress, cinched with a wide white belt at her petite waist. The front of her dress is all buttoned up to her neck. She sits in one of the two upholstered chairs in the living room.

My wet bloomers and halter top cling to my body. I slink into the living room, look down at the floor, and avoid looking at the teachers or at my mother. I rock back and forth on my bare feet and clasp my hands in front of me. I'd like to disappear.

It's time to start talking to Jesus.

Momma sits in the other Goodwill chair. She lights up a Lucky Strike. "Would you like a cup of coffee?" she asks the teachers. She pats her rounded stomach, bulging under her skirt with our new baby; she's five months pregnant. She smiles at the teachers and tells them how much I help her around the house, especially now that she has her sight back and is so busy with her art lessons.

"I've only had my eyesight for one year now, and I'm working on the Famous Artists School lessons," Momma says. She points to her bedroom, where her art table and easel are set up and where she's been drawing all morning while I've been doing the wash.

"We need Beverly to come to school today," the older teacher says to Momma. "She's the best speller in our school, and we need her to represent us in the Dade County spelling bee."

"Oh, I didn't know there was a spelling bee today," Momma says.

I stop rocking and stand perfectly still. The young teacher looks straight at me. Our eyes meet and hold for the longest time. She knows what's going on here. I feel safe in her presence, even protected, if only for a moment.

"Be not forgetful to entertain strangers, for thereby some have entertained angels unawares." Hebrews 13:2 (King James Version), one of my favorite Bible verses, repeats in my head.

"Beverly is the only student representing Little River Elementary School," the blonde teacher says. "She beat out all the other students at our school, even the fifth and sixth graders. She'll compete against the spelling bee winners from all the other elementary schools in the county. She can come back to school with us, and we'll take her to the contest this afternoon. We'll bring her back home after it's all over. I know you must be so proud of Beverly." She's my new heroine.

Momma turns to me. She takes a long drag of her cigarette and blows out three smoke rings that hang in the air, awaiting the verdict.

"Go clean up and put on your Sunday dress," she says.

My heart pounds with joy. I rush to the bathroom, wash up, and put on my plaid dress with the round white collar and my newly polished black-and-white saddle shoes. My clothes were waiting for me right where I laid them out last night.

• • •

Strong Beverly is a winner today.

The blonde teacher takes me to the area high school, where we check in with the other fifty spelling bee contestants, mostly fifth and sixth graders. I slip a big sign over my head. It has my name, school name, and contest number on it.

The blonde teacher and I walk on stage to find my seat. She places her hands on my shoulders, and looks me straight in my eyes, "You can do this, Beverly. You are a terrific speller. Stay calm, go slowly. Get a picture of the word in your mind before you start to spell it. You will do a great job." Then she takes a seat in the front row so she can see the big, happy, confident smile on my face.

The contest goes fast. Kids misspell one word after another. Soon, there are just ten contestants on stage. I'm one of them.

"Chauffeur," the judge says.

"Chauffeur," I repeat.

"The chauffeur drives us to the spelling bee," the judge says.

"Chauffeur," I say. "C-h-a-u-f-f-e-u-r. Chauffeur."

"Correct."

The blonde teacher gives me a huge smile and a thumbs-up. I'm going to win this contest.

After several more rounds, there are only four of us left on stage.

"Archaeology."

"Archaeology," I repeat.

"The archaeology professor shows his class some human bones."

"Archaeology," I say. "A-r-c-h-e-o-l-o-g-y. Archaeology."

All of a sudden, everything in the room moves in slow motion. The lady sitting next to the judge picks up her right hand and holds it over the bell. My eyes burn. Before I know what is happening, the blonde teacher is beside me. She puts her arms around my shoulders and escorts me off the stage.

"You were outstanding," she says. "Everyone at Little River will be so proud. You were one of the final contestants. Good for you. I am very proud of you, Beverly. You were fearless."

"Fearless?"

"Yes. You were one of the youngest and smallest contestants. But you were not afraid. You just got up there and did your best. You out-spelled most of them. Confident. Brave. Promise me you'll always be fearless."

"I promise, I'll be fearless," I tell my teacher. I don't tell her I can't be fearless all the time. Only at school.

• • •

Momma is fixing dinner when I arrive home. I change out of my good clothes, and Momma tells me to set the table and make up a plate for each of us kids. There's no talk about the laundry, the teachers, the spelling bee, or my staying home from school.

"Did you win?" Momma asks me right before bedtime.

I want to tell Momma, *I was fearless*. But I don't.

Chapter 10

MOMMA IS FAMOUS

By the time Momma has our sunshine baby in August of 1951, she's on the brink of fame. Michael Dennis is the first of her five children she's been able to see at birth. Nevertheless, she runs her hands all over his face, just like she did with me. She learns as much about his features by touch as with her new eyes. We call him Mikey so we don't confuse him with *the baby who died*, Mickey.

Aside from having a normal-size head and chubby legs, Mikey looks a lot like Mickey: bald, with milk-white skin. He's a healthy, good-humored, happy baby who loves to eat and smile. I'm glad to have another little one in the house, because that means I have diapers to change and formula to heat. Even though Momma can see now, we line up all the baby food jars and organize our linen closet just like we did when she was blind. It's still my job to keep everything in its place.

• • •

"I'm calling from the New York Lighthouse for the Blind," the man on the phone says to Momma a few weeks after Mikey is born. "We at the Lighthouse are launching our two-and-a-half-million-dollar fundraiser. We would be honored if you'd serve as a volunteer. We hope you'll agree to help us out. The Lighthouses sponsor surgeries like yours all around the country. We want to expand the work of great doctors like Dr. Bascom Palmer."

That's all Momma needed to hear. If it weren't for Dr. Palmer and the Florida Lighthouse, Momma would still be blind and would be only imagining drawing again. The Florida Lighthouse paid for Momma's surgeries and gave her a Famous Artists' Home Correspondence Course so she could develop her talent and become a commercial artist. It was Momma's course application that caught the eye of Al Dorne, one of the artists who, along with Norman Rockwell, started the Famous Artists course.

"During my time in darkness, I bore four children, made most of their clothes and delayed my dream of becoming an artist," Momma writes. "Thanks to Dr. Bascom Palmer and two selfless cornea donors, I can now see. I can see my children and my husband, and I can return to my art and to the career I always dreamed of having."

In August 1951, the Famous Artists featured Momma's story in their newsletter. From there, one thing quickly led to another. Newspaper reporters around the country wrote stories about Momma, her successful corneal transplants, and her remarkable life story.

Now the New York Lighthouse for the Blind has a plan, a way she can help others see. They want her to appear on several popular radio and television quiz shows produced in New York City. She'll be a specially invited guest, there to raise money for the Lighthouse. She'll tell her personal story as the "hook" to winning over the audience. The more audiences like her, the more prize money she'll earn for the Lighthouse. She won't keep any of the money for herself.

That's fine with Momma. This is a chance to spread her story and win the adoration of viewers. This will be Momma at her best: she loves to have an audience. She's poised, eloquent, and has an inspiring story to tell, one she tells with emotion and animation. She loves the idea and spreads the word to Mrs. Kinnard and to all our neighbors at Victory Homes.

• • •

In the early summer of 1952, Momma and Ron Radzai leave me in charge of the kids and go to New York City for ten days. Sharon's seven, Ronnie's four, and baby Michael is almost a year old. I've babysat before, many times. I know just what to expect, and I'm not looking forward to the responsibility.

It's easy to take care of Mikey: feed him, give him a bath, get him dressed, put him in the playpen. That's a cinch. Ronnie and Sharon, though, are another matter. As soon as Momma and Ron Radzai leave, they are wild. They run through the house, scream, and wrestle each other. I sit on whichever one is on top of the heap, pull on arms and legs to disentangle them. The only way I can get their attention is to become my mother. I smack them. They cry and hit me back. It's a madhouse. I don't want to hit them, but I don't know what else to do. I don't know how I'm going to do this for ten days.

Momma appears on a blitz of radio and television programs, including *We the People*, *It's News to Me*, *Broadway to Hollywood*, and *Strike It Rich*. On each program, she tells her story, and money pours in for the Lighthouse Association. Television is *the* most popular household product in the 1950s, and quiz shows are popular for their voyeuristic opportunities. Viewers enjoy peeking in on the lives of contestants. Many of the shows feature people who are down on their luck and have risked their savings to get to New York, stand in line, and pray they'll be selected as a contestant.

Of course, we don't have a television. There's only one

neighbor who does. She invites us in to watch *Strike It Rich*, so I get the kids ready and we march over to sit on the floor in front of the neighbor's fifteen-inch black-and-white Zenith television.

"Look, there's Momma!" I point at the screen, trying to get Ronnie's attention. He's wandering around the neighbor's living room. Mikey is sprawled across my lap, and Sharon is sitting on the floor beside me. Several of the neighbors sit behind us, their kids also roaming through the tiny home.

Warren Hull, the emcee, has randomly picked a few women out of the large studio audience. "I'm pleased to introduce our special guest, Mrs. Alett Radzai," he says. "She's here as a spokesperson for the New York Lighthouse for the Blind. I can't wait for you to hear her inspiring story. Mrs. Radzai, come on out."

All the neighbors clap when Momma walks onto the stage. She looks pretty in her tight black sweater, tucked into a full flowered skirt that hits her legs mid-calf. In spite of her inch-and-a-half heels, she's the shortest person on the stage.

Strike It Rich is a show of woe. All the contestants have a sad story to tell. One woman tells about not having enough money for a life-saving operation; another has a husband who can't find work and the family's about to be kicked out of their apartment. Then it's Momma's turn.

"Before I went completely blind at age eighteen, I liked to draw and hoped one day to be an artist," she says. "During my ten years in darkness, I had four children, made most of their clothes, and took care of the family. Then I met Dr. Bascom Palmer, who said I was a good candidate for a new technique called the corneal transplant. In 1950, he took the cornea from a living donor and transplanted it onto my right eye. I was so lucky. Soon, Dr. Palmer had a second cornea for me and operated on my left eye. My vision is now 20/20. The Florida Lighthouse for the Blind paid all my medical expenses. I can now see my family and resume my art career. I am so thankful. The Lighthouse and Dr. Palmer can help more people like me if we help them raise money."

The audience roars. Women have tears in their eyes. A man in the audience jumps up and shouts, "I'm so impressed by this woman's story that I will personally write a check to the Lighthouse so that she can keep her prize money."

People love Momma's story. She performs like an actress on this big stage right in the heart of New York City. Like me, she has her public and private personalities. On the stage, she is confident, capable, vivacious, eloquent, calm, poised; in private, she is silent or full of rage. The people in the audience wouldn't recognize her at home, wouldn't believe this is the same woman who beats and curses her daughter and is angry much of the time.

After he sees Momma on television, Robert C. Ruark, author and syndicated columnist, interviews her and writes an article, "Gift of Sight Restored," that appears in many local newspapers around the country (including the *Buffalo Courier Express*, September 21, 1952). He ends his column: "I went away into the rain thinking what a wonderful thing it is that a woman can be blind for ten years—and then, due to the marvel of modern medicine, not only can see her visually unknown family, but entertain again the hope of being an artist."

Ruark's article and the public's interest in Momma generated by the television shows result in many more newspaper articles. It's this publicity that leads to the major magazine features that are in the planning stages as Momma wraps up the television shows in New York City.

Before she leaves the Northeast, there is one more important stop to make: Westport, Connecticut, the home of the Famous Artists' School. There, something happens that will change our lives forever.

Al Dorne, one of the most prolific and popular illustrators of the time, and one of the founders of the Famous Artists' School, takes a particular interest in Momma. He has his own rags-to-riches story, plus a solid reputation, one he would not jeopardize lightly. He thinks Momma exemplifies the American Dream. She has that same spunk, that spark, that he sees in himself. He identifies with her and predicts that she will become a successful commercial artist in three years if she works hard at her lessons.

Dorne suggests that the Radzai family relocate to the Stamford, Connecticut, area so that Momma can study directly with him and the other famous artists. He tells Momma that they'll help Ron get a job at the Pitney-Bowes factory in Stamford and that they should come as soon as possible so we children can begin school at the start of the new academic year.

• • •

"We're moving to Connecticut," Momma announces when she and Ron Radzai return from their long trip. The huge smile on Momma's face and her very good mood tell me she's excited about our move and optimistic about her new life. "You kids can start bagging up your clothes and toys right away."

"But school starts in a week," I say. I'm looking forward to being in sixth grade and seeing all my friends and old teachers at Little River Elementary. I can't believe we're moving. I'm not interested in this idea. Where is Connecticut, anyway? I hurry to find a map.

"We'll wait to register for school until we get settled in our new home," Momma says. "You and Sharon will just miss a few weeks of school. We have some things to do here before we can leave. We're going to have two special visitors next week. A reporter and a photographer from *Woman's Home Companion* magazine will be here all week, taking photos and interviewing me. Once they leave, we'll pack up and head to our new home in Connecticut."

The next day, Momma gets a call from *Mademoiselle* magazine. They have named her "Homemaker of the Year" for 1952 and want her to send them a photograph and approve the citation they'll print in their January 1953 issue, in which the merit awards will be highlighted. They read the information to Momma over the phone: "Housewife Alett Radzai was a promising art student before she became totally blind at eighteen. During the ten sightless years following, her indomitable spirit created a normal family life—she married, raised four children, did the sewing, cleaning, cooking herself since money was scarce. Now, her sight restored by corneal transplants, she has seen her husband for the first time and resumed her commercial art studies. A top commercial artist stakes his career on her making good in three years."

"Oh, yes, I approve that," Momma says.

• • •

The same day that school starts in Miami is the day Stanley Frank, the writer, and Joseph DiPietro, the photographer, show up at our front door. These two men make me laugh so hard I just about forget about school. They interview Momma and take hundreds of photographs at home and outside in the yard. I get to be in most of the photos. The best part is that I'm wearing my pink skirt the day Mr. DiPietro takes us to Food Fair. We recreate scenes of my reading chicken soup labels to Momma. She tells the men, "Before surgery restored my sight, I'd do my shopping with Beverly, who led me along the aisles, kept me from bumping into people, told me what was on sale. Beverly was my Seeing Eye."

We go back home and Mr. DiPietro takes more photos, one of me changing Mikey's diaper, another of me serving dinner to Ronnie. Sometimes we all laugh so much he has to take the photo several times to get one he likes. Back when we lived in Yonkers, Sharon and I posed for photographs every six months, but this is the first time since then that we've been professionally photographed. We are all smiles.

Momma's in a great mood. She doesn't pinch or smack me in front of company and even when the men leave for the evening, she's happy. The week goes by too quickly. The men tell us that the article will appear in their upcoming January issue. By then we'll be settled in our new school and our new home in Stamford.

Now it's time to get ready to head north to Connecticut, where Momma will fulfill her dream.

She'll become a great artist.

Chapter 11

IN PURSUIT OF THE DREAM

September 1952

Everything we own is in the car. The trunk of our 1951 beige Chrysler New Yorker—bought, in part, with money Momma won on *Strike It Rich*—is full of blankets, dishes, toys, baby supplies, and clothes. Momma's paintbrushes, oils, pastels, charcoal pencils, drawing paper, and completed lessons for the Famous Artists' School course are carefully packed, the white box nuzzled into a stack of sheets and towels. Her art table and easel, the most important things of all, are disassembled and the pieces lie on top of everything else.

"Hurry up, you girls," Momma hollers from the living room.

"I don't want to go to Stamford," Sharon whispers.

"Me either," I whisper back.

We're sitting on the mattress in our bedroom, chins in palms, elbows on knees, staring at our oak dresser. We wear matching blue-and-white-striped bloomer shorts and triangle halter-top sets. It's only been a few days since Joseph DiPietro and Stanley Frank left town and took our laughter and joy with them.

"Go through the drawers one more time and make sure we have everything," I tell Sharon. I get up and check the closet for the tenth time. "It's going to be okay," I reassure her. "Come on. The sooner we get there, the sooner we'll go back to school." It's hard to maintain my role as big sister when I'm so sad myself, but I have a special responsibility to watch over Sharon and I take it seriously. After all, I'm trying to convince myself that moving is a good idea.

"Hurry up—we're leaving," Momma shouts.

Sharon and I run out of the house and scramble into the backseat. As the oldest, my place is in the middle, to keep the peace between Sharon and Ronnie and to serve as the conduit between the front and back seats, the easiest transfer point for food and the baby. All our clothing and food are in bags on the floor and on the back-window shelf. I straddle my legs over the hump and nestle my right foot on a sack of clean diapers, my left on a bag of groceries. Momma hands a chubby, sleeping Mikey to me. Every inch of the backseat is taken up by us kids, six bare legs glued together by sweat and the anxiety of what's ahead. Our baby, sprawled across my lap, is oblivious to it all.

"Give our furniture to some other family who needs it," Momma tells Mrs. Kinnard, who's come over to see us off. We're leaving everything here: the chairs, tables, mattresses, dressers, sofa, and lamps. Most of it was given to us by local churches or various social service agencies. We're also leaving the grocery crates. I'm sure the Famous Artists will have a furnished apartment ready for us once we arrive.

"We'll miss you," Mrs. Kinnard says. She hangs her head in Momma's window and blows kisses back toward us kids. We laugh and blow kisses at her and the neighbors who cluster around the car, waving and shouting, "Good luck." With all the excitement, I think moving might be a good thing, after all. But I already miss my friends, teachers, school, and my church here in Miami.

"Mr. Dorne says we'll have a better life in Stamford," Momma reminds Mrs. Kinnard why we're leaving Victory Homes. "I'll continue my art lessons with him. Thank you for everything." She reaches out the window to give Mrs. Kinnard a final hug and kiss.

Ron Radzai guides the long Chrysler out of Victory Homes, past the playground with my favorite monkey bars, past Little River Baptist Church with its deep baptismal pool I never got into, and past my magical Little River Elementary, with all my angel teachers, the grassy courtyard, James Lashe, and all my other friends. It's early in the afternoon, about the time my classmates would be in science class, with the sixth grade teacher I'll never meet. That funny twitch starts in the bridge of my nose but I fight back my tears. *We're going to have a better life*, I keep telling myself. In any case, if I wake the baby, I'll never keep the backseat quiet.

I'll just put something new in my mind. I roll my tongue around my mouth. When it rests on one of the empty spots, I think of the dentist who comes to Little River every four months or so to inspect each child, looking for rotten teeth. Like most of the other kids from the project, I've never gone to a dentist. Many of us have adult teeth that have gone bad. The school dentist has only one solution for me when he finds a bad tooth: he gives me a numbing shot, pulls the tooth, puts a big cotton roll in the empty spot, and sends me back to class.

I stick my tongue through the four holes in my mouth, one for each of my years at Little River. Pulling teeth instead of saving them has lasting effects on Housing Project kids, including me. A good deed gone sour.

Ron Radzai turns onto US Route 1, our two-lane path along the Atlantic Ocean coastline. Some 1,400 miles later, we'll be in a different home and settled into a new life. I try to imagine my new school and my teacher: what she'll look like, what I'll learn, how well I'll do in her class. The windows of the Chrysler are all down, the wing windows cracked. The hot Miami breeze kicks up the temperature of the sauna inside the car. Momma's Lucky Strike smoke goes out one window, back in another; the tobacco haze fills the car. I squirm under Mikey's weight, his wet diaper and sweat-soaked body, trying out subtle variations on the placement of my feet and legs. It's 1952—there are no disposable diapers, seat belts, air conditioning, or interstates. Of course, we don't know about such things, so we don't miss them. Even so, I know this is going to be a very long trip.

We've traveled on Route 1 before. In June of 1951, a few months before Mikey was born, we made our way to Warsaw, New York, for one of the Robinson family reunions. Momma hadn't seen her mother or siblings since she ran away from home in 1940 to marry Dad. But now that Momma's photo was in even the Warsaw newspapers, alongside the story of her miraculous corneal transplants and her great artistic talent, she'd become a local celebrity and was welcomed back into the loving arms of her family as if nothing had ever torn them apart.

The car's more crowded for this trip; this time we're not coming back to Miami and now we have Mikey, sound asleep on my lap. Everyone inside the car is quiet, lost in our own thoughts, until Momma passes peanut butter and jelly sandwiches to us. For the time it takes to eat the sandwiches, we spring to life. Before long, though, everyone in the backseat is asleep except me.

I count cows until they disappear into the darkness. Our headlights illuminate the billboards and the red signs that pop up every mile or so. *Violets are blue/Roses are pink/On graves/Of those/Who drive and drink/Burma-Shave.* That's funny. Before long, there's another, and then another. I play a game with myself and try to figure out what the next red sign is going to say. *The ladies/Take one whiff/And purr . . ./It's no wonder/Men prefer/Burma-Shave Lotion.*

Welcome to Georgia.

Ron Radzai speeds up, passes a slow-moving car, and ducks back into our lane just as the headlights of the oncoming car blind me. I cringe and think we're all going to die on the way to our new and improved life. My stomach cramps, and my body aches. There's a sharp knife in the pit of my belly. I transfer Mikey to Sharon's lap, groan my way onto the hump, and push my fists into my stomach.

"What's wrong with you?" Momma asks.

"I'm sick. My stomach's killing me. I think I have to throw up."

"Use these. We're not going to stop." Momma passes me a handful of paper towels.

Ron Radzai announced before we left that we'd drive through the night and only stop for gas breaks. During the morning rush-hour, we'll park in a rest area so he can sleep for a few hours. Then we'll be back on the road. Those are the rules, no matter what emergencies may arise. He says we'll be in Connecticut in two days.

• • •

When we finally stop what seems like hours later, all of us kids and Momma follow the urine stench into the gas station bathroom.

I use the toilet first. What's this brown stuff on my underpants?

"I'm bleeding," I whimper.

Momma comes into the stall, inspects me, and says, "You have your period. You are now a lady."

She goes out to the car and comes back with one of her sanitary napkins.

"Put this in your pants," she tells me. "And stop crying, you bitch."

The pad's big and clumsy. I walk bow-legged out to the car. By the time I get settled in the backseat, it's made its way up to my waistband. I stick my hand into my bloomers and pull the pad back to my crotch. I have no idea what's happening to me. No one's told me about becoming a lady.

As we drive on in the dark, I remember some of the older girls at Little River whispering about something out in the courtyard. About pain and napkins. So this is what they were talking about. I don't know if being a lady is a good thing or not. And I don't want to think about it right now. All I want is to get out of this car and into my new school. And get rid of this awful ache in my belly.

• • •

We arrive in Stamford late the next night. Ron Radzai parks in an empty lot, leans his head back, closes his eyes. Momma curls up across the front seat and lays her head on his lap, lovey-dovey-like. During the drive, she scooted close to him and put her arm across his shoulders.

Momma and Ron Radzai have made this trip in virtual silence. That's nothing new. They are silent most of the time at home. Only now, instead of playing gin rummy, they're driving into the unknown. He's going to a new job and she to a new career. She'll have the opportunity of a lifetime: studying with some of the country's best commercial artists with the hope that she'll become one too. It should be an exciting time for them. But it's hard to know just what they're thinking and feeling. They show little emotion, excitement, or anticipation of what's ahead. Since they seldom talk out loud to one another, I assume they have a secret communication code. Maybe they send messages with their tender touches, like they're doing now.

Whatever their feelings, they keep them to themselves. Is Ron Radzai looking forward to his new job? Will Momma take lessons directly with some of the top artists like Norman Rockwell, Al Dorne? I don't know. There's no talk about what will happen once we arrive. Is there a place for us to live, just awaiting our arrival? They haven't told us kids, so I expect everything's been arranged. What planning they've done, I'm sure, has been done in the quiet of their bedroom, not in front of us. Right now, I have no reason to doubt that they have a plan in mind. I only hope that the promise of *a better life* means Momma will be happy and return to her good-natured Yonkers self. That will make my life better. Aside from that, I just want to get back to school.

• • •

At daybreak, Ron Radzai pulls the Chrysler into a gas station and fills it up. The rest of us trudge over to the bathroom. I smell bad and need a bath, but a few quick splashes at the sink will have to do. Momma gives me a new napkin, and I stuff it in my panties, wash out Mikey's bottle, and fill it with formula while Momma combs her hair, puts on fresh lipstick, and smoothes the wrinkles out of her blouse and shorts. She buys a local newspaper and two steaming cups of coffee, and we all climb into the car. Momma hands me a jar of baby food, then opens a tin of Vienna sausages. We each get one. Breakfast.

When Momma turns to the Apartments for Lease want ads and reads the possibilities out loud to Ron Radzai, I begin to worry about *the plan*. Ron Radzai says "good" after each listing and Momma writes the phone number and address on her pad. Then she finds the streets on the local map that's spread on her lap. I've never heard Ron Radzai say "no" to Momma, or "I'm not going to do that," or "I don't like that idea," or even "Why don't we do this?" He goes along with everything she suggests, like I do. I wonder if he does this to placate Momma, to keep her in a good mood—to keep the peace, like I do.

We're off to find ourselves a new place to live. I'm about to get my first glimpse of Stamford.

• • •

We drive down wide, tree-lined streets. Large homes, set far back from the street and sidewalks, rise up like castles at the horizon, framed by huge, neatly trimmed, grassy lawns. Multi-colored flowers bow their smiling faces along the front porches and down the long driveways. Everything is big, luxurious, prim, and proper, perfectly maintained.

Ron Radzai stops in front of a white, two-story mansion with green shutters. Two tall columns hold up the porch roof. Beside the house is a second building that's a replica of the main house except there's a two-car garage on the main level and an apartment upstairs. This may be where we're going to live.

Momma and Ron Radzai trudge up the long, steep drive-way. She's wearing her short shorts and white heels. Ron Radzai hasn't changed his clothes since we left Miami and the early morning sun highlights the wrinkles in his shirt and pants. Two girls come out the front door and pass them midway down the driveway. Their blue-and-white-checkered, pleated skirts sway an inch above their knee-high white socks. Black-and-white saddle shoes, perfectly polished, guide their quick steps; their white blouses are starched and tucked in. Their arms hold stacks of brown paper–covered textbooks. One girl has long blonde braids, perfectly plaited and tied with tiny ribbons. She's my age. The other, also blonde, is younger. Sisters. Talking about school, or the fun they'll have this weekend.

I slink down so the girls don't see me. My hair's greasy and I'm still in my striped bloomers and halter top. There's a chill in the Stamford air. All of us are dressed for autumn in Miami. These girls live here. I wonder what their bedrooms look like. What they'll have for lunch. What their teachers are like.

I don't really want to be one of these girls or even to live in their mansion. But I do want a bed. I want to be in school, to be around teachers and my new friends. I'm ready to get back to my normal life, to be able to carry my books home from school, do my homework, raise my hand in class, and spout off the correct answer. Seeing these girls makes me miss school and my teachers all over again. I imagine walking down Little River's sun-filled corridors, greeting my teachers, getting an A on the spelling test.

I look up toward the mansion. A woman's talking with Momma and Ron Radzai in the open doorway. In minutes, they're back in the car.

"Well, how much money *do* you have?" Momma screams.

"It wasn't big enough for us, anyway," Ron Radzai says.

"You bastard," Momma sneers at Ron Radzai. She pinches his arm. "You good-for-nothing bastard." I've seen Momma pinch and holler at Ron Radzai many times before but I've never seen him raise a hand to her.

Ron Radzai looks straight ahead and doesn't say a word to Momma. He always does that whenever she hits him. All of us kids know enough to keep our traps shut and get invisible real fast. The shit's about to fly—and the sooner Momma forgets she has four kids in the backseat, the better.

This is about the time I get to worrying just how much money they do have, because it looks like Stamford is going to take a lot of it. I worry if they have any idea how they'll navigate this upper-class community. Are they so caught up in Momma's dream that they've forgotten we're poor? I wonder if Ron Radzai worries about how much money we'll need to live in Stamford and if he's made a conscious decision to not rock the boat. Just go ahead and do what Momma wants—to move to Stamford, study art, and work in the Pitney-Bowes factory. I guess he thought all the details would just fall into place.

Ronnie, Sharon, and I are mute for the rest of the day. Even the baby knows it's better to be silent. Ron Radzai and Momma go in and out of one huge home after another. The drama in the car repeats with each new rental possibility. The dialogue is the same—just more intense, the actors more agitated, as the day progresses. Sharon and I nudge each other to indicate our concern but we don't dare say anything or show any expression on our faces for fear Momma or Ron Radzai will see us. Stamford is very far from Victory Homes in more ways than one. To me, the town is intimidating—too rich, too grown up, too overwhelming. I don't like anything about it.

• • •

By nightfall, we've not found a place to live. Ron Radzai drives out of town and pulls into another parking lot to sleep. Momma lets us kids get out to walk around and pee in the woods surrounding the lot, empty except for our car. We're all dirty and smelly. I daydream about taking a bath and washing my hair. My body hurts from sitting so long, from sleeping sitting up, from not being able to run around and get some exercise, and from having my first-ever period. I pray we'll find a new apartment soon so we can get back to our *normal* life, even if that means sleeping on a mattress on the floor.

School. School. I need to get back to school.

Momma opens a can of spam, cuts pieces, slaps them on saltine crackers, and passes them to me for distribution.

"Sharon's hitting me," Ronnie complains.

"I am not," Sharon says. "*He* hit *me*."

"Can't you keep things quiet back there, Beverly?" Momma snaps.

I elbow Sharon and hiss under my breath, "Shut up."

We spend the next two weeks driving around Stamford looking for an apartment, sleeping in the car each night, washing up in gas stations, and eating pork and beans and Vienna sausages out of cans. I hate that I'm sitting in the backseat of our car instead of being in school. I hate Stamford and everyone who made all these promises to Momma. Why doesn't one of the Famous Artists find an apartment for us?

• • •

One day, Ron Radzai drives in a new direction and pulls off at the Yonkers exit. He weaves around narrow streets with four-story brick apartment buildings all built out to the sidewalk. No grassy front yards. He parks and we pile out of the car. He grabs the baby and Sharon, Ronnie, and I follow him and Momma into an old apartment building. We climb a flight of stairs and walk down a dark, musty hallway. He knocks at a door.

"Mom, we need to stay here tonight," Ron Radzai says to the round, gray-haired woman who answers the door.

She looks shocked at the sight of four kids, her son, and the married woman he left Yonkers with more than five years ago.

"Here are your grandchildren, Ronnie and Mikey," Ron Radzai says. He plunges Mikey into his mother's unsuspecting arms. The woman babbles something in Polish and hollers out to her husband. She backs away from the door and gestures for us to come in.

Smells of cabbage and mildew fill the apartment. Several large, overstuffed chairs with hand-crocheted doilies on the arm rests and backs emerge from the dark living room. Sharon jumps into one of the big chairs. Her sticky fingers land on a crisp, starched doily. Momma grabs her arm and pulls her out of the chair.

"I don't have room for all of you," the woman says.

"We'll sleep on the floor," Ron Radzai says. "We have to get out of the car for a night and we all need to take a bath. Children, this is your grandmother," he says, turning to Sharon, Ronnie, and me.

This is a surprise to me. I've never considered the fact that Ron Radzai might have parents and maybe even siblings. He's never mentioned his family. Since he talks so little, I realize I have lots of questions about him now that I see he has a mother and father. Here they are, right in Yonkers.

Grandma offers us cabbage and Polish sausage. I'm so happy to have a hot meal I forget how dark, dank, and smelly the apartment is. After dinner, we each take a bath, shampoo our hair, lay a blanket on the floor, and fall asleep. I'm so relieved to be clean, to smell fresh, to have a change of clothes and a full stomach. It's enough to make me hopeful that we'll soon find a place to live, I'll be back in school, and all will be well.

The next day, after cereal and milk, we pile into the car and drive back to the Stamford area to look for an apartment we can afford.

• • •

Before I know it, it's the end of October. We've lived in the car for six weeks and have looked for an apartment in all the towns between Yonkers and Stamford, including New Rochelle, Eastchester, Scarsdale, Port Chester, and even some across the Hudson River in New Jersey: Fort Lee, Hoboken, Clifton, and Paterson. About every two weeks, Ron Radzai drives us back to his mother's apartment for a hot meal and a bath. He finally has to call the manager at Pitney-Bowes to tell him that he can't show up for work because we haven't found a place to live. The Stamford newspaper runs this story:

STAMFORD JOB MAY WRITE HAPPY END TO FAMILY STORY

A job is waiting for an Army veteran now living with his wife and four children in an automobile.

The job at Pitney-Bowes, Inc. has been open to him since September, but Roland Radzai can't find a place to live.

In spite of the newspaper's appeal, no one comes forward with an apartment for us.

The car is now our home.

• • •

"Take the girls and me over to Smart Avenue," Momma says to Ron Radzai during one of our Yonkers visits. "Beverly, you and Sharon get washed up and find something clean to wear. We're going to see your aunt Marion and uncle Frank."

Uncle Frank, my dad's older brother, owns a landscaping company in Yonkers and runs it with the help of his two adult sons and his wife, Marion. The nursery and the main home are part of the several-acre Armento compound that includes two other homes for family members, greenhouses, and lots of potted shrubs and trees.

As we drive up to the imposing white clapboard home, I remember being here before—many times—back when I was a little girl, back when we lived in Yonkers. Before the fight. My eyes follow the vertical lines of the turret to its church-like spire, pointing toward the clear blue autumn sky. I forgot how much I loved to look at this six-sided tower that juts out from the rest of the home, with its bay window on the main level and its steep, triangular, shingled roof, the highest point of the home. If you count the basement, the house is three stories tall and has three different roof lines. Limestone columns line the street, and limestone steps bring you into the Armento world. Six Smart Avenue looks like it belongs in Stamford.

I smile as I recognize Aunt Marion, and she envelops me in her garlic bosom. It's been six years since I last saw her.

"How are you, *bambina*?" she asks. "We miss you and your little sister. Look at you girls, all grown up now. You both look just like your father."

"Where is their father?" Momma asks. "I know you're hiding him. He hasn't paid any child support all these years. He owes me money."

"I have no idea where he is," Aunt Marion lies, looking squarely at Momma.

We stand in the foyer of the big house, next to a staircase that leads to the second-floor apartment where one of our cousins and his wife live. The aromas from both kitchens fill my pores with good memories. Pork chops, peppers, garlic, sausages, tomatoes. Aunt Marion is the boss of the big house, making sure her daughters-in-law stay in line, that the hired hands are well fed, that her sons work hard, that her husband has everything he needs, and that all their Yonkers connections never go hungry.

Maybe she'll offer us some dinner.

Aunt Marion motions to Momma to follow her. I guess she wants to talk in private. That gives Sharon and me the chance to run around and play tag outside with one of our cousins who has been standing in the living room, just staring at us.

• • •

By the time we head back, Momma is out on the sidewalk, pacing back and forth. Aunt Marion stands on the porch, her hands on her hips, looking none too happy.

"Where have you two been?" Momma hollers.

"Just playing," I say.

"Did you see the chinchillas?" Momma asks.

"What chinchillas?" I ask.

"The filthy chinchillas they're raising," Momma screams, loudly enough so that Aunt Marion can hear.

Thankfully, at that moment, Ron Radzai appears in the Chrysler. We drive back to his parents' dark cabbage-and-kielbasa apartment. I'm so hungry. I wish Aunt Marion had offered us some Italian food. That evening we pass a spoon and a can of pork and beans around the table.

"Your goddamned father's not paying for you girls to eat," Momma hollers as the spoon comes around to me. She pinches my arm, smacks me across my face. "They're hiding him. I know it. Have you seen him?" she asks me. "Do you know where he is?"

"No, no," I say. I cower and raise my arm to hide my face from her next blow. I wish she'd left me with Aunt Marion.

How would I know where my father is?

I put the spoon back in the can, pass it on to Sharon, walk away from the table, wrap myself in a blanket, and lie in a corner of the living room. I wish I did know where my father was. I have so many questions for him. I need to know why he left me. I need to know why Momma is so angry with him.

And why she's so angry with me.

Chapter 12

LODI'S NOT STAMFORD

December 1952

Long after the trees turn their brilliant reds, oranges, and yellows and lose their leaves, long after the cold nights force us to huddle into each other in the backseat, after I stop imagining what my sixth grade teacher will look like, after the Stamford newspaper implores the community to rent us an apartment, and after a Thanksgiving of Vienna sausages, pork and beans, and potted meat, Ron Radzai drives one more time over the George Washington Bridge into New Jersey and he and Momma finally find us a place to live in Lodi, a gritty, blue-collar, ethnic Italian town just minutes outside of New York City.

We've lived in the car for ten weeks.

Ron Radzai parks in front of an aging, three-story, red brick building. The bricks and the front door start where the sidewalk ends. No Stamford grassy front yard, colorful flowers, or columns grace the front porch. There is no front porch. Every building along the street is built right into the sidewalk, just like this one. There's no garage for the car and none of the kids who play hop scotch and ride bikes in the middle of the street wear a school uniform.

"We're going to live in the basement apartment, down at the end of the hallway," Momma says. "Help your father unpack the car."

I grab a handful of diapers, a few bags of clothing, and walk down a long, dark hallway. There is a door to my right, and another to my left. I open the one on my right. Smells like urine. I run my hand along the wall until I find the light switch. A lone, bare bulb screwed into the tall ceiling sheds a dim light on a dirty toilet. A skimpy roll of toilet paper sits on the floor. That's it. No sink. No bathtub, no shower. No mirror.

By now, the rest of the family has disappeared through the doorway across the hall. I pause at the open door to view our new home. It's one big, square, freezing room, with cinder-block walls and no windows. Off to my right, just inside the door, are two gray aluminum utility sinks, attached to the wall. I walk over and stand on my tiptoes to reach the faucet. The edge of the sink cuts into the top of my chest. These sinks will soon become the center of all our washing: dishes, clothes, and our bodies. Next to the sinks is an old gas stove, grimy and caked with remnants of food. In the center of the room, two large wooden beams rise from the floor to the ceiling. Beside one of the support beams is a white appliance. It's about as tall as I am, with two doors, a large one on top and a smaller, rectangular one below. I clasp the silver latch and open the top door. Cool air escapes. The two clear plastic shelves are empty. A large cake of ice sits on the lower, grated shelf. Water runs off the ice block and plunks into the large aluminum pan below. *Drip. Drip.*

"It's an icebox," someone behind me says. "Hello, I'm Jack," says the tall, thin, dark-haired man who thrusts out his hand. "I own the building. I had a new block of ice delivered today."

Jack shakes Momma's hand, then mine.

"Welcome to Lodi. I've been waiting for you. Here are the extra keys to the apartment." He hands Momma two keys. "Here's the door you open to get to the pan of water." He turns back to the icebox and opens the lower door.

Emptying the pan will be one of my jobs. I envision hoisting it up to the lip of the utility sink and hearing the whoosh as the melted water cascades down the drain.

"The ice man comes once a week, on Monday mornings, to deliver a new block," Jack says. "Garbage day is Monday too. The can's over there in the corner. Just put it out on the sidewalk by seven in the morning. The folks upstairs share the toilet. You need to supply your own toilet paper. First come, first served in the bathroom. I'm going to bring you six cots and blankets in about an hour. I know you said you don't have any furniture. It gets mighty cold down here. I'll have the heat turned on later today. Say, do you have any coats for the kids?"

"We just moved from Miami," Momma says.

That means no. We have no coats. Jack knows how to translate.

"My wife can get you connected with one of the social agencies," he says. "But since it's Saturday, I'll ask her to bring you some things from the church."

• • •

Later that day, Jack's wife comes to meet us and makes guesses about our sizes. She returns early in the evening, her arms full of winter clothes. There's a jacket for everyone, and long-sleeved shirts and pants too. I'm grateful. My existing wardrobe—my Miami school clothes and lots of bloomer and halter sets—was not going to get me through this cold weather.

I'm familiar with the generosity of churches and the good work social agencies do for poor families. In Miami, several women made regular visits to our home, bringing clothes, furniture, and staples—food, diapers, school supplies. At Thanksgiving, there was always a turkey and cranberry sauce, and at Christmas, gifts for all us kids. Even though I was embarrassed to see the women arrive, I will forever be thankful for the goodwill that was showered on us over the years.

"Where's the school?" I ask Jack's wife. I can't wait to get back to school and meet my new teacher. I'm sure she'll be just like all my Miami teachers—smiling, encouraging women who think I can do anything I try to do. She'll make me work hard but treat me like I'm a genius no matter how scruffy my clothes or how bruised my arms.

"Columbus Elementary is just up the street," Jack's wife says, pointing in the direction of the icebox.

• • •

"I couldn't sleep last night," Sharon says. We're bundled in our new jackets, walking down the block to Columbus Elementary School. We've missed the first twelve weeks of school.

"I couldn't either. Can you turn over in your cot?" I ask. I can barely get out of mine. My body sinks down almost to the floor. To get out, I swing my legs over the edge and hoist my butt onto the wooden frame. The first time I tried it, I turned the whole contraption over and toppled onto the floor.

The only other furniture in our new apartment is Momma's art table and easel. The six cots are scattered about the room. I chose a corner, and Sharon plunked her cot down near mine. Momma, Ron Radzai, Ronnie, and baby Mikey's cots are in the far corner.

"At least you can't kick me." Sharon laughs.

"That's crazy," I say. "You're the one who kicks me."

We laugh. We're at our new school already.

• • •

I give the envelope with our birth certificates and report cards to the school secretary. Pretty soon Sharon is safely in the hands of her second-grade teacher, Mrs. Cimiluca.

Now it's my turn. Mrs. Matthews, the principal, takes my hand and we walk down the hall to my sixth-grade classroom. I'm so excited I can hardly control myself. I want to skip down the hall. Instead I walk tall and proud. I'm ready to meet my new teacher.

Mrs. Matthews opens the door and motions for Mrs. Veronica Hull to come out and meet her new student.

Mrs. Hull is just as I've imagined: a smiling, gentle, pretty young woman with curly brown hair down to her shoulders. She ushers me into the classroom, her arm around my shoulders.

"Class, we have a new student. Let's welcome Beverly Armento."

My new classmates clap. Tears well up as I take the seat Mrs. Hull indicates is mine. I can't believe these kids are happy I'm here. I want to tell them how excited I am to finally be back in school—where I can be myself, where I can talk, where I can feel my strength.

The room looks a lot like my Little River classrooms: wooden desks and chairs, all one piece that you scoot into and hide under when the air raid drill sounds. The top of the desk opens at a 45-degree angle to reveal a roomy place for your books and pencils. The desks are neatly lined up, one row after another, all facing the front where a cursive alphabet banner runs along the top of the room-long blackboard. Six chalk-filled erasers rest on the tray. An American flag hangs behind the teacher's desk, which is kitty-cornered between the windows and the blackboard, close to the second row, where I sit. Student art covers the two bulletin boards along the side and back walls. Another board displays handwritten essays, the teacher's A's and B's in red marked boldly at the top of each. Pretty soon my work will be up there too.

The kids sitting near me smile and say, "Hi." I smile back but I really want to hug each one, be their friend, thank them for welcoming me to their class. I slip into my desk, put my notebook on top, and place my pencil in the hollowed-out groove at the top of the blond wooden desk.

It's second period. Time for English. Mrs. Hull calls the names of four kids. They stand spaced out at the blackboard, where she has written four different sentences across the top. Each child picks up a piece of chalk and draws a horizontal line. They write the subject of their sentence on the line. Okay. I get that. Then they draw more lines—vertical lines, slanted lines, lines connecting to other lines. Lines, lines.

My tears come. What in the world is this? I've never seen anything like this before in my life. I know how to find the subject, verb, and direct object in a sentence and I know my prepositions and what adverbs and adjectives are. But these drawings are foreign to me. My body trembles. How can I get out of this school? I want to run away from this place. I want to be back at Little River Elementary, where I have friends and normal-looking sentences.

"Good job everyone," Mrs. Hull says. "Now, how would we diagram this sentence with a compound direct object?" She's written a new sentence on the board: *Mrs. Smith asked Antonio and Susana about their homework.*

Everyone bends over their desks, drawing away. I pick up my pencil but don't know what to do, where to start. I'm scared. Feel stupid. So, this is what's been happening all the time I've been sitting in the car. I stare at the paper. Draw a horizontal line. Perhaps a solution will magically appear on the page.

Suddenly, Mrs. Hull is beside my desk. She kneels down so that she's at eye level with me. She smiles. I try to smile but I'm all puckered up, ready to bawl.

"Have you ever diagrammed sentences, Beverly?" she asks.

"No, ma'am," I manage to say.

"Here, let me show you. What's the subject of this sentence?"

. . .

Before long, I'm diagramming complex sentences at the board and leading the class as we take on the more challenging examples. I have trouble with arithmetic and social studies too. But Mrs. Hull always pops up beside me and says, "Let me show you how to do this."

My angel teacher. It feels so good to be back in school, my safe place, where Strong Beverly lives.

I am finally home.

Chapter 13

HOLLYWOOD: HERE WE COME

January 1953

"Can you keep a secret?" Ron Radzai whispers, his long, pale face close to mine. I'm on a stool washing the cereal dishes in the utility sink, making us eye-to-eye. This is the first time I've been so close to his wavy blond hair and sad eyes.

"Oh, yes," I say. I'm all ears to hear his secret.

"Once I tell you, you can't talk about this," he says. "You can't let on to your mother or Sharon what's happening. Can you do that?"

I realize Momma's out in the hallway bathroom, the baby's asleep on his cot, and Sharon and Ronnie are racing around our big, mostly empty room, hollering "tag" every few minutes. Ron Radzai has picked the right time to tell me a secret.

"Sure." I nod, my eyes wide. This sounds serious. I turn off the water and turn my body toward him. I can't imagine what's so important that Momma and Sharon can't know about it.

"Your mother's going to be on a television show in two weeks. She thinks she's going out to Hollywood to be on *Queen for a Day*, but the real reason for the trip is that she'll be the star on *This Is Your Life*. We're all going to fly to California to be on the program with her. You and Sharon will have to miss about a week of school."

He holds out two pieces of paper, folded in half. I blot my hands on my shirt and take the notes. Did he say we're all going to California? This is such good news. I'm relieved I'll not have to stay home and babysit this time. We're all going to be on television. Oh, wow. I can't believe my ears.

"These letters are for your teachers," he says. His lips hardly move when he talks. Maybe he's trying to hide the empty spaces where he once had teeth. "I want you to get clothes ready for the trip. You kids need your best outfits for the program. And good clothes for the airplane rides and for the three days we'll be in California. I'll borrow two suitcases. Decide what we need for Mikey."

Right about then, Momma comes into the room. Ron Radzai quickly moves away from the sink. I hide the notes under a dish towel and finish the dishes like nothing's happened.

· · ·

I grab my social studies book from the heap of textbooks stacked under my cot and open to a map of the United States. Using my pinky, I measure the distance from Miami to New Jersey, then from New Jersey to California. Well over twice the distance. We're going all the way across the country. My first airplane ride. My first television program. I'm bursting to tell Sharon, but I have a promise to keep.

I remember seeing Jack Bailey holler out, "Would *you* like to be Queen for a Day?" last summer when we watched television at our Miami neighbor's home. Like all the other quiz shows Momma's been on, this one is a program where a woman with a sad story is awarded a bunch of prizes and made to feel like Cinderella—or, in this case, a queen. Using the applause-meter, the audience votes for the lady with the best hard-luck story. A crown on her head, a fur-trimmed robe over her shoulders, her arms full of a dozen roses, the winner is escorted to a big, fancy throne where she learns how her life will change. I hope all us kids will get to see Momma named Queen for a Day in the magical Moulin Rouge dinner theater, where the program is taped.

Most of the quiz show contestants I've seen are shy, frightened women who are embarrassed to tell the audience their sad plight in life. Momma is different. Her life is hunky-dory. She's a miracle with two new eyes that can now see. She's going to be a great artist. She walks on stage with confidence, holds her head high; her voice is clear and strong. She's doing a good deed—raising money for an important cause. I imagine Momma telling her story on *Queen for a Day* and *This Is Your Life*—which, I figure, is just what the name suggests, a program that features one life story.

Momma's version of her life just appeared in the January 1953 edition of *Woman's Home Companion*. "Love at Second Sight" is a six-page spread, full of photos of our family. A half-page bust shot of Momma's beautiful face adorns the first page, along with this quote from her: "I knew I'd lose my sight one day, and at eighteen it happened. For ten years I was blind. In those years I fell in love, married, and bore four children. Then, suddenly, a miracle happened. Two kind people left their eyes to me and I could see."

Right on the heels of the *WHC* feature, the *Mademoiselle* magazine issue highlighting Momma as the Homemaker of the Year also appears. Our phone rings off the hook with reporters who want to interview Momma. She's famous again, and that means she's happy more of the time. I'm hopeful all this fame will bring back my Yonkers Momma—one more time.

• • •

Now that we're settled in our Lodi apartment, Momma's back at work on her art lessons, spending time each day at her art table and easel, which are set up in a corner of the big room. Even though we're not in Stamford, Momma concentrates on her lessons, sends in her assignments on time, and eagerly awaits feedback from one of the artists.

"I'm going to California to be on a television show," she says one day, turning away from the drawing she's working on.

I've kept the secret for a week now, just waiting for the next bit of news. Here it is.

"Oh," I say, acting surprised. "What show?"

"*Queen for a Day*—the Braille Institute wants me to help them raise money," she says. "I'll be gone for two days next week. I need you to stay home from school to watch Ronnie and Mikey."

"Sure," I say. "Which days?"

Ron Radzai and I are doing a good job keeping our secret. Momma has no idea she'll see all of us kids in California. I just play along and tell Momma I'll be glad to miss school to help out. I iron Momma's clothes and help her pack a suitcase she borrows from the landlord. Then, early one morning, a limousine comes to pick her up.

The rest of us have to be ready to leave that same evening. I make sure all our clothes are tidy and pack plaid dresses for Sharon and me, a white shirt, bow tie, and suspenders for Ronnie, and Mikey's cutest outfits. I set out clean clothes and get everyone dressed for our big adventure airplane ride. Now that Momma is safely out of the house and on the airplane, Ron Radzai tells Sharon the secret.

• • •

"Give me the baby while you eat your meal," Ron Radzai says.

We're about an hour into our six-hour Trans World Airlines jet ride to Los Angeles, and it's dinner time. *That's really considerate of him,* I think as I pass Mikey across the aisle to him. He has said more to me over the last few days than he has in the six years he's been part of our family. There's a lot to do to manage three kids, and he knows we have to work together. We take turns holding Mikey and changing his diaper. He usually grabs Ronnie's hand when we're walking, and I grab on to Sharon. He speaks softly and never gets angry like Momma does. We make a good team. I wonder if he knows how Momma treats me. I wonder if I should tell him.

A glowing white sun sits atop a band of dark clouds at the horizon and wraps its red and golden arms around the mountains. A sprawling city appears out our window, spread far and wide in the valley, like a geometry buff's Tinkertoy model. Rectangular city blocks, framed by the dark lines of roadways, stretch until they merge into the mountains. Pretty soon office buildings, homes, swimming pools, then cars, streetlights, and people come into view, closer and closer, like looking at the veins of a leaf through a microscope. Here we are, in Los Angeles, on the other side of the continent from Lodi.

• • •

A man in a black suit waves a sign that reads THE RADZAI FAMILY at us when we arrive at the baggage area. He grabs our suitcases and leads us to a white stretch limousine stocked with bourbon, glasses, and snacks. We pile in.

"We're going to 7000 Hollywood Boulevard," Ron Radzai says to the driver.

"Oh, yes, I know," the driver says. "The Hollywood Roosevelt Hotel. It's one of the oldest and best hotels in Los Angeles. You're going to enjoy your stay." He points out some of the popular sights on our quick trip to the hotel. Everything's new, glitzy. I wonder which movie stars we'll see.

• • •

My eyes can't blink fast enough once we get to the hotel: the chandeliers, the sophisticated women, the handsome men, the fancy clothing. I look up, down, all around. People in the hotel lobby look like they just walked off the cover of a fashion magazine. Everyone but us. We look like a band of ragamuffins. Ron Radzai, the only man in the lobby not in a suit and tie, stands out. I want to hide our scuffed-up suitcases, our screaming baby brother, the spot on my shirt where I dropped some of my airline dinner. Sharon wanders away from me and touches everything in sight—the lamps, the pillows on the soft chairs. She kneels on the rug and traces the pattern, then strikes up a conversation with some men standing nearby.

Ron Radzai finally gets us checked in, I corral Sharon, and we're off to see our home for the next few days.

Another man in a dark suit escorts us to adjoining rooms, one for the boys and one for the girls. Sharon and I have our own room with two double beds made up with crisp hospital-cornered sheets and a plump white coverlet, too pretty to touch or to sleep under. I stare at my bed. It's a real bed, with a mattress and box springs. It has legs, a headboard. It's a far cry from my cot in Lodi, or the backseat of our car, or our mattress on the floor in Miami. I haven't slept on a real bed since we lived in Yonkers. Back when I was five.

I toss off my shoes, jump on the bed, and snuggle under the covers. "I'm queen for a day," I proclaim. Sharon and I laugh, hard and loud.

I jump out of bed and grab Sharon's hands. We twirl around and around until we're dizzy. We're in Hollywood!

We even have our own bathroom. I walk in and turn on the lights. The chrome fixtures, the shiny countertops, a white porcelain sink and bathtub—everything glistens. Soft, fluffy, huge white towels, bars of soap, and small bottles of shampoo, conditioner, and body lotion fill the shelves and wicker baskets. There's even an extra roll of toilet paper. Sharon and I giggle and hug each other.

"Is this all for us?" I ask.

Sharon's too busy to answer. She's smearing lavender body cream all over her arms and legs.

• • •

This evening, a babysitter comes to the hotel room to watch the boys, and Ron Radzai, Sharon, and I go to the lobby to meet Grandma Robby and Aunt Lena, who arrived from New York City a few hours after us. It's easy to find Aunt Lena in the crowd. She looks just like Momma—same face, same nose, same smile, even the same hairdo. Aunt Lena embraces Sharon and me, pulling us into her full, flowered skirt.

Grandma's silver short hair is tightly curled, her wire-rim glasses set atop her jagged nose. She grabs us for a hearty group hug.

"You girls are so grown up," Aunt Lena says. "I remember when I took care of you, Sharon. You were only two."

"Oh, did you visit us in Yonkers?" I ask.

"No, no. Your mother brought you and Sharon to Warsaw on the train," Aunt Lena says. "Don't you remember? You stayed with Bernice Greene, your mother's best friend, and Sharon stayed with me. Your mother took the train back to Yonkers to have kidney surgery. She said the surgery would save her eyes."

I hesitate, trying to think back that far. "I don't remember that. I didn't know Momma had kidney surgery," I say to Ron Radzai.

"No, I don't remember that," he says, a scowl on his face. "We need to go into the restaurant now. We have a busy day tomorrow, so we need to get to bed early tonight."

Ron Radzai doesn't want to talk about 1946. He tries to change the subject. Aunt Lena, though, wants to talk about the past, and I've got lots of questions for her.

"Wasn't that about the time you met Alett?" she asks Ron Radzai.

We follow another man in a dark suit into a sea of white cloth–covered tables. All the diners are decked out in their Sunday finest. I'm seated between Aunt Lena and Grandma. I put my hands in my lap and stare at the silver and china extravaganza in front of me: two forks, two spoons, two crystal glasses, a gleaming white plate on top of larger white plate. *What do you do with all this stuff?*

"You know your mother ran away to marry your father," Grandma Robby says to me.

"That was a long time ago," I say. Momma's told me her mother didn't like Dad and was angry with her for leaving home. I wonder how Grandma feels about Momma now that she's famous.

"Alett had just turned eighteen," Grandma says, reaching for the bread basket. "I thought she was too young to get married, but she was determined. She left on her birthday and never said good-bye. I was so mad I never opened all the letters she sent me. I just let them sit in a basket on the dining room table."

Oh, my. I wonder what Momma thought when she never received a return letter from her mother. That's sad. I'll bet Momma was upset about that.

"I was surprised when your mother called me six years later and said she needed me to watch you girls for a week or so," Aunt Lena says. "She said her kidney surgery would restore her sight."

She's come back to this topic. This is curious to me. I've never heard this story before. I'm all ears.

"Funny thing, though," Aunt Lena continues. "Your mother kept extending the time, saying she wasn't well enough yet to take you girls back. Beverly, I had to give you to Bernice Greene. You stayed with her. I had my hands full with my own son and with Sharon."

My head swims with all this news. I try to do some fast math—how old was I then, what was happening in my life?

Five. Oh, yes. Yonkers. The fight. The Blond Man. My missing toys. My missing father. No wonder Ron Radzai doesn't want to talk about 1946.

"Turns out, you and Sharon stayed with us for well over a year," Aunt Lena says. "Just about a year and a half."

"We stayed with you for a year and a half?" I ask in a loud voice, startling a couple at the next table. "Did I go to school? I don't remember this." I'm unsettled over this news. How come I don't remember any of this? Who is Bernice Greene? Is she coming to be on *This Is Your Life?*

Ron Radzai tells the waiter we're ready to order. I want to know the rest of this story. I like sitting next to Aunt Lena and Grandma.

"What happened to your arm, Beverly?" Aunt Lena touches the black and blue marks that peek out from the sleeve of my blouse.

I move my arm away. No one's supposed to see under my clothing. "I bumped into a door," I say.

"My arm looked just like that when I was a kid," Aunt Lena says. "Your mother pinched me every time she was mad at me. And she was mad at me a lot. She'd grab a piece of skin, twist it, and hold on forever. I was black and blue all the time."

"That must have hurt," I say, pretending I have no idea what she's talking about. I can't believe Momma used to pinch her own sister. That's exactly how Momma pinches me. Maybe I should tell Aunt Lena what really happened to my arm.

• • •

"Surprise! Happy Valentine's Day, Beverly," Ron Radzai says the next day. He stands beside me in the hotel lobby, his hands behind his back. Suddenly he thrusts a corsage toward me, a cluster of a dozen miniature pink roses tied with a pink ribbon.

"Mrs. Hull wanted you to have this for the program today. She said to tell you that your entire sixth grade class will be watching. She even asked me the color of the dress you were going to wear so the flowers would match," he says as he pulls the long pin from the corsage.

How did Ron Radzai keep this secret from me? I wipe my tears as he comes closer to pin the corsage on my best plaid dress, the one with the bolero stitched on to the blouse. My classmates will see me on television tonight, and they'll see the flowers they sent! I have the greatest teacher and classmates in the world. I've never had a corsage. I love my teacher and my new friends.

Everyone nearby claps, including our large *This Is Your Life* group. All the folks who will surprise Momma on television have arrived. There's Mrs. Mattie Lou Kinnard, the manager of Victory Homes, wearing a black, full-skirted dress with a scooped-out neckline that shows off her pearls. She swirls a long shawl around her shoulders and walks like a movie star. Mrs. Kinnard likes to talk. She hasn't stopped since we all gathered in the lobby to await the two limousines that will take us to the El Capitan Theater for the program. Mrs. Diehl, Dr. Bascom Palmer's secretary, is here, in a smart dark blue suit and white blouse. Ron Radzai embraces her before introducing us kids. Mrs. Kinnard and Mrs. Diehl, their dark brown hair freshly coiffed in tight curls that frame their faces, are tall and regal. Mrs. Christine M. Oser, her silver hair glistening under the chandelier, takes my hand in hers, bends close to me, and shows me her glass eye.

"I think it's wonderful what you did for my mother," I tell her as I stare into her eye, remembering the first day I saw Momma with Mrs. Oser's cornea. "Thank you. All of us kids are so happy Momma can see now, thanks to you."

Aunt Lena pins my corsage on my dress. I grab Mrs. Oser and Aunt Lena's hands and head toward the limousines.

We're ready for our television debut.

Chapter 14

THIS IS YOUR LIFE

February 11, 1953

"Alett Radzai, after ten long years in darkness, thanks to the miracle of corneal transplants, you can now see and return to your art career. Alett Radzai, of Lodi, New Jersey, *This Is Your Life*," Mr. Ralph Edwards proclaims, his voice filling the historic El Capitan Theater.

Hundreds of women in their finest dresses, hats, and gloves and men in suits and ties break into applause as Mr. Edwards takes Momma's arm and escorts her to the stage while the theme music plays. Backstage, the ten of us who will soon walk through the portal to say a few words and hug her are seated in the order we'll be called to the "magic curtain," as Sharon has named it—the curtain that will part to allow us to enter the even more magical world of live television. On the screen in front of us, we see the action in the theater and our mother who looks tiny on the loveseat, her legs dangling above the floor, her voice soft and demure—a voice I seldom hear. One of her many voices.

The fact that we are all here—Grandma Robby, Aunt Lena, Ron Radzai and the four of us kids, Mrs. Kinnard, Mrs. Diehl, and Mrs. Oser—is totally surreal. I have the same feeling I got a few weeks ago when I read the feature story in *Woman's Home Companion*. It was then that I realized there are different versions of Momma's life. There are her version, my version, and I'm sure each of the others who sit beside me has their own take on who Momma really is. On the quiz shows and for her magazine and newspaper interviews, Momma tells the story in her own words. But tonight, Ralph Edwards is in charge of the script—and one reason his show is so popular is because folks love to hear secrets about famous people. As I look at Momma's face on the screen, I see a calm woman who expects to hear an inspiring story from the man behind the kind voice. I wonder if he has any surprises for her.

• • •

Momma's birth date flashes on the screen and Mr. Edwards says, "After five boys, finally a girl is born. A healthy girl."

"That's what we thought until we found out . . ." Grandma Robby's voice comes from backstage.

Grandma Robby, elegant in a new blue satin blouse and long black skirt, walks on stage to embrace the daughter she disowned when Alett left home to marry an Italian man. Mother and daughter embrace like they'd never had a serious disagreement. Momma even asks Grandma Robby to tie the bow on her blouse sleeve that's come undone. Momma is a great actress. I wonder if she knows her mother never opened any of the letters she sent home after she was married by the Warsaw justice of the peace and moved to Yonkers with Dad.

Backstage, Aunt Lena bends toward me and whispers, "Good luck." Jane, Mr. Edwards's assistant, motions for Lena to come to the curtains.

"That's when we found out Alett had real talent for art," Aunt Lena says from behind the curtains. On the screen, some- one turns the pages of the tiny sketchpad Momma used as a teenager, the one she pressed into Dad's hands at the CCC dance. The pages reveal one luminous portrait after another, the details exquisite, facial expressions well articulated, clothing fluid and perfectly appointed.

Momma greets Lena like she's her favorite sibling. Truth be told, Momma likes each of her six brothers more than her only sister. As children, the two girls vied for their parents' attention, and after their father died, Grandma favored Lena. "I was the one who had to iron my brothers' shirts," Momma has told me. "And Lena was the one who got the bicycle." But on live television, Momma and Lena act like they're the best of friends. Lena bends close to Momma and the camera reflects mirror images: same profile, noses, facial structure, even hair styles. They could be twins.

Jane motions for me to come to the curtains.

"It's 1940. You drop out of school," Mr. Edwards continues. "You reach out and meet a boy. Fall in love. Was it a happy marriage?"

Backstage, I see Momma on the big screen. She squirms in her seat, appears shocked at such a bold question. I am also. Somehow, I never imagined we'd talk about Dad on *This Is Your Life*. The movie of the fight plays in my mind. A twitch makes its way across the bridge of my nose and works its way into my eyes. I can't cry just as I make my television debut. Why am I crying? This is supposed to be a good story, a "Made in America" story where a miracle is laid at the doorstep of an average person and she becomes a wonder woman, a hero, a successful artist, the Housewife of the Year. The irony of it all smacks me in the face. Momma has two lives. Tonight, on national television, we'll see the life Momma presents to the world: competent, accomplished, loving, a brilliant mother and wife, much admired, a woman who has overcome tragedy and who will prevail. That's the only story Ralph Edwards knows—the façade of our lives. Mr. Edwards hints he knows there's more to this story, but he also knows he can't push his guests so far that they break.

"Well . . . no," Momma says, hesitating.

Mr. Edwards wants to press the issue but it's clear Momma doesn't want to talk about Dad and her failed marriage. I don't know what he wants her to say. I'm uncomfortable for Momma, being made to talk about something that's long over and something that ended with so much trauma. It's rude to make her—and me—remember Dad. After all, what should she say? Should she confess that the failed marriage was her fault? That she took on a lover, that she was not loyal to Dad? I'm not willing for the charade to be unraveled, at least not on national television. People don't really want to know the truth—the dysfunction, the beatings, the rage, the delusions. Stick with the story line. What good would come from anyone knowing the truth? This is supposed to be a happy story.

"Maybe there's something others can learn. Did you feel that a person—sightless—had to save her pride?" Mr. Edwards persists, oblivious to Momma's discomfort. He has got his own answer to the question, one he obviously arrived at after reading the *WHC* story, especially the part where Momma said Dad was the reason for their breakup, that he was the one who cheated on her. Mr. Edwards wants her to confirm it all on live television. I'm sure he thinks the *WHC* story is all true.

The part of the Yonkers movie-in-my-mind where Momma strikes Dad replays. I blink hard to make the images and my tears go away. The fight movie now has a real-life sequel: beatings, biting, pinching. This time, I'm the target, not Dad. I see Momma in her yellow nightgown.

The scene dissolves into Momma as the star of *This Is Your Life*, with one version of her life. I'm about to be a central character in this pretense. But I've forgotten my lines. *Hurry and get into your role. Stop crying. You're supposed to be the happy oldest child, the seeing eye girl, the one with a wonder-mother, a medical miracle, a great artist, a loving mother.*

"In 1946, the marriage ends," Mr. Edwards says, finally moving on. "There are two children—two little girls—Beverly, now twelve, and Sharon, seven. Where are they now?"

Of course, Momma thinks we are still in Lodi.

The curtains part. This is it. It's my turn. I hand my wet tissue to Jane and walk onto the stage. But I'm not ready. My face is all puckered up from crying. I'm still stuck in the movie playing in my mind. Momma embraces me like I'm her dearest child. I hug her like she's the best mother in the world. I remember my part, enact my role. Momma never notices my tears.

The moment Momma lets go of me, Sharon runs on stage, full of giggles, her cut-too-short bangs and dark hair framing her beaming face, her best plaid dress with the white piping bouncing, as her energy bursts on stage. She's got a story to tell and has been waiting for an audience. I'm glad to have the camera off me and onto my gregarious sister. Sharon shows off her TWA wings to Momma, who puts a finger to her lips, hoping Sharon will get the clue and stop babbling. But Sharon has more to tell. She's wound up. Ron Radzai was right—we had to keep the secret from Sharon.

Mr. Edwards motions for us get off center stage and sit on the bench beside Grandma and Aunt Lena. I'm relieved but can't stop sobbing. This is so crazy—Ralph Edwards knows only part of the story, but that's the part that makes for good television.

"Ten sightless years," he says. "Alett Radzai. Your life is an example to others. We all have hardships to overcome."

That's right. Momma is an example to others.

Mr. Edwards sketches the rest of Momma's life and with each story, another person from her past walks on stage to embrace her. The story weaves from World War II and Ron Radzai's army paratrooper jumps at the invasion of Sicily and

Nijmegen, Holland, where he was injured. Then on to Miami and the birth of Ronnie, the move to Victory Homes and Mrs. Kinnard's story about our moving in with no furniture. Mrs. Diehl talks about Dr. Palmer, Momma's successful corneal transplants, and her current near-perfect vision. Ron Radzai brings in baby Mikey, and finally it's time for my favorite person—the one with the glass eye, the saint.

• • •

Mrs. Oser walks on stage, her silver hair, her halo. She and Momma hug. Momma points to her right eye and the audience bursts into applause.

"I was to lose my eye anyway, and Dr. Palmer told me about Alett," Mrs. Oser says to Mr. Edwards.

"You didn't expect to be paid, did you?" he asks.

"Oh, no, Mr. Edwards. What God has given cannot be sold. I'm thankful I could do something for another human being."

"Alett Radzai. *This Is Your Life.* You have said, 'Affection is the only thing not scarce in our house,'" Mr. Edwards says.

The twitch in my nose returns.

• • •

A month after our television debut, our *This Is Your Life* gifts start to arrive at our Lodi apartment. A twelve-foot-tall, sparkling white Amana home freezer, full of Snow Crop frozen vegetables, sits in the middle of the big room next to the four-foot-tall icebox, its block of ice still dripping nonstop into the stainless steel bowl. The new Tappan gas range can't be hooked up because the grungy old one is connected to the only gas outlet and Jack the landlord doesn't want to unhook it, so the two ranges sit side by side also. Our very first television, a twenty-one-inch black-and-white Westinghouse, in its handsome dark wood cabinet, is plugged into a corner electrical outlet, a two-pronged antenna on top. We move it around and around to clear up the fuzzy reception.

After school, Sharon and I sit on the floor in front of the television and watch *American Bandstand*. We know the names of the best dancers and all the words to the popular songs. We sing along and mimic the dance moves in the empty spaces between our cots. Our new Encyclopedia Americana is packed in three cardboard boxes and stacked in another corner. When I need to look something up for my science and social studies projects, I dig through the boxes for the right burgundy-and-gold-bound book, and when I'm done I return the volume to the box for safe storage.

The big Saturday finally arrives. All of us kids are cleaned up and dressed in our best outfits. We're bundled in our Goodwill jackets, mine a size too small, faux-fur collar with a zipper-up front that's exactly like Sharon's except hers fits. We're lined up at the door, waiting for the word.

"Let's go," Ron Radzai says. He wears the cream suit jacket, tie, and good shoes he wore on *This Is Your Life*. Momma is in her white turtleneck sweater and black jumper with her checkered jacket.

We run out to the car. We're off to the Schwinn shop in Paterson to pick out our new bicycles.

A photographer meets us at the store to document this happy day. There are so many choices. Bicycles and tricycles hang from the ceiling, line the walls, and fill the showroom floor. Sharon, Ronnie, and I run around the store. We hop on one bicycle after another and make sure our feet reach the pedals when we sit on the seat. Finally, we narrow down our choices. Sharon picks out a shiny red two-wheeler. I choose a blue one with brakes on the handle bars—just squeeze and stop. Ronnie gets a blue bicycle with training wheels, and Momma picks out a green tricycle for Mikey, who'll grow into it. Each of the two-wheelers has a large headlight on the front so we'll be able to ride at night.

"We'll deliver everything on Monday," the store manager says.

"I can't wait until Monday," Sharon squeals.

Everyone laughs.

We stand beside our bicycles. Ron Radzai and Momma stand behind us, Mikey propped on Ron Radzai's hip. The photographer snaps a dozen photos before we drive back to Lodi.

• • •

I've not had a bicycle since we lived in Yonkers; then, it was a tricycle that I rode all around Mulford Gardens. I daydream the rest of the weekend about the fun I'll have on my brand-spanking-new two-wheeler with hand brakes and a shiny blue horn the manager said he'd install.

On Monday, I can't concentrate in school. All I can think about is my new blue bicycle and how I'll fly down our street to explore places I've never seen.

When school is finally over, Sharon and I race each other home. Our bicycles are there, parked in the middle of the apartment, clustered around the Amana and the icebox. Sharon and I walk our bikes out to the sidewalk for our inaugural rides.

This is the first time Sharon has ever ridden a bicycle. With perfect timing and balance, she sails down the street and disappears.

My inaugural ride, in contrast, is a disaster—but by Friday, I've finally gotten the hang of it. My hair blows in the cold breeze, my nose is wet and runny, and open bruises on my knees and elbows burn, but the bicycle and my body have finally found our rhythm.

Day after day, I venture farther and farther from home, exploring new neighborhoods, new homes, seeing new people. I smile at everyone I pass, calling out greetings to folks I've seen before like they're old friends.

I'm free.

Chapter 15

WHAT'S IN A NAME?

1953

Sharon's cries welcome me home from school that sunny April day. It's warm enough to stay outside longer and ride my bicycle without a sweater. All afternoon I've dreamed of the new streets I'd explore, the new people I'd see, the good times I'd have when school was over.

As soon as I open the door to our apartment, I see why Sharon's upset.

There's an empty space beside the icebox where the Amana upright home freezer sat this morning and another blank space for the Tappan gas range. But the deepest black hole is where the four bicycles were parked when I left for school, just after I rubbed my palm across the handlebars of my own blue beauty, the way you'd pet a dog, telling her how much fun we'll have this afternoon.

Sharon, still in her school clothes, lies facedown on her cot, gripping the wooden frame and kicking her feet into the cotton muslin. "I want my bike I want my bike!" she screams. Ronnie lies curled up on the floor in a whimpering ball. Momma sits slumped in our one upholstered chair, Mikey asleep on her lap, an ashtray precariously balanced on the arm of the chair. After a long drag on her Lucky Strike, she lets out three perfectly formed zeros. They drift up into the dark room before disappearing into the damp and mold of our basement home. The smells close in on me.

"Where's my bicycle?" I ask Momma.

Drip, drip, the ice block says, plunking into its bowl.

"I sold it. We need the money," Momma says. "Your father doesn't pay the rent. You don't need a bicycle. Anyway, you don't even know how to ride."

I turn and walk out of the apartment. I walk down the dank hall. I walk until I can no longer hear Sharon.

I sit on the curb and hide my head between my knees, stare at the dirt at my feet. Numb. I huddle into myself. A wave of sadness, loss, and helplessness comes over me. My sobs come in long gasps. When I try to stop, a new, deep burst of grief engulfs me. I'm afraid I won't ever be able to stop. I'll be on the edge of the cliff of despair, with no way off. I know I can't get lost in my tears, my anger, my fear.

I've built a boundary around my emotions. I need to protect myself. Over the last five years, I've learned how to lie—to tell myself things aren't as bad as they seem, that I don't hurt as much as I do, that I'm not as despondent as I am. I shove my pain down and cover it over with smiles and compliant ways of responding to Momma. I know how to become my real self, Strong Beverly, in school and my guarded self, Weak Beverly, at home. So this day, the day our bicycles disappeared, is just another day. I have to realize, once again, there's nothing I can do about it. I have to stay strong, to save my energy for the things I can control.

A cool breeze nudges me to my feet. I walk the streets I rode yesterday, smile at the folks I've waved at, and stop to chat with the old Polish lady who sits on her front stoop each day waiting for the sunset, greeting her friends and neighbors, passing the time of day, her time. This is her life.

This is my life.

May 1954

My seventh grade school year is about over when Momma and Ron Radzai move the family to a three-bedroom tenement in a red brick building off Passaic Street in Passaic, just a few blocks from the United States Rubber factory where my stepfather has a job on the assembly line. I hate to leave all my friends at Columbus Elementary, but I'm glad Sharon and I will have our own bedroom again. And there is a full bathroom. Except for our three days at the Hollywood Roosevelt Hotel, none of us has had a bath for a year and a half, not since we've lived in Lodi. The first evening we fill the tub so many times we run out of hot water.

• • •

"Radz-EYE," the principal calls out in the crowded front office of Woodrow Wilson Junior High School.

"Radz-EYE," she says again, more loudly, looking straight at me. I'm sitting on a bench because, with only six weeks left in the school year, I've just given the principal my sealed manila envelope with my school and vaccination records so I can enroll in this grades-seven through-nine junior high school. Back in Lodi, I was an upperclassman in our kindergarten-to-grade-eight elementary school. Here, I'll be one of the youngest.

Lots of kids hang out in the office. They've already gotten into trouble or are late for homeroom. Black kids, white kids. I've never been this close to a Black person. All my schools and neighborhoods so far have been segregated. I've not seen a COLORED ONLY sign in New Jersey, like I did in Miami, but all of the neighborhoods I've seen in the north are segregated. Even though I'm now thirteen, I've never participated in a classroom discussion about race at school or at church. I've not studied about slavery and I don't know that in just sixteen days the US Supreme Court will rule on Brown v. Board of Education, stating that "separate educational facilities are inherently unequal." In New Jersey, several school districts voluntarily integrated, and Passaic County is one of them.

I remember our bus rides in Miami when Black mothers and their children walked to the back of the bus even though there were empty seats up front. I know that was wrong. Now I'm sitting next to a Black girl. I want to say, "Here we are, sitting on the same bench. Look at that. What's so wrong with this?"

"Oh, are you calling me?" I ask when I realize the principal's staring at me. I jump up and hurry to the counter. Mrs. Stephens, the principal, shoves my cream-colored Lodi report card toward me. She's a tall, stately woman dressed in a dark blue suit and white blouse, her hair tied up in a bun. All business. She's in a hurry and I'm a minor distraction. There's an office full of kids who need late slips, a talking-to, or detention. *Why's this kid entering school in May, anyway?* she must be thinking.

"Is this your report card?" she asks.

I stare at my name, Beverly Armento, written on the pupil line. Someone has drawn a line through *Armento* and written *Radzai* right above it.

"Yes," I stammer. "But that's not really—"

• • •

"Okay, Miss Radz-EYE, let's get you to your homeroom. It's almost time for first period. You'll be in Mrs. Leach's homeroom class. Room 210. Bring these papers with you. Here's your class schedule. Now go on, Miss Radz-EYE."

"It's RAD-zee," I say loudly. I gather the papers and turn to find my way through the long hallways.

The bulletin boards are bare: no artwork, no student essays, nothing. This doesn't look like any of my other schools. Everybody's in a rush. Bells ring and then ring again. The hallways are lined with silver lockers, one row on top of another, all with combination locks. Welcome to junior high.

"How do you say your name?" Mrs. Leach asks when I enter her classroom and hand over the paperwork.

"Beverly RAD-zee," I say.

That's not my name, I want to shout. But I don't say anything. I go along with the new name Momma has given me. I've been Beverly Armento since I was born. That's who I am. I'm Italian—my father's daughter. I guess that's why Momma wants to assign me a new name. She's destroyed his photographs, now his name. Perhaps she can get rid of her Tony Armento memories now.

"Take that seat in the middle row, Miss Radzai," Mrs. Leach says, pointing. "It's almost time for the bell for first period."

All the kids look at me as I slip into my new desk. No one claps to welcome me. But most of them—Black kids, white kids, sitting next to one another—do smile at me as they look me up and down to see what they can figure out about me.

The middle row? I'm used to sitting in the front row—near the teacher, near the chalkboard. I'm used to being first: first when the roll is called, first in line, first to have my hand up to answer a question. Now this teacher is putting me smack dab in the middle of the classroom. I want my name back. I don't belong lost in the middle.

"Sharene, you have the same schedule as Beverly," Mrs. Leach says, her glasses resting low on the bridge of her nose as she examines my class plan. "Please take her with you to your classes today. Make sure she meets all her teachers and gets her books."

Sharene, her hair all braids and tiny barrettes, blocks my view of the blackboard. She turns around and gives me a big smirk like she just got a stomachache because the teacher picked her to be my helper. Now she's stuck with me all day.

"Here's her locker and combination," Mrs. Leach says, handing Sharene a piece of paper, as the bell rings. "Teach her how to use it."

• • •

Between homeroom and math, Sharene takes me to my locker. It's on the bottom. I bend down to try out the combination lock. Seventh, eighth, and ninth graders swarm out into the halls. Big kids. Lots of kids. All go to their lockers. Everyone talks, shouts. Bodies push other bodies. Someone steps on my skirt. I stand up, look around. I don't see Sharene. I'm lost in this swarm of sweaty, smelly humanity.

Suddenly, someone grabs my hand. Sharene.

"Come on, we'll be late for math," she hollers over the crowd.

She's not much taller than I, but she knows how to navigate the hallway traffic. I hang on. We weave in and out, below armpits and around football players.

The morning goes fast. First math, then science, then music. Bring ten dollars for a flutophone. Every time we change classes, Sharene grabs my hand so she won't lose me in the hallway. Now we head to the cafeteria. The smells of hot dogs and macaroni and cheese hang in the air, and the noisy, large room set up with long tables is crowded with seventh graders by the time we get there. For a moment, I'm overwhelmed by this strange experience. In all my other schools, we simply ate our lunch in our homerooms, at our own desks.

"You can sit with me at lunch," Sharene says.

I'm relieved to have an invitation.

A Black girl, her hair pulled back from her face and wrapped into a bun on top of her head, leans across the table. "What's your name?" she shouts at me over the lunchroom hubbub.

"Today, it's Beverly Radzai," I say, unwrapping my peanut butter sandwich.

"What do you mean, *today?*" the girl next to me shouts, laughing and pointing at me. All the girls at the table turn and look toward me. I'm the only white girl at the long table. The table next to us is all white kids. Then there are more tables of only Black kids. Guess the cafeteria is segregated. I'm a little self-conscious, but not uncomfortable. My table is louder than the white girls' table next to us, but aside from that and the skin color and hair style differences, I'm thinking, *These girls are friendly and nice,* and *They like me and I like them.*

"What was your name yesterday?" one girl howls from down the table.

I laugh too. I didn't think it was funny all morning, But now, all of a sudden, it's hilarious.

"Yesterday, I was Beverly Armento," I say, laughing. "Today, my mother changed my name to Beverly Radzai."

"I want my mother to change my name to JoElle," Sharene says. "You want one of my cookies?" She offers me a home-made oatmeal-raisin, and I accept.

"I want to be Shirley," another girl says.

All the girls scream out what they want their names to be. Sharene hits me on my back, pumps my hand, and congratulates me on having a new name.

"You can sit with us tomorrow," Lasette says as we finish lunch. "Maybe you'll have another new name."

• • •

After lunch, it's time for gym.

"I'll introduce you to Miss Ellis, and then I have to hurry and dress out for class," Sharene says as we walk into the coach's office.

Coach Ellis, dressed in a crisp white cotton shirt buttoned down the front, white shorts that come down past her knees, white sneakers, and a red whistle on a red cord around her neck, extends her hand. We shake. Sharene introduces me and scurries off.

"Tomorrow you need to bring ten dollars for your gym suit," Miss Ellis says. "Come on, I'm going to give you a tour and explain some things. But first we need to go into the gym."

Where am I going to get twenty dollars by tomorrow? We haven't lived in Passaic long enough for me to get any babysitting jobs. I'll have to ask Momma for money. There will be a scene about that tonight, I'm sure. I'll worry about this for the rest of the afternoon.

About fifty girls, decked out in white sneakers and blue one-piece bloomer uniforms with neat small belts at their waists, are lined up in five rows in the gym. A group of boys, all in blue uniforms and white sneakers, are lined up on the other half of the gym. A student stands in front of each group, taking attendance.

"Okay, girls," Miss Ellis says. "We have a new student, Beverly Radzai."

"Beverly Radzai *today*," several girls chirp. I grin at my lunch-table friends, stifling a giggle. I'm going to like junior high, after all.

Miss Ellis raises her hand to quiet the group. "I need a few minutes to show her around. Annette, finish up with attendance and then I want you girls to start your warm-up exercises until I return. Josie, you're the captain of Team A, and Sandra, Team B."

Annette calls out names again and Miss Ellis leads me into the dressing room. There are three aisles, a long wooden bench down the middle of each. The walls are lined with long, narrow, black lockers.

"You need to bring a combination lock tomorrow," Miss Ellis says. "You'll lock your street clothes in a locker during class. Overnight, you can store your gym clothes in your regular locker, but you must take your uniform home on Fridays to wash and iron it. The only time you're excused from physical education is when you have your period. Then you can 'sit out.' Only one day. Otherwise, you're expected to dress in your uniform and be on the court by the second bell, lined up and ready for class."

"After class, everyone takes a shower," Miss Ellis says as we walk through the changing rooms and into the steamy area where group showers line both walls. "This is mandatory."

Faucets and shower heads, evenly spaced along the white ceramic tiles, stretch to infinity. I squeeze my eyes shut. I'm going to pass out at the thought of being naked in a shower with forty-nine seventh grade girls.

"You'll use these towels." She unfolds one from the tall, white stack on a table outside the showers. It's barely large enough to cover the front of me, to say nothing about hiding the bruises and belt marks across my back and legs. What happened to recess, back at my elementary schools, where we played double Dutch, hopscotch, kickball, and tag in our regular school clothes?

• • •

The last two periods of the day combine social studies and language arts. The teacher hands me a page with five story-openers, a pad of paper, and a timer. "Go sit in the back of the room and take the next forty minutes to write an essay on one of these topics so I can see a sample of your work," she says.

When the timer rings, Mrs. Jones walks to my desk and picks up my story. She stands beside my desk and critiques it out loud. Several kids turn around and watch. I pretend I don't see them. I've written a story about a girl's first day in school; I based it loosely on my first day at Columbus School in Lodi.

"I like how you open the story, Beverly, going right into the classroom and leading straight away into dialogue between the main character and the teacher. This is good. Colorful imagery.

Coherent scene development. Surprise ending. You make me want to know what's going to happen to your character. Good job on developing your story. No problems with grammar or spelling. Nice work."

One kid who has been listening the whole time gives me a big grin. I grin back.

"I'm going to recommend you for the school newspaper, *The Wilsonian*, next year," she says when she finishes her summary. "Would you like that?"

"I'd love that," I say to my new angel-teacher.

• • •

Sharon and I arrive home about the same time. I dropped her off at her new school, McKinley #8, early this morning at seven thirty. She was clutching her own sealed manila envelope so she could enroll in third grade. When I see her now at four, her eyes are wide and glassy, as if something has frightened her.

"Momma changed my name," she whispers.

"Changed mine too," I tell her.

"What does that mean?"

"Sharon, you're the same person you were yesterday," I say like I know what I'm talking about, like I've figured it all out. "Momma can't take that away from us. She wants to let us know we're not Dad's kids anymore."

"But we are, aren't we?" Sharon asks.

"Sure we are," I say. "It doesn't matter what we're called. We know who we are, and that's the only thing that's important. Right?" I really have no idea why Momma changed our names, but I need to convince Sharon as well as myself that it's not a big deal.

There's one thing I do know for sure. Like Momma selling our bicycles, having a new name is something we can't change.

Chapter 16

GUINEA HILL AND POLACK VALLEY

BEVERLY MOVES TO CLIFTON

Beverly Radzai, managing editor of The Wilsonian, *has moved to Clifton. We all wish Beverly good luck in her new school and hope she gains as many new friends as she had here.*
—The Wilsonian, *front page story, March 28, 1956*

I'm heartbroken. A month after our middle-of-the-night walk to the Most Holy Name of Jesus Slovak National Catholic Cathedral, Momma talked Ron Radzai into leaving our Passaic apartment that was plagued with communists and chinchillas, radiation and danger. I had to say good-bye to all my friends, leave my leadership roles at school, and forego ninth grade graduation with teachers and classmates I loved.

We rented a sweet little bungalow in Clifton and I enter another junior high, also named Woodrow Wilson. I wasn't there long enough to complete a six-week grading period when we moved again, this time to Garfield. Now I'm a freshman at

Garfield High School—entering, once again, at the worst time: the end of the academic year.

May 1956

Guinea Hill and Polack Valley. That's how the kids on our street describe our new city. We fit in perfectly with our two blond Polish boys and two dark Italian girls. Our tiny apartment, situated above a luncheonette, next to the railroad tracks and in the heart of the main commercial corridor in Garfield, is the place we'll live for the next six years—the longest we'll ever live anywhere.

Garfield is a two-square-mile village a short fifteen-minute drive from New York City. It's bounded on the west by the meandering Passaic River and on the south by a long, winding ethnic street market that links Lodi, Garfield, and Passaic. That's where we live: on Passaic Street, on the southernmost fringe of the city, near the big dip in the road at the train trestle, dug out years ago so the horse-drawn trolley wouldn't have to cross the railroad tracks. That was back in the days when textile mills and chemical plants polluted the river and tainted the air.

The Garfield train station is one building away from our apartment, which is right above Milly's Luncheonette and across the street from Mae's Sweet Shop. Small, family-owned shops line both sides of Passaic Street selling just about anything you might want, from pork chops and kielbasa at the butcher's to fresh fruit and vegetables at the farm stand to a bottle of milk at the general store to a full meal at the luncheonette. Many of the proprietors live above their stores, but above Milly's are four unrelated families who fill the tiny apartments on the second and third floors of the red brick building, the tallest on our block. Sandwiched between the luncheonette's large glass windows and a barber shop is a white wooden door with three diamond-shaped cutout windows set about six feet high. The brass numbers, 89, centered above the windows, announce our address: 89 Passaic Street.

• • •

The first time I see the apartment is the day the movers unload our stuff. Ron Radzai has picked up the four of us kids from school—our last day in Clifton, where we've lived less than two months. But here we are, in front of the white door—yet another place to live and more new schools to attend. Ron Radzai opens the door and all of us kids cram into the narrow hallway. On my left, four black metal mailboxes are set into the wall. *Radzai* is already printed on the first box.

Up we go. "Sixteen, seventeen, eighteen," I count out loud. We have eighteen glistening white marble steps in the hallway. Then we open another door. Our apartment is to the right. The door stands wide open. Momma is inside, directing the placement of our furniture.

We maneuver around two men who've hoisted the sofa bed above their heads and around the big white refrigerator that butts up to the front door. They pivot to the right, into the living room. We follow the men, eager to see the new place.

"You can put the sofa right up against the half wall," Momma says. The half wall separates the shallow, rectangular living room from the kitchen. Our *This Is Your Life* television is already on, positioned kitty-corner from the sofa's new spot, near the two windows that look out to Passaic Street, the trestle, and Mae's Sweet Shop; its snow-covered black-and-white screen conceals Dick Clark's face but not his universally recognizable voice.

"This is going to be your bedroom," Momma says to Ronnie, now eight, and Mikey, five. She's already figured out how a family of six will cram itself into a tiny two-bedroom apartment. The boys won't have any privacy in this open room—the place where they will eat, do their homework, watch television, and sleep until one is well into his teens and the other eleven years old.

On the other side of the half wall is the kitchen. Our round black-and-white Formica table is set up against the wall and two matching chrome-and-black plastic chairs are at opposite sides of the table. This is where Momma and Ron Radzai will sit for hours, playing gin rummy, drinking coffee, and eating their meals. All of us kids will eat with plates on our laps, hanging around the boys' room, watching television. Even though you could force six chairs around the table, we only have two, and in this apartment I will never practice setting the silverware like I learned to do in 4-H. Since we use it so often, our pressure-cooker sits on the counter between the sink and the gas stove and under the small window that looks out to the alley and the two-story bank building that blocks our kitchen view of the train station. Once, in Passaic, the pressure cooker top blew off with such force it left a huge hole in the ceiling and sent stuffed cabbages flying around the kitchen. One of us kids said something like, "The communists are back," which Momma didn't think was very funny. We then busied ourselves picking up the food, and Momma washed it off for dinner. Ron Radzai inspected the pot and proclaimed it to be "okay," so it has continued to feed us at least once a week.

I walk down the apartment's short hallway and open the folding doors on my left. Momma has set our broom, mop, and ironing board inside the closet, along with some of the boys' hanging clothes—their cotton shirts and pants. It's my job to hand wash and press their school clothes and I'll do that for the years to come—scrubbing them in the tiny bathroom sink, laying them around the tub to drip dry, and setting up the board in the hallway to iron enough to give my brothers fresh, neatly starched shirts for the week ahead.

Opposite the closet, on my right, are two doors. The first opens to Momma and Ron Radzai's bedroom and the second to the bedroom Sharon and I will share. Momma's double bed is set up, the headboard against the other side of the kitchen wall and a tall dresser on the side of the wall that butts up to my bedroom. There's also a built-in closet, where Momma hangs her fancy, strapless party dresses and the collared knit shirts that Ron Radzai wears to work on the assembly line each evening. Soon after Momma was featured on *This Is Your Life*, she bought the first of many cocktail dresses; absent any party invitations, she wears them to the grocery store, the post office, and our Robinson family reunions in western New York, where Aunt Lena and Grandma Robby greet her arrival in their gravy-stained aprons and all our cousins ooh and aah at their "famous" auntie Allie.

The bedroom I share with Sharon is at the end of the hall, right next to the bathroom. Our double bed sits flush with the door, the headboard against the hallway wall. My side of the bed is right inside the door, so I'm the first one Momma grabs when she comes looking for Sharon and me.

At the foot of Sharon's side of the bed is a tall, narrow window with a crank opener. Because there's no screen, we can crank open the window and step onto the back porch. This window will be our secret exit—the way Sharon and I will sneak out of the house and run down the alley and across the street to buy a candy bar at Mae's.

The tiny bathroom at the very end of the hallway has a toilet, sink, and tub with shower head and plastic curtain. There's a window with another crank opener, right above the toilet. Over the years, our various cats will come and go through this window, bringing in live gifts for us humans.

The bathroom's and our bedroom's windows lead to a concrete landing with steps up to the third-floor apartments and steps down to the gravel yard that doubles as a parking lot for the renters and the employees of the chemical plant next door, its blue and yellow metal drums lined up in front of the one-story cement building's loading dock. Strange smells waft into our apartment and linger in the parking lot where we play, but we'll soon acclimate ourselves to these odors and carry on like normal.

. . .

We never put chairs on the back porch but occasionally sit on the concrete and play jacks or marbles. The boys play catch on the gravel yard and all four of us often play tag or kickball, but we girls are getting too old for such games and our enthusiasm to run around with our little brothers soon wanes. They eventually find a few boys in the neighborhood and get up games that last until Momma calls them in—usually well into dark.

The hours we spend on homework increase. Since the living room is actually the boys' bedroom, there isn't a common area for everyone to gather. What little cohesiveness we had as a family unit becomes even more fragmented during the Garfield years, with the boys relegated to the front living room, the girls to their bedroom, and Ron Radzai and Momma splitting their time between their bedroom and the kitchen.

We have our own version of Guinea Hill and Polack Valley right in our little apartment. The boys look just like their Polish father—blond and fair-skinned, with blue eyes. We girls are cut from our Italian father—brown-haired, dark-skinned, and square-jawed. The fact that the four of us have the same mother isn't easy to detect in our physical traits. I think of the boys as my brothers, but now the separation between us grows—in part because of the geography of our apartment, and in part because of the different ways Momma treats us.

Perhaps because of Momma's anger with our Italian father, her rage is selective, directed only toward us girls. I never see Momma raise a hand to either boy. But she does beat their father—often enough that the police arrive at our Garfield address on many occasions only to hear Ron Radzai say, "Everything's okay, Officer."

The best family times are when we visit relatives. We drive over the George Washington Bridge to Yonkers to see our Polish relatives—Ron Radzai's parents, his two sisters, his brother, and their families. Momma never again suggests that we visit any of our Italian relatives in Yonkers and I soon forget all about Uncle Frank, Aunt Marion, Cousin Margaret, and my godfather, Michael. For our weeklong summer vacations, we drive to western New York to attend Robinson family reunions, where we visit with Grandma Robby, Aunt Lena, and Momma's six brothers and all their families. By now I've forgotten the secrets Aunt Lena told me in Hollywood, so I don't remember to ask her more questions about my childhood. Uncle Bud, one of Momma's favorite brothers and the youngest of the eight children, usually hosts the reunion picnics. Each time, Momma insists we stay at Letchworth State Park for the week—in Cabin C-10, a rustic log cabin with bunk beds and no running water. The cabin area is at the Lower Falls, where the CCC camp was based and the Friday night dances held. We cook out on the grill and traipse over to use the group bathrooms. Many years later, I will remember Dad's CCC days and wonder if Cabin C-10 held special memories for Momma and if she still savored those thoughts in spite of her fury with my father.

Momma's art table and easel disappear when we move to Garfield. This is big. Momma was supposed to be the *next great commercial artist*. This was the reason we moved from Miami. Being an artist was what Momma wanted, what she dreamed about, what she worked for. Momma started her Famous Artist's correspondence school lessons soon after her sight was restored in 1950, when I was nine, and has worked diligently until now, in 1956.

For six years, Momma regularly sent in her work and received lengthy critique letters, along with a professional artist's hand-drawn corrections, done in red ink on see-through paper that sat atop the original drawing she submitted for the lesson. The artist-critics in Stamford taught Momma how to draw the human body by re-drawing her work—showing her, element by element, what she should be doing. Momma seldom shared these drawings with me or discussed her work, but I saw the corrections sitting on the kitchen table and noticed her grades when we lived in Miami, Lodi, and Passaic: B, B-, C+, C. Momma put all the feedback into a folder and started on her next lesson, one on perspective. She drew a barn. The return mail included another overlay with the "correct" way to draw a barn. Momma never said this to me, but I imagine she was disappointed with her poor grades, her slow progress, and all the red-ink corrections.

Momma's art lessons were made more difficult by her increasingly diminished vision. I did notice around the time Momma thought communists were shooting radiation at us that she was spending less time at her art table. Rather, she spent her evenings listening for chinchillas at the black kitchen pipe. By the time we moved to Garfield, her eye disease had fully reinfected both corneas, and the doctors told her she'd need another round of transplants. For the last two years, she has had to move her chair closer and closer to her canvas to see what she was drawing.

As a teenager, Momma was a portrait artist. But her Famous Artist lessons included few portraits. Instead, there were lots of human bodies in action poses, animals, buildings, and outdoor scenes. Momma never had formal art training; she's an intuitive, self-taught artist. Her early drawings of women—sensitive, expressive, and detailed—are what inspired several artists to encourage Momma, to predict her success, to urge her to move to Stamford, to take a risk on her. However, once we moved to New Jersey, there was no further word from any of the famous artists. There were no phone calls to praise her, no letters, no promises, no encouragement. I wonder if any of the famous artists noticed how poorly she was doing in her lessons or that by March of this year, soon after our long walk to the Catholic Cathedral and after her eyes clouded over again, Momma stopped sending in her lessons.

Momma will never talk about this, but she will never again doodle new drawings or take out her old illustrations to admire. She will never again raise her easel. Her art career is over.

She always seemed happy to be at her art table. I'm sad to see that it is no longer in her bedroom, disappointed to see this opportunity for Momma disappear along with her dreams of becoming the "next great commercial artist in the country." I don't know how long Momma thought about quitting her lessons or how discouraged she was. She kept all these feelings to herself. What is obvious to me is that ever since she stopped drawing, her behavior has become more delusional, more rageful, more erratic, and more bizarre.

Giving up her dream of becoming an artist may have been a major turning point for Momma.

It certainly is proving to be a turning point for our family.

November 1956

"You communist son of a bitch," Momma screams at Ron Radzai from the bathroom. The flush of the toilet echoes in my bedroom. It's Momma's new medicine, heading to the sewer.

"Damn bastards. Trying to poison me. You're all crazy," she hollers, her voice filling the tiny apartment. "I'm not taking these pills."

For good measure, she stops off in my bedroom.

"You goddamned communist," she screams, pinching my arm. "Are you in on this?" There's something terribly wrong with Momma's mind. Now it looks like Ron Radzai thinks the same thing. He took Momma to a doctor today, but she is not a willing patient. She insists nothing is wrong with her. All the rest of us are crazy. She refuses to return to the doctor and refuses to take any medicine. It's all a conspiracy to harm her, and we're all in on it.

Ron Radzai never talks with me about Momma, so I will never learn what the doctor said or if there is a diagnosis. I don't tell him about our late-night adventures either. I don't know if he knows about the radiation, the chinchillas, the night we spent at church, or even that Momma beats us girls. He is home for much of the screaming. But he never comes to rescue me, or to take away her weapons—the broom, the belts. Much of the chaos happens at night, after he's gone to work—but not all of it.

When we moved to Miami and the beatings began, I thought Momma was just mean—angry with Dad and us girls. Now, her rage colors our lives and takes on new forms every day. Her behavior is not just mean, it's delusional, irrational, and unpredictable. Momma knows how to be normal—and she is any time folks come to visit or when we visit relatives. Social workers and women from the local churches used to come over with clothes and food. Sometimes they'd come just to talk with Momma because they found her interesting, talented, expressive. Most everyone who meets her comments on how sweet she is, such a creative artist and wonderful person. Momma's behavior on television shows suggests that she's a well-balanced, intelligent, calm woman, a person who loves her family and is a capable mother and wife. But that's only part of the story, the public face of Momma.

Behind the scenes, she's out of control, violent, prone to sudden episodes of anger and rage. Her delusions about communists and Guineas are more frequent and frightening now. I don't dare tell my friends about Momma's behavior. I'm not sure they'd believe me if I did. The Momma they know is a completely different person.

All these secrets I keep to myself.

Chapter 17

THE WONDER OF IT ALL

December 1956

Multicolored bubble lights on our two-foot-tall artificial tree draw my attention as I enter our apartment. Class was dismissed early today because it's the last day before Christmas recess, and it looks like I'm the first one home. The tree sits on a table in the middle of our living room window that looks out to Passaic Street. From Mae's Sweet Shop across the street, you can get a perfect view of our family's proclamation that the holidays are here.

Four lights aren't bubbling—too bored after sitting in a dark cardboard box these last eleven months to muster up the energy, I think. I run my hand along the lowest branches, reshaping the wires. I wind up with a handful of plastic. Even fake trees lose dead needles.

As I sit and stare at the little tree, I remember Christmas in Miami, when we had real trees decorated in blues, silvers, and gold—trees full of shimmering tinsel that we gingerly placed, strand by strand, on just the right branch so that all the decorations were perfectly balanced no matter where you stood to admire the tree—and I sigh. After the tree dried out and Momma decided it was time to be done with Christmas, we'd replace each ball in its special cardboard compartment. Then, one by one, we'd lay the icicles on a flat cardboard, ready for the next year.

When lit, our Miami trees took my breath away. They created a stillness, a silent-night kind of quiet—the reverence the holiday was due.

That was a long time ago, I remind myself.

• • •

The Christmas I remember most is 1950—the year Momma regained her sight and we lost our baby, Mickey. What a year that was—miracles and joy, loss and sadness. It was the year Momma started drawing again after a decade in near-total darkness.

As she promised, I was her first subject. Her lesson called for her to draw a complete human figure. She seated me sideways on a chair, facing her, my left arm resting on the Formica table top and my left hand crossing my body to reach my right wrist. She told me to cross my legs at my ankles. I wore my favorite bloomer and halter set and had my locket on a thin chain around my neck. When she finally got me settled just the way she wanted, I had to sit perfectly still for hours while she worked with charcoal pencils until she thought the sketch was perfect.

When I looked at her drawing, I cried. I knew I was beautiful in her mind. I had a huge smile on my face as I hugged her and said, "Thank you, Momma." I stood and stared at my face, my body, as seen through Momma's new eyes. *That's just how I look*, I thought. *How did she do this?* I was so proud of my mother. "You're a great artist, Momma."

Momma also had a big smile on her face as she packaged the drawing and sent it to the art school. When she received the professional critique about a week later, however, her smile disappeared. On see-through paper attached to her original drawing, the artist had completely re-drawn me in red pencil to illustrate the correct way to represent a human figure. He highlighted where the muscles and joints were and how the artist should employ this knowledge. In the margins, he drew enlarged versions of my face, eyes, hair, mouth, and leg to teach Momma how she should have portrayed these elements.

Momma was very quiet as she studied the drawing and read the long letter the artist had written, explaining the human body in detail and reiterating the lessons he wanted her to incorporate in her future drawings. She stored everything in her folder and went to her easel to start Lesson Two.

I told her I liked her drawing of me better than his but that didn't seem to make her happy. Her drawing looked exactly like me—she'd captured my eyes, my serious nature, the true shape of my face. This was her first opportunity to represent me on paper, the first time she'd actually studied me long enough to draw me. That was the wonder of it all. I was nine years old, and my mother could finally see me. That meant the world to me. The professional artist had never met me, didn't know my face, my personality. He may not even have known that Momma had been blind all of her life. Even though he was technically correct in his revisions, Momma had drawn me as the sweet, shy girl she saw, and it was perfect. The teacher missed the miracle.

That year, 1950, everyone was looking forward to Christmas. I'd seen Momma whispering to the church ladies about gifts she thought we'd like. I'd hinted for some time that I wanted to learn how to twirl a baton, but I would never come right out and ask for something that extravagant and totally unnecessary. I did need a new dress for church, so that's what I asked for. Sharon wanted a new doll and Ronnie needed a playpen and some blocks. Ron Radzai's meager salary was enough to keep us in basics, but not enough to buy extras. Somehow, the "social ladies," as we called them, always came through for us kids and the family.

Our tree was particularly beautiful that Christmas. Momma orchestrated the decorating, sitting on the floor with Ronnie, Sharon, and me as we put together the crèche while singing carols with Frank Sinatra, Bing Crosby, and Bob Hope. She talked non-stop about the details on the carved wooden wise men, how small yet distinct the features were on baby Jesus, and how the light reflected off the many shiny balls on the tree. It was the first time in her life that she could clearly see the magic in the blue, silver, and gold tree that had been part of her life since childhood, when her own mother and her siblings decorated their trees year after year in blue, silver, and gold.

As usual, Sharon and I went to Christmas Eve services at our Baptist church. When we arrived home, we found Momma, Ron Radzai, and baby Ronnie sitting in the dark living room, the only light the quiet peacefulness of our tree. We tiptoed into the room and sat with them, soaking up the magic of the baby Jesus's birth, the marvel of Momma's new eyes, and the secret of the new baby growing within her.

Finally, Momma broke the silence. "Now, you girls need to get ready for bed. In the morning, you can go to the bathroom if you wake up early. But you need to wait for your father and me to get up. Then we'll go to the living room together." With a big smile, she added, "This is going to be a wonderful Christmas."

Every time Momma was in such a good mood, I'd convince myself that my Yonkers mother had returned. So that Christmas Eve, I lay in bed and said a prayer of thanks to God for bringing her back, and told Him that I'd devote myself to missionary work if He'd make sure she kept her good humor. I'm not sure God appreciated the bribery, but that was the way I convinced myself He was listening.

Awake before daybreak, I tiptoed out to the bathroom. "There are scraps of paper all over the hallway floor," I said when I returned.

"Do you think Santa Claus left in a hurry and dropped all that paper?" Sharon asked when she lay back down on our mattress.

We didn't have long to wait. Soon we heard Ronnie's cries and Momma's voice calling us to the living room.

The tree was aglow in its cerulean beauty, the radio was playing non-stop carols, and the aroma of cinnamon rolls in the oven added to the spell of this special morning. Beside the tree, a new playpen had been assembled and was full of blocks, stuffed toys, miniature cars, and trains. Sharon ran to a large doll who sat atop a box full of tiny cups and saucers much like the ones I'd once played with in Yonkers. Several wrapped gifts were scattered around the base of the tree.

Handing me a long box, Momma said, "Something special for a special girl."

I couldn't believe my eyes: a brand-new baton! Before I could take a practice twirl through my fingers, Momma touched my arm and whispered, "Let's wait until we've all opened our presents and then you can go outside with your new baton."

I lay my baton on my lap and caressed its silver rod while I waited for everyone to take their turn. Ron Radzai held up a new beige shirt he could wear to work, Momma tried on a frilly pink blouse, Ronnie lined up his toy cars in a row, and Sharon took all the clothes off her new doll. Finally, Momma turned to me and said, "Have you noticed all the paper on the floor?"

Of course I'd noticed. Scraps of paper ran the length of the hallway and into each of our bedrooms. Our home was always neat and tidy, so this was highly unusual. "Sharon thought Santa left a mess," I said, laughing.

"Well, Santa did," Momma said.

She was playing a joke on me. She knew that I knew all about Santa, but she had something up her sleeve. Ever since I'd surprised Momma with the red pepper, she'd been playful— that is, on the days she was in really good spirits, like today.

"Here's a paper bag. Take your sister and follow the trail to look for a hidden treasure. Pick up the paper as you go. Once you find your surprise, bring it back here so everyone can see."

Sharon and I took off on our little Christmas adventure, giggling as we filled the bag with the pieces of paper Momma had torn from the local newspaper. We followed the path into the bathroom, into and around the bedrooms, and back to Momma's closet. I opened the door and there, hidden behind some shoes, were two gifts wrapped in white tissue paper.

"We found the treasure," I hollered as Sharon and I scooped up the large boxes and ran back to the living room.

Everyone pitched in to help me open my packages. In the first was my new all-white majorette outfit, a short, pleated skirt with bloomers and a short-sleeved blouse. I could tell immediately that it would be a perfect fit. In the second box, glistening with sassy red tassels, were my brand-new white leather marching boots. I was so happy I sobbed out loud.

"Stop blubbering before you get your new uniform all wet." Momma laughed and patted my shoulder. "Go put it on so we can see our majorette."

For the rest of Christmas day, I high-stepped all around Victory Homes, showing off my extraordinary new gifts and the few tricks I'd taught myself with the baton. I couldn't wait to strut with the other majorettes in the Little River courtyard and learn new routines.

• • •

These are all distant memories now, six years later, as I stare at the bubbling lights in our Garfield apartment. I can't remember a time since I was nine when Momma has created a surprise for me or has touched me lovingly.

Well, yes, there was one time. In 1952, when I was eleven and the *Woman's Home Companion* editor and photographer spent a week with us, they set up one of my favorite photos.

Momma was seated in her comfortable chair, her head reclining against the head rest, her eyes closed, as I read a book to her. I sat at her feet, and she rested her hand on my shoulder. I can still feel her touch.

Our family had put on a great show that week, and I think the WHC team came to believe we really were a loving family. I'm sure they and the readers of the published article thought the photos represented typical family behaviors. The truth of the matter was that we were great actors.

My baton, majorette outfit, boots, and all the Christmas decorations were among the many things we left in Miami when we packed the car to head toward Momma's dream of becoming a famous artist. We asked Mrs. Kinnard to find another deserving family and I imagined some nine-year-old girl strutting around in my boots and twirling my baton. We haven't had a blue, silver, and gold tree since then, and I doubt we'll ever see one again.

Everything in our lives now revolves around Momma, and nothing happens without her say-so. We each know where we stand and when to get out of the way, when to disappear. The boys are consumed with their sore eyes and the knowledge that they'll lose their sight one day. The girls escape to school and to church, and Ron Radzai to work. Sharon and I conspire, in whispers, in our bedroom or on our long walks to church. We purposely lie to protect one another. But when Momma starts in on one of us, it's every girl for herself.

On Christmas Day, Sharon and I will walk the mile down Passaic Street to the First Methodist Church and if everyone is in a good frame of mind, Ron Radzai will grate some potatoes and onions and make us a pancake lunch.

We'll each get an item of clothing. The girls will go to our room to read and the boys will watch TV. Momma and Ron Radzai will play gin rummy.

And that will be Christmas.

Chapter 18

MEN, MEN, MEN

January 1957

"So, do you have a boyfriend?" Joe asks me. He sits at the foot of the double bed Sharon and I share, facing me, caressing the part of my right leg that sticks out from beneath my pink flannel nightgown.

I'm propped up against the headboard, my lap covered in textbooks and papers, my pen poised above my composition pad, ready to get back to work. Joe rubs my legs and talks with me most evenings he comes to see Momma. At first, I was frightened of this strange man, but over the last few months I've gotten used to his presence and to Momma's new behavior. What choice do I have? Adapt, do your homework, make the best of it. That's what Sharon and I try to do. We talk about it. A lot. And we're relieved every day to get to school. But at night, we have few options.

I don't know where Momma met Joe, but soon after her second round of successful corneal transplants in June 1956, he showed up. *Wife Sees Husband Again after Two Year Blindness* was the local newspaper headline. "Oh, he looks so good," Momma gushed when she saw Ron Radzai after her surgery. It didn't take long, though, before Momma had eyes for more than Ron Radzai.

"You ask me the same question every time you're here, Joe. You know I don't have a boyfriend," I whisper. I still haven't figured out if I like this ugly, hairy, little guy with a big nose on a square face or if I can't stand him. Tonight, I'm annoyed that he and his men are here, well after midnight. I still have at least an hour's worth of English homework to finish and I'm trying to keep the bedroom quiet for Sharon, who's sound asleep next to me, bundled in our blue blanket like a mummy, her back against my left leg, covers pulled up over her face to block out the light.

"I'm going to get a cup of coffee and give you time to finish up your homework. Then I'll come back to see you." Joe winks at me like I'm his girlfriend. "Can I get you a cup of coffee?"

"You know I don't drink coffee." I smile at him and pat his arm as he walks past me to head out to the kitchen. At first, I didn't like that he came so often to visit Momma. I didn't like that he came into my bedroom, that he touched me. He was creepy, and I was scared of him. But after a while, having him here, stroking my legs, passing the time—it all just seemed normal. I don't pull my legs up and away from him now like I did during the summer. I have to concentrate to get my homework done while I entertain him with conversation, but most evenings I manage just fine.

For the first two months, Joe came alone. Then he brought others. This was all new to Sharon and me, and we were shocked to think about what happened on the other side of our bedroom wall.

The men come most Mondays and Wednesdays, soon after Ron Radzai leaves for the night shift at US Rubber. Usually two men. Sometimes three or four. Most all Italians. And always, there is Joe, his legs made even by a big, black orthopedic shoe on his right foot. Sharon and I make up stories about what might have happened to his leg. Maybe he was shot in the war or had a factory accident where his foot jammed in a machine. Perhaps he was born that way, with a short leg. I've never gotten up the nerve to ask him. The men take turns. When one's in the bedroom with Momma, the others sit in the kitchen drinking coffee or they sit on the bed and talk with us girls. The kitchen crew is usually quiet because Ronnie and Mikey are asleep on the sofa on the other side of the half wall that separates the kitchen from the living room.

Sharon and I are supposed to be sleeping too. That doesn't stop Joe or the others from coming into our bedroom. Most of the time the men sit on the bed and ask us about school and if we have boyfriends. We ask them if they're married and have children. They're all married, and they all have children. Some even have grandchildren, though most are about Momma's age, thirty-five. They all seem nice enough as they wait patiently for their turn.

I strain to hear what's going on in Momma's bedroom. Even though our apartment building is old and in disrepair, the walls are thick. All I ever catch is an occasional laugh. No one has set me down to tell me about the birds and bees. Sharon and I have figured out the basics from what we've picked up on the playground and from books we've found on the subject. It took us a long time before we knew how a baby gets inside the mother—that sex is all about babies and what's in your panties.

It's hard to imagine all this sex going on right here in our apartment with four kids sleeping nearby. I wonder what the boys think and if they stay awake worrying about Momma. I worry. That she'll get pregnant. That she'll get some disease. That Ron Radzai will come home early, like my dad did that night so long ago.

I worry that I'll be just like her one day.

When Joe touches me, I'm afraid he'll slide his hand up my leg and into my panties. Maybe I want him to touch me all over, like he'll do with Momma when he finally gets into her room. The more Joe rubs my legs, the more I have these strange feelings in my crotch, like when I was younger and used to sit on the monkey bars and rock back and forth. That's when I worry that I am weak. That I'll eventually let Joe move his hand up. That I'll indeed become my mother.

That's when I vow that I'm strong. That this will not happen.

Finally, my homework is done. I clear away my books, turn off the bedroom light, and get under the covers. *Clunk . . . thuh . . . clunk . . . thuh . . .* Joe's coming. He scoots up on the foot of the bed, places his hand on my leg—now covered by a sheet and blanket—slowly, rhythmically rubs. Right where he left off a few hours ago. It's about two in the morning and I have to be up at six to get ready for school. I'm tired, but I do like the attention. None of the boys in school notice me unless they want to see my Latin or geometry homework.

"Joe, I need to get some sleep," I say. "I'll see you next time."

"Go on to sleep. I just want to sit here a little longer."

March 1957

"Stay up tonight. I want you to go with Joe and me after the kids go to bed," Momma says. She comes to my bedroom to tell me this, dressed in her yellow chiffon strapless dress and her clear plastic heels, her bleached blonde hair framing her face, after Ron Radzai leaves for work at eleven thirty.

Momma has never asked me to go out at night with her before, but last summer she did ask cousin Connie, seven years older than I, who had come with her four-year old daughter for a visit. When Momma was a teenager, she babysat for Connie, one of the first of Grandma Robby's grandchildren. So when Connie needed marital advice in 1956, she came calling on her favorite aunt Allie, whom she trusted and loved. She and her daughter stayed here for a few weeks. The four of us girls figured out how we could all fit on our double bed, and we giggled into the nights, telling family stories.

"There are a bunch of men out in the kitchen," Connie told me one night before we closed our bedroom door.

"Yeah, that happens," I said.

In the same way I lie about my bruises, I lie about what goes on at home. I'm embarrassed for Momma. For myself. I want to cover it all up, ignore it; I wish it would all go away. I closed our door during Connie's visit so Joe would stay out. I felt I must keep this part of our lives hidden from my cousin. In our tiny apartment, though, the parade of men was not going to be a secret for long.

"That's weird," Connie said.

"Yeah," I said. "It is. Very weird." I was ashamed of Momma's behavior. I wished she'd ask the men to stay away while Connie was visiting. But even in front of company, Momma now shows her true self, the way we know her.

Connie's daughter had already witnessed Momma chasing me through the apartment, beating me with the broom. This frightened her so much, she screamed uncontrollably for hours. Now, this. Sharon and I were used to the parade of men, but this was very strange to our cousin—most unusual. She was shocked.

"Oh, my," Connie said.

In spite of the closed door, Joe came into our bedroom to chatter with us girls. Connie, an outgoing, effervescent soul, regaled Joe with stories of her childhood. Before you knew it, we were all up on the bed, laughing out loud, bantering with Joe like he was an old friend—just one happy family.

When Momma suggested that Connie accompany Joe and her out one evening, Connie says, "Sure." Like me, Connie felt comfortable around Joe. Certainly, her aunt Allie would protect her.

Connie crawled into bed about four that morning. In tears. We hugged. She sobbed.

"What happened?" I asked.

"I can't talk about it."

The next day, Connie couldn't get on the bus fast enough to return to western New York.

Now Momma wants me to go out with her. Trouble is, I won't be able to take a bus out of Garfield if I don't like what's going to happen. There's no way out for me.

"Sharon, we're going to leave for a few hours," Momma says.

That's Momma's way of telling my twelve-year-old sister she's babysitting the boys. I've gotten really good at reading between the lines to figure out just what Momma means when she does have something to say. Most of the time, though, she's silent, as though she's in a world all her own.

Silence shrouds important topics, like sex and just what these men are doing in our apartment—or what they are doing coming into our bedroom or how any of us kids feel about it. No one in the family talks about their feelings or even about what's happening in our lives—like how hungry we are or how sad we are when the cat dies or when Momma beats us. Silence and rage dominate our home; there's nothing much in between except the cryptic commands and statements we use to communicate with one another.

"We're going to Yonkers": Momma's announcement implying that we should get dressed and head to the car for our periodic trip to see the Radzai family.

"Make a plate": when it's time for dinner.

"We're leaving for a few hours": when Momma needs someone to mind the kids.

I pull on a skirt and blouse and Momma and I walk out of the apartment, down the hallway, and out to the gravel parking lot behind our building, where Joe waits in his black car. He greets me as I get in the backseat, but both he and Momma are silent as he drives out of Garfield. Joe's greasy black hair, slicked straight back, glistens like strands of licorice as we pass under streetlights. I can't imagine why I'm in this car going somewhere strange with Joe and Momma. I remember Connie's face when she returned that night, the fear in her voice. "I have to get back home as soon as I can get a bus ticket," she said.

Joe drives down one residential street after another and finally stops in front of a large two-story white home, set back from the street. No one is on the street at one in the morning and most of the houses we pass are dark, but there are several cars parked near this house. We walk up a dirt path to the front door. Joe pulls a small flashlight out of his pocket, shines the light on the door, unlocks it, and ushers Momma and me into a large, smoke-filled room.

There are oversize black leather chairs along the wall, two lamps on end tables, a few ashtrays full of cigarette butts. Two men stand in the shadows across the room. This is really creepy. I want to run, just run, out of here, out the door I entered. Where is that door? There are doors everywhere. The room closes in in me, the stale smoke chokes me. My heart races.

"Beverly, you can wait here," Joe says. He turns and leads Momma through one of several doors that open off this main room.

I don't want to wait here.

"Joe," I gasp out. "Are you coming back?"

Joe and Momma disappear. My heart pounds. I think it will pop out of my chest. Oh, God. Why am I here?

Suddenly, one of the men is at my side. He smells like cheap cologne and cigarettes. Now he's in front of me, his hands on my arms, stroking me. Like Joe strokes my legs. Up, down, up—slowly. Up farther each time, until his hands are on my shoulders, my neck, my face. My body is a slab of concrete.

I can't move. I'm suffocating. I need to run. Get out of here. I should have known something awful would happen. *Push him. Hit him. Run. Oh, God. Help me get out of here. What is happening?*

The man cups my face, pulls me into his hot, sweaty body. I pull back. His grip on my chin tightens. He kisses me on my forehead, my cheeks. His lips are hot on my mouth. His fingers pry my mouth open. Wet. His tongue thrusts into my mouth. This is so foul. I'm going to gag. I'm trapped. I have to kick him. *Run.* I pull away. He's strong. Big. He grabs me. *No.* I'm stronger. Hit him. I have to get out of here, away from this danger, this horrible, nasty man. *Fight, fight.* But I'm frozen. My arms are weak. I have no strength. I think I'll crumble to the floor.

He pushes me into a leather chair. Kneels in front of me. Unbuttons my blouse. Fumbles behind my back and unbuckles my bra. My breasts tumble out. His mouth, hungry. His tongue makes loud, lapping sounds on my nipples. I'm going to lose this fight. He's overpowering me. I can't lose. I can't do this. I don't want to do this. I have to punch him. Hard. I have to do it. Now.

Even though I'm sixteen, I have only vague notions about what sex is all about. I'm shy about my body. No one has touched me like this, used such force against me, invaded me in this way. I don't know exactly what is happening, but I do know that it's not right and I don't like any of it. I know this is what goes on with Momma and all the men who make their way to her bed. But she's willing. I'm not. I'm not willing. I'm not willing.

"Oh, so beautiful," the man groans. "Don't be afraid. I'll be gentle with you. Here, let me see you."

"No, no," I say, my voice hoarse, weak. It comes from the other side of the room. I push him with all my strength. There's no contest. He grabs my arms, pins them down, lays his body against my legs, forces his body onto my chest.

His mouth has latched onto my breast. His hand goes up my skirt. He pulls my panties off. His fingers. So big. He's hurting me. His breath is heavy, hot, wet. He pants. Suffocates me. *Me.* I'm Beverly. I've got to get out of here. Now. I have to hit him. My mind races, but my body can't get the message. My arms are weak against his power.

"No, no!" I scream. This time my voice is alive, loud, confident. I've found it.

"What did you say?" he asks.

"I said no. No. No. I don't want to do this." *I am not my mother*, I want to scream.

"I don't understand," the man says. "This will be so good. So good for you. Joe said it was time for you. You were ready. I promise. You'll like how I'm going to love you."

"Don't touch me." My voice is calm, deep, certain. "Joe is wrong. Get off me."

He does.

I lie there, in shock. I can't believe this is over. He walks away.

Was it my tone of voice? Was it something I said? Did I actually say, "I am not my mother"?

I'm exhausted from this struggle, from the fear, from the helplessness of it all, from my vulnerability, my weakness. At this moment, I don't feel strong. Don't feel that I've "won" anything. I've been attacked. Viciously. By a friend of Momma's. Of Joe's. They've betrayed me. Taken advantage of me. Misjudged me.

I'm angry. At everybody. Including myself.

•　•　•

No words will ever be spoken about that night, or about Connie's traumatic night and sudden flight from Garfield, or about the day Sharon will come home to an empty apartment to find a man in our bedroom—a man she'll kick so hard when he tries to mount her that she'll knock him out—or about the men who will continue to visit Momma for the seven years we live in

Garfield. Nothing will ever be said. Such matters will simply evaporate into the air—to be processed by each one of us in whatever way we can.

It will take me a while to realize that Joe groomed me for this experience, that he and Momma agreed to bring both Connie and me into these dangerous situations. I can't figure out what they had to gain or why they'd think we would be willing participants. Perhaps I led Joe on, was too willing to allow him to touch me, was too nice to him. I've conditioned myself to be compliant with Momma to minimize her rage, so I was compliant, willing, naïve with Joe too—all to be polite, to avoid a scene. Quite possibly, to curry his favor. To have his attention. I was clueless about the consequences. Now my eyes are open.

I know one thing for sure now, too. I don't want any part of Momma's life for myself.

I refuse to become my mother.

Chapter 19

THE CREAM PUFF

April 1957

I become a food thief when I'm sixteen.

No, that's wrong. I've been stealing food for years.

It started when I picked out all the raisins from the cereal box and scooped extra spoonsful of chocolate ice cream fudge. Momma accused me of doing these things. I told her I didn't do it. She hit me anyway.

I'm a liar and a thief. Not proud of it.

My petty crimes turn into larceny the day our apartment staircase becomes a delivery destination for Milly's Luncheonette.

The sweet aroma of freshly baked bread fills the hallway as soon as I open the door to get our newspaper at six in the morning. A single light bulb hangs from the ceiling, casting an orange glow on the eighteen white marble steps—my evidence that this crumbling building was once a grand place. The newspaper sits midway down the staircase, but my gaze skips to the third and fourth steps. In my stocking feet and pink nightgown,

I tiptoe down the steps, past the newspaper. I peer into three brown paper bags. Each conceals a still-warm loaf of long, crusty Italian bread.

A large tray sits on the step below, filled with two dozen pastries: chocolate-covered cream puffs, cinnamon swirls, blueberry muffins, apple turnovers, jelly-filled donuts, apple fritters, and even a few cannoli. I want to eat them all. First, the cannoli with its thick, sweet, white cream cheese and chocolate bits and yellow and red chunks of dried fruit. Then the apple fritter with its chewy dough, all sticky and hearty. On and on I'd eat. I'd devour the muffin next, its big, fat blueberries bursting in my mouth. Last, the cream puff. But no, I want the cream puff first. That's the one I want.

I'm dizzy with the sweet smell of baked apples and berries, of chocolate and cinnamon. Whipped cream, pudding, cream cheese—they flow in and around the berries, the pastry dough, the chocolate, and swirl together in my brain. It's a Christmas feast set out for my pleasure in April.

There's just enough room on the third step for the pastry tray and my skinny body. I squat down and stare at the chocolate-covered cream puff. Its thick, white whipped cream overflows the golden housing that struggles to contain it. A crunchy, dark brown topping, flaked ever so lightly with specks of confectioner's sugar, pulls me closer.

I didn't come into this cold hallway wanting a cream puff, or even thinking about cream puffs. But now I fixate on this beautiful creation.

I want it. I'm going to take it.

Am I nuts? I'm a good girl. I get good grades. My teachers like me.

I'm the president of the Methodist Youth Fellowship. My minister respects me.

But no one will know.

Take it. Eat it. Be done with it.

For as long as I can remember, Momma's steady stream of venom for Dad has been the extra serving with my every meal. Her gift of guilt. Guilt for having things Dad isn't paying for—my food, clothes, school supplies—all tainted with the qualification that I don't deserve it, that I'm a burden, an ungrateful, additional mouth to feed, a mouth that isn't paying her own way.

I'm tired of taking the blame for my irresponsible father.

I'm tired of feeling guilty about eating too much.

But it's a sin to steal.

If I take it, I could move the apple fritter a little and make it look like the tray is full.

I deserve this cream puff.

No one will miss this cream puff.

I fight back and forth with myself, until it becomes evident which Beverly is going to win this battle and my internal struggle quiets.

The airy pastry evaporates as soon as it hits my tongue. The crisp chocolate topping crackles. I close my eyes, let the cool cream fill my throat. Then I remember where I am. I jump up. A little confectioner's sugar dots the front of my nightgown and the fourth and fifth steps. I lick two fingers, jab them into the marble to erase the clues I almost left behind. I grab the newspaper and rush back to our apartment to get ready for school.

• • •

It's all I think about all day.

I see it in geometry class.

I'm supposed to be finding the areas of ten equilateral triangles but all I can think about is my chocolate-covered cream puff. I've washed my hands a dozen times, yet my fingers still smell like chocolate. I run my hand beneath my nose and inhale. The aroma brings back this morning's pleasure—and my guilt.

In Latin class, my thoughts wander.

Here I am in a college prep track—Latin, Spanish, geometry—but I know I'll never go to college. There's no money. Momma wants me to go to work when I graduate to help support the family, to pay back the debt for my care all these years. I don't know why I'm taking up space in these advanced classes.

Now I'll be caught stealing cream puffs. I'll never get the college scholarship Mr. Tengi, my English teacher, wants me to apply for. No school will admit me if I'm a convicted thief. My concepts of right and wrong, good and evil, were formed early and reinforced by my Baptist and Methodist Sunday School classes. There's no doubt in my mind that I've done wrong.

I can't stop thinking about it. It was so good. The cool cream, the thick, sweet chocolate, the pastry so light. I loved it, this little moment of joy, of warmth, of love. But I wasn't really hungry. I ate it just because it was there. Because I could. Because I was mad—mad at Momma and Dad. Now I'm mad at myself.

Maybe Momma's right. I don't deserve nice food. I don't deserve cream puffs.

I'm not a good girl. I'm a girl I don't respect. A girl I don't like.

It's hard to concentrate in Latin class. I scribble in my notebook:

Pater, da mihi veniam. Miserere mei.
(Lord, forgive me. Be merciful to me.)

• • •

The next morning, I wake early to get the newspaper. Yesterday was a once-in-a-lifetime event. Surely the baker won't leave pastries in the hallway again.

"Please, Jesus—no temptation today," I say before I open the stairway door.

The unmistakable fragrance of freshly baked bread fills the air. I'm frozen at the top step.

Today there are two large trays of pastries and three loaves of bread.

I hesitate, but only for a moment. I race down the stairs, grab an apple fritter, hide it behind the newspaper and run back up the steps. My heart pounds. I puff loudly, try to catch my breath. I hold the newspaper and fritter in my left hand, hurry past Momma's bedroom and into the room Sharon and I share. I close our door without making a sound.

I prop myself up against the headboard and tear the fritter in half. I wave the larger half in front of Sharon's nose. She's barely awake. Her eyes get big. She sits straight up. We devour the sweet, soft, forbidden fruit.

"Where'd you get this?" Sharon asks, licking her fingers.

"In the hallway. Don't ask me any questions. Let's just get ready for school."

Now I'm corrupting my little sister. What's wrong with me?

· · ·

For the next week, the hallway's empty except for our newspaper. I'm relieved. I can get back to my schoolwork. Then, one day, I'm jolted back to reality. The world of hard choices, the world where temptation dangles a pastry in front of my face and my knees buckle—that world comes back to taunt me.

Weak Beverly takes an entire loaf of freshly baked, sliced white bread.

"You got a whole loaf of bread?" Sharon asks. She props herself up on the bed with her right arm. Her long, straight, silky black hair falls over her arm and onto the pillow. Every morning, she eagerly awaits my return from the newspaper run.

I plop the loaf in the middle of our bed, then sit on my side.

We pull back the wrapper. We each take a few slices of still-warm, soft, fragrant bread. Peel off the crusts, wad the pliable bread into hard balls, and bite in. We look at each other, smile, and take another slice. It *is* delicious. We *are* hungry.

"Let's put the rest under the mattress," I say. "Tonight, we can have more."

. . .

Early that Sunday morning, Sharon and I walk out of our apartment onto Passaic Street, turn right, and walk past the big glass windows of Milly's Luncheonette. We look straight ahead. We cross the Passaic River, walk past Sixth Street where we once lived, past the US Rubber plant where Ron Radzai works. We cross Main Street in Passaic and trudge up the steep hill and take a left on Paulison Avenue. We walk well over a mile to get to the brand-new First Methodist Church of Passaic, where I ask for forgiveness. I'm a devoted sinner, and church is an important part of my life.

I bow my head and ask God to forgive me, to give me the strength to stop stealing. God put a test in front of me, and I flunked it. I keep flunking it. It's so easy for me to steal the bread and pastries. The cream puff gives me immediate joy, a feeling of warmth and satisfaction, a little jolt of love. Love, like the way I felt when Momma and Dad put their arms around me and kissed me—a long time ago. The cream puff fills me up. For a moment.

But the warmth I get from the pastry doesn't last long. All too soon I'm hungry again, ravenous, empty. I have to have another, and another. But the stealing doesn't feel good. I'm jittery all the time—afraid I'll be caught and mad at myself because I can't stop. I know I'm becoming a bad person. I'm afraid people won't like me if they discover my true sneaky, lying self.

I worry about all these things. But I keep stealing food. Why am I so good at it?

I'm leading my little sister into bad habits.

I tell God I'll turn over a new leaf. This is it. I'm not going to steal ever again. Ever.

Please, God, give me the strength I need.
The next day I take two pastries.
And the next day and the day after that.
I never get caught.
But I still pay penance, all these years later.

June 1957

Mashed potatoes fly around the kitchen. They land on Ron Radzai's blond hair, slop down his face and onto the black-and-white Formica kitchen table. Momma smacks him again with the masher and blood flows down his forehead, mixes with the potatoes stuck to his cheek, splats in big red and white blobs onto the white linoleum floor.

"What the hell are you doing?" he screams. He grabs her arm and holds it taut. His large upper-arm muscles bulge through his tight baby blue pullover.

I've never seen Ron Radzai hit Momma, but he tries to protect himself when she attacks him—which is often, but not nearly as often as she beats me. I never hit Momma either. But I do shield my face and body, as Ron Radzai's doing right now. Momma will fly into a rage and beat me even more if I fight back. Ron Radzai and I placate her, sweet-talk her, try to keep her calm and happy, do what she wants, and don't rock the boat. I've been doing this so long I don't even think about it anymore. Once things get going and Momma is out of control, it's impossible to calm the waters, to get things back to normal. Ron Radzai and I both know that and act accordingly.

"You, fat bastard—get out of here." Momma turns her attention from Ron Radzai to me.

This is the first time Momma's called me "fat." I guess she sees that I'm gaining weight.

"You girls take your dinner plates and go eat in your bedroom," she tells us. "Your stepfather wants to stare at you."

Momma sees things no one else can imagine. It's funny to think Ron Radzai would do anything wrong. Over all these years, he's only talked directly with me a few times. He almost never looks at me and certainly doesn't look at me in inappropriate ways, as Momma is suggesting. It's ironic that Momma accuses Ron Radzai of harboring sexual intent when it is she who brings nightly visitors into the apartment. I wonder if Ron Radzai has a clue about what goes on at night after he's gone to work. Maybe I should tell him.

Ron Radzai holds Momma's right arm upright. The masher drips potatoes on the floor. She struggles to free herself. While they are frozen in this tableau, I dish a scoop of potatoes from the pot and stick a fork into one of Momma's famous hard-as-a-rock hamburgers.

Instead of going to the living room to watch television with the boys, Sharon and I take our plates to the bedroom, close the door, and sit up against the headboard, our legs spread out in front of us to balance our plates. We look at each other, straight-on. I give Sharon a wink and a smile. She lifts her chin in agreement. We speak a silent language born of survival instincts—one of the many adaptations we've made over these ten years and the countless hours we've spent together, especially on our common bed.

Momma's hamburgers are barely edible. We ate them in the past because that's all we had. Tonight, we have an alternative. We tear the little rock-burgers into tiny pieces. I gather the meat in my left hand, hop off the bed, open our bedroom door, and go into the bathroom, only a step away. I close the bathroom door, flush the hamburger pieces down the toilet. Then I do the same with the potatoes.

Back in our bedroom, I pull up the mattress and grab the loaf of bread I stole this morning. Sharon and I eat our loot for dinner.

Eating in our bedroom has its advantages. Old secrets remain buried, and new ones can be hatched.

Sharon and I eat in our bedroom for six years. From the time we arrive home from school, the boys essentially live in their room—the living room—and we girls live in our bedroom. We take meals separately, do homework, and sleep apart from the boys. Except for the times I clean the apartment, wash the dishes, or iron the clothes, I'm in my bedroom. Our parents sleep most of the day while we're at school. Then, after Ron Radzai leaves for work, Momma reads audio books for the blind or, more recently, entertains her men friends.

Even though I changed their diapers, dressed and fed them, and watched over them as infants and toddlers, now that the boys are both in school, my main interaction with them is to care for their clothes. The distance between their lives in the living room and our lives in the back bedroom grows wider each year. They don't come into our bedroom to chat on their way to and from the bathroom, and we don't linger in the living room after we wash the dishes. Two sets of lives pass each other in the hallway, continuing the patterns of silence Momma and Ron Radzai have instilled in our home.

Chapter 20

NATIONAL HONOR SOCIETY

May 2, 1958

"I pledge to maintain my high scholastic standing . . . To hold as fundamental and worthy, an untarnished character," I repeat, my right hand raised at my elbow. The wide waistband of my plaid pleated skirt strains to hold in my flabby belly fat, the bulging button reminding me of the polishing work needed to fulfill my oath.

It's not until I stand on the Garfield High School auditorium stage with the other twenty-four juniors being inducted into the National Honor Society that I see Momma in the audience. I squint into the sea of faces made hazy from the spotlights. Momma is in an aisle seat about ten rows from the stage. All my mixed-up, confused feelings about Momma well up: pride, fear, love, hate, embarrassment. Above all, I'm in a constant state of anticipation, always on edge, waiting to see what she will say, what she will do, what kind of a mood she's in. Momma's behavior has been increasingly unpredictable these many years since we left Yonkers, but in many ways quite predictable. She's volatile but capable of being calm and rational. She's sweet in public but violent at home. Somehow,

I hold on to hope that things will improve and my Yonkers Momma will reappear. I look for clues that my optimism isn't totally in vain. Today, I have a clue. I can't think of another school event she's attended for me. But she's here today to celebrate my academic achievements.

About a month ago, when I received the letter saying I'd been selected for membership in the NHS, I waited for just the right moment to tell her.

I chose a night when Momma had made stuffed cabbage in the pressure cooker. That was a sign she was in a good mood.

"I just found out I've been selected for membership in the National Honor Society," I said when I went to the kitchen to dish up plates for Sharon and me. "'Twenty-five juniors were chosen by the teachers on the basis of our grades, leadership, character, and service,'" I read from the letter.

"That's good," Momma said.

"The ceremony will be in the school auditorium on May second, at nine," I told her. "All the parents are invited. Can you come?"

"We'll see."

That was that. Momma never said another word to me about it. So, last night, I reminded her, "Tomorrow is the National Honor Society induction ceremony at nine. Can you come? Do you want to take the bus with me in the morning?"

"I don't know," she said.

She was still in her bedroom when I left home this morning so I went to school alone.

I blink again and stare into the darkened auditorium. *Yes, it's Momma.*

We complete the pledge, and Dr. Rozema, the school super-intendent, gives each of us our pin and membership card.

"It's a joy to celebrate your achievements, your leadership, and your outstanding character," he says. "This is also a time to reflect on the oath you have taken to maintain your high standards and to go into the future as a leader. I want to thank your parents and teachers for the roles they've played in raising such fine young people."

The NHS president lights a candle from the chapter torch and each of the new junior members lights our candle from his. As the ceremony ends, the auditorium lights dim and we file down the aisle, candles glowing.

I smile at Momma as I pass her. I'm happy she's here for my special day. She's tiny in her seat, a wisp of a woman. Her pink strapless gown overflows into the aisle, her white sweater covers her shoulders. She'll stand out among the tailored suits and shirtwaist dresses worn by my classmates' parents, but today I don't care. The important thing is that she's here. This is a good sign. She's my mother, and I still love her.

The senior NHS members lead us into the cafeteria and the folks in the audience follow. By the time I've blown out my candle, Momma's clear plastic heels are click-clacking behind me.

"I'm so glad you came," I tell her.

"I have something for you," she says. She thrusts a glossy white package into my hand, its gold ribbon as wide as the small box. "Open it," she says.

I lead her over to a cafeteria table and place my candle, membership card, and program on it so I can concentrate on Momma's surprise. I untie the gold ribbon and take off the glossy white paper. The tiny white box fits in my palm. I look up at Momma and smile. I can't believe she got me a present.

"Open it," she urges, her voice full of excitement.

I slide off the box cover. "Oh, Momma, it's beautiful." It's a compact. The gold rectangular case catches the cafeteria lights, and the eight stars etched on top twinkle. I take the compact out of the box and open the top. Inside, a mirror and a small compartment for pressed face powder.

"What do we have here?" Mr. Tengi, my favorite teacher, asks as he comes up behind me. He clasps Momma's tiny hand in both his large ones, pumping hard. "Mrs. Radzai, I presume. It is so good to see you here today to celebrate Beverly's accomplishments."

"Momma, this is Mr. Tengi, my English teacher," I say. I look into his gentle eyes, magnified by round, scholarly, dark-rimmed glasses.

"Look on the back," Momma says, a bit annoyed at the interruption.

I turn the compact over and read aloud the four engraved lines:

Honor Society
Garfield High School
Beverly Radzai
May 2, 1958

Momma has kept a big secret from me. She's proud of me; she still loves me. She has planned this surprise. My optimism is warranted—my Yonkers Momma may yet return. Her gift is my second clue today that I'm not a total fool to hold on to hope. I'm on the brink of tears, but my friends cluster around to look at my gift. I blink hard and show off the engraving and my shiny new compact.

"Oh, Momma, it's truly beautiful," I whisper and hug her, the big smile on my face mirrored on hers.

"I know you're so proud of Beverly," Mr. Tengi says to Momma. He holds my gift and inspects the engraving. "Now, this is something you will treasure forever as a memory of this day, Beverly."

• • •

A few months ago, Mrs. Miller, the guidance counselor, called in the juniors, one by one, and asked us what we wanted to do after high school. I said I didn't know. Maybe a missionary. Maybe a newspaper reporter. She gave me a career inventory to fill out.

"Turns out you should be a teacher," Mrs. Miller tells me a few weeks later.

Of course. Why didn't I think of that? I love all my teachers and always try to be like them, but I've never translated that desire into a career option. While I'm in an advanced track in high school, I've never truly envisioned going to college. I have no idea where the money would come from, and I'm not good at long-range planning—but now that I'm a junior, it's time to give serious thought to my future. Why couldn't I be just like all the teachers who have encouraged and nurtured me over the years? I could do the same for my own students, pay back my teachers by passing on their lessons to others.

Yes. The idea fills me with joy, purpose, and hope—hope that there will be a tomorrow. I'll be a teacher, a teacher who makes a difference in the lives of my students.

Mr. Tengi took an entire class period to talk with us about why it's important for girls as well as boys to have a career. He said that we girls might need to work while raising our children and that working helps you keep your mind alert. He said the state colleges in New Jersey are good places to get an education and that there are scholarships that paid your tuition. They are hard to get, but if you have a good academic record and can prove your financial need, you can apply for one.

• • •

"I've encouraged Beverly to apply to Paterson State College," Mr. Tengi tells Momma.

She smiles at Mr. Tengi. *Good start*. But I know exactly where this conversation is taking us.

"Beverly is very smart," Momma says. "But we don't have any money for college. You know, her father never supported her."

I cringe.

"There are lots of scholarships and loans," Mr. Tengi says. "I hope you'll encourage her to get a college education. I think she'd qualify for enough money to pay for her education. If she becomes a teacher, I just know she'll be a terrific one. Let me know, Mrs. Radzai, if you would like to talk more about this. I'm counting on you to support this idea for Beverly."

• • •

The reception is over, and it's time for Momma to take the bus back to Passaic Street. It's time for me to get to my dreaded third-period class: typing. I'll never use typing. I don't want to be a secretary or stenographer like so many of the girls do. But the counselor suggested that I take typing so I squeezed it into my schedule.

I'm the only upperclassman; all the others are freshmen. I'm the only one who types twenty words a minute, still persever-ating over a-s-d-f-j-k-l-;. The others type well over forty. Their fingers fly over the keyboard, as they do now, their *click-click-click*s seeping through the closed door, as I approach the room.

I open the door, walk into the classroom. In unison, every girl stops typing and stares at me, standing in the doorway.

"I didn't know you were smart," Mrs. Travers says, look-ing up from a student's desk.

Any other day, that comment would have kicked me in the stomach. Not today. Even though I can't type, I'm in the advanced track for a reason. I'm going to college. Right this moment, I know I can do anything. Even though no one has invited me to the junior prom or to the local pizza joint, I've been invited to the National Honor Society. I might not be great at typing, but I get A's in Latin. When I become a teacher, I'll never say anything hurtful to a student.

• • •

During study hall, I go to see my guidance counselor.

"Mrs. Miller, can you help me apply to Paterson State College?"

Chapter 21

PATERSON STATE COLLEGE

November 1958

Momma has no choice but to let me go to college. Early in my senior year of high school, I'm accepted to Paterson State College, an easy thirty-minute commute from Garfield. I receive one of the coveted New Jersey State Scholarships that guarantees all my tuition for four years if I maintain a B average. On top of that, I'm awarded a Rotary Scholarship that pays for my books the first year.

"Where do you think your clothes and food are going to come from?" she asks the day I tell her the good news. It's clear she's not happy about this turn of events.

"My babysitting and Two Guys from Harrison salaries will be enough for my other expenses," I say. "I'll give you the rest for the household." I've worked for Two Guys, a large discount department store on Passaic Street, for years, during the summers and after school, mainly in the boys' clothing area. I've passed most of the money on to Momma, only keeping enough for basic school supplies.

"How much is that going to be?" Momma can never let me forget that Dad abandoned Sharon and me and left her with no child support. She reminds me with every new outfit I get, with every meal I eat, and with every extra school event that involves money. This time, though, I'm not going to let her sabotage me and I'm not going to allow my guilt to consume me. School has been my refuge for years. I can't imagine not being in classes, not spending every weekday with caring teachers. I know that having a college degree is essential to my becoming a teacher, missionary, or newspaper reporter—my three top career choices, in that order. No matter what it takes, I'll attend Paterson State.

• • •

"In spite of my scholarships, I worry about having enough money for college," I tell my Mrs. Miller soon after the conversation with Momma.

"Congress just enacted the National Defense Education Act Student Loan Program," she says. "It's for people like you who are strong in mathematics and who plan to teach. If you teach for five years, up to half of your loan can be forgiven. Do you want an application?"

I apply for the maximum amount—money I know I'll contribute to the household in exchange for Momma's blessing.

That seals my fate. I'm going to be a teacher.

September 1959

"Oh, my gosh. Is that you, Beverly?" Catherine asks when she picks me up in front of 89 Passaic Street in her 1951 gray Chevy for the first of many rides to Paterson State College. "I don't recognize you. You look great. How much weight did you lose?"

Catherine and I haven't seen each other since Garfield High's June graduation. I'm feeling sassy in one of Sharon's size five dresses, a far cry from the tens and twelves I wore just months ago. My short hair grew out over the summer and is now about to my shoulders. I sleep on hard-plastic pink curlers so I can turn it up on the right side and under on the left, where I tuck it behind my ear, just like the popular girls did in high school. My sleeveless white dress shows off a deep tan, baked in after soaking in baby oil and lying on a towel, face to the sun, for hours out on our gravel-covered parking lot/backyard.

It may have been that *Mutt and Jeff* photo in the Retrospect 1959 Yearbook where I looked like a blob climbing the ladder next to the tallest boy in the senior class that convinced me it was time to lose weight, or maybe it was the fact that I was down to two outfits that fit. I'd certainly had enough of those stolen pastries and was tired of feeling stuffed all the time. Most of all, I was sick of being at the bottom of the social scene.

No boy ever pinned a corsage on me or took me to a football game, the prom, or the drive-in movies in high school. There were no Friday night dates at the local pizza joint where all the teenagers congregated every weekend. I was determined to make my college experience different. For that to happen, I had to be thin.

"Yeah, I've lost almost forty pounds," I say as I slip onto the front seat. "But I have another ten to go to get to ninety. That's what I want—to be ninety pounds. Then I'll be happy."

"You're kidding—forty pounds?" Catherine says. "I can't even lose ten. How did you do it?"

"I just worked really hard," I lie. I don't know her well enough to tell her I haven't eaten a thing all summer, except for a few bites of carrot and saltine crackers. At graduation, I decided I'd eat as little as possible all summer and lose weight fast. It was really easy for me to flush all my dinners down the toilet, since our bedroom was right next to the bathroom. At first I felt so hungry I thought I wouldn't be able to follow through on this starvation plan. But after a week, I didn't crave food. Just water. Lots of water.

"Sharon, do you want my dinner?" I asked one hot June evening as we sat on our bed, legs outstretched, balancing our robin's egg blue Melmac plates on our laps, a tiny, black hamburger and a mound of mashed potatoes staring up at us.

Sharon was busy creating a smiley face on her potatoes with hamburger chunks and had just popped on the nose. She turned to me and grinned, pointing to her artistic creation. "Are you kidding?" she asked, laughing.

We had lots of practice cutting up those burgers, throwing a few pieces and a glob of potatoes into the toilet, flushing, waiting for the toilet to refill, and then disposing of more. Sometimes it took five flushes to get rid of our unwanted food. In times past, though, we always had a stash of bread or cheese Danish hidden between the mattress and the box springs. Since Milly had stopped the early-morning deliveries, we no longer had a backup to Momma's dinners. It was this or nothing. For Sharon, it would be a few spoons of potatoes. For me, nothing was what I wanted. I filled up on water and dreamed about where the needle would stop tomorrow when I stepped on the scale at Two Guys.

• • •

"You're going to lose ten more pounds?" Catherine asks. "Why don't we go on a diet together and we can each lose ten?"

"Great idea," I say. I decide not to tell her my body has stopped working.

• • •

"This is so good—try some," Sharon said a few weeks ago as she ate the stuffed pepper Momma had prepared for dinner.

I picked out a spoonful of the rice and hamburger mixture, mushed it around in my mouth, and swallowed. I gagged and motioned for Sharon to get me some water.

"I haven't had my period all summer," I told her, out of the blue, once I regained my composure.

"You're kidding. Are you pregnant?"

"Of course not, dope. You know I don't have a boyfriend."

"Well, then, dope, what's the matter with you?" Sharon glared at me, her hands on her hips. "You need to eat something. How much have you lost, anyway?" she scolded.

"I'm *trying* to eat," I said. I put another spoon of rice in my mouth. This was the first hot food I'd eaten for more than three months. *Chew, chew. Think about it. Swallow. One more now. Chew, chew. Swallow.*

"I haven't pooped all summer, either," I confessed.

"Oh, damn. What are you doing to yourself?"

I wondered that too. My fat had rolled away, but my body was rebelling. My summer starvation experiment was coming to a screeching halt. How could I seduce my body into working again?

• • •

"What kinds of things are you eating?" Catherine asks me. Her thick, shoulder-length brown hair is combed in a pageboy flip. Her soft curls bob every time she turns to look at me in the passenger seat.

"Oh, I just sort of eat less of everything," I lie again.

Catherine and I hardly know each other. I'm not going to start off our driving arrangement with a lot of confessions. She and I weren't in any classes together at Garfield, and she's only here driving me to college because we live within a mile of one another, both of us have been accepted to the Elementary Education program, and only one of us has a car. The plan is that I'll split the cost of gas with her.

Catherine wasn't very popular in high school, but she was a lot more popular than I. She even belonged to one of the girl-clubs and wore a boxy white sweater with the club's insignia on the pocket. She seems nice enough. Since I have no other way to get to college, I need to make a good impression.

"Look at these signs," she says as we pull off Pompton Road onto the hilly, heavily wooded Paterson State campus and follow the arrows for freshman parking. "They've got us parking way down here, in this muddy lot. That means we'll have to hike up that steep hill to get to Hunziker Hall."

There are only three buildings on the three-hundred-acre campus: Hobart Hall, the college president's mansion; the student union, the gathering place for eating and club meetings; and Hunziker Hall, the two-story brick building where all our classes are held.

"It'll get us in the dieting mood," I say. We laugh so hard we hold our stomachs as we huff and puff our way to our first-ever college class.

• • •

"I feel bad, not badly. I feel bad, not baaaad-leee, I feeeeel baaaad, not badly . . ." Catherine and I shout-sing and carry on all the way home from classes. It's a snowy, late-February afternoon and our voices fill the Chevy with variations of Dr. Don Edwards's chant for the day. Each rendition is louder and more raucous than the one before as we bounce higher and higher on the beige leather front seat.

Our last class of the day is Advanced English Grammar and Composition with our favorite teacher, Dr. Edwards, a tall, lean, handsome chap with a full head of curly black hair and a playful yet serious demeanor. He's about a half-dozen years older than his students and we're awestruck around him.

Today he jumped up on the window ledge of the newly installed portable classroom building adjacent to filled-to-capacity Hunziker Hall. Suddenly, all we could see were the soles of Dr. Edwards's shoes. We ran to the window just in time to watch him do a handstand on the ground, his fingers imprinted in the freshly fallen, wet snow like a child's clay gift to his mother. He took off running and disappeared around the building. While we were still craning our necks out the window, he popped through the door, along with a gust of winter wind. "Lord, what fools these mortals be!" he sang out with a Shakespearean flourish as his freshman class, mostly girls, giggled and tried to figure out what lesson he was demonstrating today. He adjusted his tie, buttoned his suit jacket, and positioned himself in front of the class. It was time for Act Two.

This is his way of modeling dangling participles and run-on sentences. Of course we all know about such things, but he likes to get us into the tough topics with a good laugh. His three-hour tests and his pop write-an-essay-in-the-next-thirty-minutes activities are no laughing matters, though. No one has earned an A from him yet.

But today, when he passed back the papers we wrote yesterday in class, Dr. Edwards paused at my desk, looked down at me, and said, "Such good work, Beverly. Would you revise this and turn it back to me, please?"

My heart pounded. I turned over my essay and saw an A-/A at the top of the paper.

"Oh, my heavens," Catherine said, gawking over my shoulder. "You got the first A!"

"It's an A minus," I whispered, still in shock. I read the comments he'd scribbled on my paper—"promising," "a good opening," "you make your points clearly." I was so proud I could hardly breathe. I was a little embarrassed, though, because no one else in the class was smiling.

Catherine kept poking me in my back. I turned to see a huge smile on her face. We broke out laughing—silently, of course, our hands cupping our mouths.

To get encouraging comments from an English teacher I admire means a lot to me; it feels like confirmation that all the hard work I did for years writing for the school newspapers in junior high and then at Garfield High was worthwhile. Dr. Edwards reminds me of Mr. Tengi, except Edwards has a better sense of humor and is much younger. Both men have high expectations, make me stretch and work hard for a grade. And when the A finally comes, I know I deserve it.

"Let's stop for a slice of pizza to celebrate your A," Catherine says as we drive closer to Sam's, where we often enjoy fat slices of thick-crust pizza topped with loads of sweet sausage, pepperoni, and onions. Thick crust—my favorite, and Catherine's too. There's almost nothing better than sinking your teeth into rivers of hot mozzarella cheese, especially after a long day of classes.

"Great idea. But it's an A *minus*," I insist.

No longer am I afraid to eat, and pizza is one of my many new favorites. By now I've figured out how to get rid of it all and keep my weight low: my trusty laxative pills.

When I started to eat solid foods again last September, I had to relearn how to swallow. I soon conquered that, but the rest of my digestive system refused to cooperate. So I had the bright idea to buy some chocolate laxative. After a week of gagging on that awful, chalky stuff, I discovered the little pills. Easy. No taste. Just swallow them. Five. Fifteen. Whatever it took to get rid of the food I ate that day.

Bobby Darin croons out from the car radio. Catherine and I sing along as we each finish off a huge slice of pizza.

"Mmmm. That is so good, I could eat another one," Catherine says.

I nod. "Me too. Let's do it!" We hop out of the car and pop back into Sam's.

Lately, I can't get enough to eat. I'm hungry all the time—never satisfied. It helps to know I don't have to worry about gaining weight. I have my little solution tucked into my purse, so I can eat whatever I want to, guilt-free.

My weight hovers around ninety pounds.

Eating is one of my favorite activities.

Purging is my second favorite.

• • •

"So, let's calculate the magnetic field created by two currents going in the same direction," Dr. Felix Yerzley says as Catherine and I scurry onto our stools at the back of the lab.

We're late for physics again. Dr. Yerzley tips his balding head and gives us a jowly smile as we settle in. For some odd reason, he loves the two of us. We're not only late most days for this eight-in-the-morning class, but neither of us has the slightest idea what he's talking about. Nevertheless, he spends endless hours trying to knock some scientific sense into us, as he will do today after class when he tutors the two of us, step by step, on the concepts most of the rest of the class easily grasps.

We're now in our second year of classes, and Catherine and I are great pals. I like her low-key, straight-talking, Jersey-girl personality. She's pretty and popular but not flashy, and definitely not stuck up.

Even though I trust Catherine more than anyone I know, I haven't divulged my eating secrets to her. I've never heard the words *anorexia* or *bulimia*, and I think my behavior is exclusive to me. I invented it. I'm certainly not interested in discussing my habits with anyone. It's my secret, and it's going to stay that way. I'm thin and popular, and I'm the class historian. I've even gone on a few blind dates that Catherine and her cute Fairleigh Dickinson University boyfriend, Lou, fixed up for me.

One day when we roll in late again for Yerzley's class, my stomach cramps. "I have to hit the bathroom," I whisper to Catherine, then hurry out the door.

Thankfully, there's no one in the restroom. I empty my bowels with a loud blast. "Oh, whew," I say, relieved to have made it to the toilet in time. It feels so good to be empty.

I flush, take a few sheets of toilet paper, and pull up the seat. I've learned to clean up the toilet and not leave any evidence of the messy explosions that are part of my daily purging. I finally walk out of the stall, only to see another student standing at the sinks.

"Are you okay?" she asks, a look of concern on her face.

I've been caught. I'm so careful to hide my toilet behavior, and now someone has heard me. But I don't know this girl, and she doesn't know me. I'm pretty lucky right now.

"Oh, yes, I'm fine," I tell her. "I just have an upset stomach. Must have been something I ate last night."

"I'm glad you're okay," she says and turns to leave.

• • •

"Hey, Bev," Catherine says to me over the phone a few weeks after the Hunziker Hall bathroom incident. "Lou and I are heading to a frat party tonight. He's got a friend who needs a date. Want to go?"

It's after six and I've already popped several laxative pills. That means I'm in for lots of intestinal noise and cramping soon.

"Oh, Catherine, I'd love to. But I have so much homework I need to finish tonight," I lie. There's no way I can go out on short notice. When I plan on a date, I don't eat all day and don't take any laxatives. That's not what's happened today. So much for spontaneity and the social life I imagined for myself now that I was cute and thin. I'm popular during school hours but socially isolated in the evenings.

Everything about eating has consequences I now hate.

There's nothing pretty about trying to stay thin this way but staying thin is paramount to me. That's the way to be loved, to be popular. I need to be in control of how much weight I gain. I have no clue how I might change anything about my obsessive-compulsive addiction, but each day I tell myself I'll not overeat and I'll cut back on the number of laxatives I pop. Deep down, though, I know that each day will be just like the day before. Even though I'm ashamed of my behavior, I make no real effort to do anything different. I'm afraid to eat, afraid to be full, afraid to be empty.

So starts my long journey into bulimia nervosa.

Chapter 22

FALLING IN LOVE

October 1961

A crystal-clear tenor voice fills the cool evening air and draws us toward the horse-drawn hay wagon, already bursting with fraternity boys and their dates. Catherine has fixed me up with a blind date, Alex. I end where his waist begins. Catherine and Lou, the good-looking Italian guy she's dated for several months, and Alex and I walk down a narrow path lit by the full moon, the evening suddenly made more magical by the night's entertainer.

At the wagon, my date grabs me around my waist and up I soar onto a bale of hay—putting me in perfect view of the baby-faced, slightly built, blond singer.

The singer smiles at me and winks. *Oh, heavens. He's flirting with me. Of all the girls on this wagon, he chooses me.* My face flushes, my heart throbs. I smile back. There's a strange magnetic force operating here tonight, a full-moon attraction. I'm completely drawn to this man. I'm going to die right here and now.

"Who's that?" I ask Lou. He and Catherine have already seen the glow on my face. They're beaming.

"He is *cute*," Catherine whispers in my ear.

"That's Johnny O'Brien," Lou says. "He's a senior. Real popular. The best voice on campus."

Johnny launches into an Irish ballad. He moves closer to me and gazes into my eyes. I imagine it's just Johnny and me on top of this wagon as the horses pull us deeper into the star-studded night. Sweet, earthy fragrances fill the air. Alex's arm is around my shoulder, but I can't stop looking at the man with the lyrical voice. We flirt all evening, until finally Lou asks, "Do you want me to give him your phone number?"

Catherine has set me up with blind dates over the last two years, but no one has given me goose bumps or even called for a second date. We usually double date—see a drive-in movie or mingle self-consciously at a frat party, make out in the back-seat, and then head home. Tonight, I can't see myself making out with Alex. I'm swooning over Johnny. Maybe it's the full moon. Or that I'm a little naughty, being with one guy and flirting with another. Maybe it's his voice. Whatever it is, I'm intrigued. I want to know more about Johnny O'Brien.

• • •

"Johnny wants me to go to a party with him on Friday," I tenta-tively tell-ask Momma on Saturday when he calls. "Can I go?"

This is the first date I've gotten completely on my own. It's not a blind date. It's a real date. I'm so excited I can hardly contain myself. But I need my mother's permission to leave the house even though I'm a junior in college, twenty years old.

The worst part isn't getting up the nerve to ask her but waiting for the answer and stalling Johnny with fake excuses.

"I don't care," she finally says when I ask again on Wednesday.

• • •

Johnny knocks at our apartment door exactly at seven on Friday evening, as he promised he would. I've been ready for a half hour, anxiously waiting in my bedroom. Soon after the hay ride, he called and we talked on the phone two separate times, just getting acquainted, before he asked me out. He's a devout Catholic, has already been accepted to graduate school at Stanford University, and will leave for California at the end of summer after his graduation in June. He's majoring in business at Fairleigh Dickinson, is on the Honor Roll, and is an only child. He lives in Hackensack with his folks and commutes to the Teaneck campus. Singing is his passion. He's in his church choir and the university chorus. He loves to be on stage. I do too. I tell him about the part I had in my high school junior play and how I used to twirl my baton on the outdoor patio stage back at Little River. I don't tell him my first grade teacher made me move my lips instead of singing out loud. I still like to sing, but I make sure no one hears me. I certainly won't be singing in front of Johnny O'Brien.

Momma and Ron Radzai are at the Formica table playing cards when I open the door for Johnny. He's wearing a starched white shirt under a dark blue crewneck sweater, khaki slacks, and loafers. His short blond hair is slicked back. I've chosen my long-sleeved white blouse and wear it tucked into a blue, loosely gathered skirt sprinkled with white flowers. My dark blue sweater drapes across my shoulders, held in place by my favorite furry-fox-face sweater clip. My hair is in a turned-up bob that rests on the back of my sweater. Johnny smiles broadly and takes my hand. I usher him into the kitchen.

"Johnny, I want you to meet my mother and stepfather," I say, stepping closer to the kitchen table. Momma takes a drag and lays her Lucky Strike in the ashtray. She looks up at my date and clasps his outstretched hand with both of hers, like he's an old friend. Ron Radzai gets up from his chair, shakes Johnny's hand, and gives him a smile and a nod.

"We're going to a fraternity party," Johnny reports, look-ing at Momma. "I should have Beverly home by midnight. Is that good?"

"Sure. That's fine. Have fun," Momma says on the long exhale.

Wow, that was easy, I think to myself as Johnny and I skip down the eighteen white marble steps to his red sports car, parked in front of Milly's Luncheonette. He holds my hand. My heart thumps, and we giggle. It feels like we've been friends forever.

Johnny sings along with Del Shannon as we weave from Passaic Street to the large, rambling fraternity house near his campus. We pass through the commercial area where I live and drive into middle-class neighborhoods where houses sit far back from the road and tall hardwoods color the lawns red and yellow. In between songs, we chatter about the classes we like best this semester. His is Effective Management Styles; mine is American Poetry and Prose.

Once we squeeze into a parking space on the street, he opens the car door and grabs my hand. Loud music and laughter spill out from the frat house next door to our destination. Johnny and I wave to the large group gathered on the porch as we pass. A few boys whistle and holler, "Hey, who's your new girl, Johnny?"

We climb the stairs onto the porch of Johnny's frat house, dense with human bodies, and wade through pats on the back, bear hugs, and introductions. We make our way into the hot party room, full of handsome couples, the women in sleek, tight-fitting skirts, cashmere sweaters, and knee-high boots. Most of the men are in sweaters and khaki trousers.

My fox-head sweater clip presses against my neck, my dark blue leotards squeeze my stomach, and the spring flowers on my gathered skirt wilt. I unclip the fox-head and drop my sweater on a chair, making sure the sweater-clip is well-hidden. *Cute. I'm cute. All the other girls are sophisticated. When will I learn to dress like the popular girls? The rich girls?*

We head to the booze table with its full lineup of bourbon, gin, rum, vodka, wine, and all the fixings. At the end of the table are platters of cheese, crackers, celery, carrots, and dip. A large blue ice chest loaded with bottles of beer sits on the floor beside the table.

"Do you want a Rob Roy?" Johnny shouts over the blaring music. "That's what I drink."

"Sure, I'll have one." I have no idea what a Rob Roy is. I've always turned down booze before; in fact, I have never tasted beer, wine, or any other alcoholic drink. I'm not interested in drinking. But I *am* interested in impressing Johnny O'Brien. I want to be cool and aloof like the other girls in the room. They're drinking, flirting with their dates, kissing off in the corner.

A man built like a football player puts his arm around Johnny's shoulder and pulls me close. "What are you drinking, honey?" he asks.

"Paul, this is Beverly," Johnny says. "Why don't you make up two Rob Roys for us while we dance? Chubby Checker can't wait." He grabs my hand and pulls me onto the dance floor.

"Heavy on the scotch?" Paul shouts.

"Light on mine," I holler into the air as we twist our way out to the middle of the dance floor, slipping between couples swinging their hips and gyrating lower and lower toward the floor. Johnny and I laugh and try to out-hip, out-dip, and out-twist one another. He sings along with Chubby, and I smile and wink at him. At the end of the song, he folds me into his arms and twirls me around. We laugh and laugh. I am free and happy, ever so happy. I think he likes me.

"Let's go get those drinks," Johnny says, and leads me back to the table. Our fancy wide-topped, long-stemmed glasses brim with red translucent liquid. Johnny hands me the one with the two cherries and takes a big gulp of his. I suck the cherries off the toothpick and savor the bitter alcohol before following his lead. The fiery lava burns my throat. I open my eyes wide, look at Johnny, and giggle. So this is a Rob Roy.

"Oh, listen—it's 'The Stroll,'" Johnny says, pulling my free hand. "Take your drink."

Everyone lines up, girls in one line, boys in the other. Beer bottles and cocktail and wine glasses stroll along. Swaying and shuffling to the Diamonds, each couple takes turns going to the center, holding hands, sipping, strolling, cutting up, spilling drinks, and laughing all the way to the end of the line. I've learned all these dances watching Dick Clark's *American Bandstand* over the last several years; Sharon and I practiced in front of the television set. Both the twist and the stroll are easy and fun to do, but you don't touch your partner much, except for some occasional hand-holding. I'm hoping now for a slow dance.

Roy Orbison answers my prayer. Johnny takes me in his arms and sings softly in my ear as we dance to "Crying." He pulls me close. My head rests on his chest. I breathe in his clean, fresh smell. Our bodies ease into the embrace, into the music, into the magic of our first date. I'm safe here in his arms, confident I can let him into my life, can trust him. I reach up and give him a little kiss on his cheek. He kisses my forehead. *I hope he asks me for a second date.*

It's eleven thirty before we know it.

"I have to get you home by midnight," Johnny whispers in my ear as he tilts his glass for the last red drops.

What the heck. I do the same. We've danced to every song and met so many new people—I can't remember all their names. Everyone knows Johnny.

During one of our slow dances, he asks me to go on a picnic next weekend with a group of his friends. I swoon, feel dizzy, giddy. Is it the Rob Roy or am I falling in love?

We drive home, our fingers intertwined. He walks me up the eighteen marble steps.

"I'll call you during the week to let you know what time I'll pick you up on Saturday," he says. "I had a good time tonight." He plants a kiss on my lips, then heads down the marble steps. Midway down, he turns and blows a kiss my way. I blow one back and smile. Then I close the stairwell door.

I touch my lips and savor the warm glow of the evening. Then, I steel myself for what's ahead.

• • •

I turn the knob on our apartment door. Take a deep breath. Here we go.

"You've been drinking, you slut," Momma screams. She's waited for me, as usual. She grabs my arm, smacks me across my face, and pounds my head against the refrigerator. I duck and run down the hallway. But she's not finished with me. She opens the utility closet, pulls out the broom, and follows me into my bedroom. *Thwack, thwack.* The hard wooden handle cracks across my back. "You bastard," she shouts. "You goddamned bastard, you. What else did you do?"

Momma uses every excuse to beat me, and going out on a date is one of her favorite reasons. She knows how to ruin my happy times, how to hurt my heart. What does she want from me? How dare she call me a slut when she brings scores of men into our apartment, when she's put me in harm's way? I'm so angry, I have to restrain myself. I want to strike her, scream back at her, call her nasty names. But I don't. She's my mother, and I know the consequences. She'll kill me if I put up a real fight. It's hard enough to protect my head, minimize the blows, not absorb her vitriol. She's intent on destroying every good feeling I have about myself, every friend, every possibility I have for a future. I work hard to not get depressed, not feel hopeless.

I have to really like a guy for it to be worth my while to sustain her abuse before and after a date. Johnny is cute, kind, interesting, and smart. He's worth it. I'm going on that picnic.

I want him to be my boyfriend. I'm not going to let Momma defeat me. She's not going to hold me hostage in this apartment, make me feel bad about myself, and make me feel guilty for things I'm not even doing.

February 1962

I like Johnny more and more with each date. We make each other laugh, and it's just easy to be with him—no tension, no disagreements. We've been together almost five months now. Neither of us dates anyone else but there's no talk of officially going steady or of a future together. Many of my friends wear their boyfriend's college rings on a chain around their necks. I stare with longing at the Fairleigh Dickinson University ring on Johnny's right hand. On my twenty-first birthday a few weeks ago, he gave me a charm bracelet with a miniature birthday cake charm. That's almost like going steady. I know he loves me by the gentle way he treats me, by our spontaneous laughter, by the way we finish each other's sentences, and by the way we caress each other's bodies—always in the dark and always through our clothing, of course—in his car or in a dark corner of the frat house after a Rob Roy or two.

One cold Saturday night, we're making out in the front seat of his car, parked outside the frat house.

"I love you, Johnny," I say. I use those words often and freely now and wait eagerly for Johnny to tell me he loves me.

He pulls my shirt over my head, unbuckles my bra, and gently caresses my breasts. This is the first time since the encounter in the dark house with Joe's friend that a man has taken off my clothing. I let it happen. I want to be close to Johnny, to feel his body next to mine, to have him caress me. This feels right. I take off his shirt, kiss his chest, his mouth. More clothing lands on the floor. My head is pressed against the hard metal door handle. One leg is under the steering wheel, the other hanging off the seat.

A sharp pain between my legs forces my butt and pelvis toward Johnny as he convulses into me. It happens fast, before I know what's happening.

"Aaaahhh," he cries, clutching me close to him, our naked bodies clammy in spite of the chill in the car.

"I need to sit up," I finally say. My crotch throbs, my head aches. A knife has sliced into me. I'm freezing, shivering. I grab at the clothing on the floor, strap on my bra, and search for my panties. I'm disoriented; my hands shake. I'm not sure what just happened.

"Are you okay?" Johnny asks.

"I'm pretty sore," I say, my voice cracking. I'm on the brink of tears, but I finagle myself back into my clothes and try to keep my composure.

"I'd better get you home," Johnny says. Dressed now, he starts the car.

"There's blood on the seat," I say, surprised, when the first street light we pass illuminates the inside of the car. Even though I know many of my girlfriends are *having sex* with their fiancés, I'm not sure of the details. I may be smart in school, but my social awareness is seriously lacking. Why I'm bleeding is a mystery to me. Even though I'm eager for a close relationship with Johnny, even though I want him to touch me, to fall in love with me, I have no idea of all that implies. What I do know is that I've gone over a threshold and there's no way of undoing that journey.

When he walks me up the marble steps tonight, he says, "I'm sorry."

• • •

The next day in church, I stay in my pew and pray for forgiveness while the rest of the congregants receive communion. I'm sad, guilty. I feel a sense of loss—but I'm not sure just what I've lost. Having sex is not so much fun, after all. All I feel is pain and guilt.

· · ·

A new problem starts to take shape in my junior year as more of my teeth rot. Except for vaccinations and the Little River dentist who pulled teeth, I've never had an appointment with a doctor or dentist. The decayed indentations in my front four teeth deepen. I have to figure out how to smile.

Cotton to the rescue. I take a small piece of cotton, twirl it in my fingers, and stuff it into each of the little C-shaped holes in my mouth. If I smile fast, no one sees the cotton. I talk, covertly hiding my teeth with my top lip or hand. When the cotton gets wet and starts to smell, I excuse myself and change out my temporary fillings. Going out on a date and having a steady boyfriend fills me with anxiety.

I'm willing to face Momma's wrath and to make any necessary adaptations for Johnny. I'm in love. I'm certain he loves me. I'm free with him—at least as free as I dare to be, with all the secrets I have to hide. We laugh, joke, and have developed a wide circle of friends. His parents love me and invite me over for dinner and a movie on a regular basis.

I see Johnny as an integral part of my future. This is the way such things are supposed to go. You fall in love, get engaged, get married, and have kids. Live happily ever after. All my friends are on this path. I think I am too.

This is the first time I've had a steady boyfriend, a guy Momma has come to know by name. She calls Johnny my pimp, says he's the one who is going to get me pregnant. It's hard for me to hide Momma's behavior from Johnny—to cajole him into bringing me home early and to make up convincing stories about the marks on my body. My fear of exposing my home life has prompted me to create impenetrable walls that few of my friends have been able to break through. I know how far I'm willing to go with the stories of my life, and it isn't very far. Not even with Johnny.

Summer 1962

From my brothers' front window, I have a full view of Passaic Street. Johnny's red sports car pulls up and I run out of the apartment, skip down the stairs, and jump in.

Johnny just graduated from Fairleigh Dickinson and we're spending as much time together as possible before he leaves for California. Today we go to his home, a comfortable two-story white clapboard colonial in a middle-class neighborhood in Hackensack. We spend the steamy afternoon washing his car in the driveway, laughing hard as we take turns soaking each other with the hose.

"Beverly and I are going to watch television in my room," Johnny says after dinner.

His parents nod; they never show any alarm when we leave for our private moments.

Since that night in February, we've spent lots of time in his bedroom, taking our relationship to new levels. This is all new to me, and it now feels so good and right. I'm in love with Johnny. He says he loves me too, but he never says, "I'm in love with you." I wait and wait for those words and for him to ask me to go steady. Maybe he'll ask me tonight.

We're soon in a tight embrace, our bodies flung across his bed, our kisses deep. His hands explore my body. He unbuttons my blouse, unfastens my bra. My large, supple breasts fall into his hands, his mouth. His tongue outlines my taut nipples. I want Johnny to touch me, to love me, to ask me to live with him forever. Soon my panties are off. He explores me with his tongue, teaching me new feelings, new sensations.

Johnny and I have agreed this is the kind of intimacy we want—not the traditional kind. Neither of us is ready for a baby. We both have more schooling to finish. My friends talk about a new birth control pill that can prevent pregnancies, but you can only get it with a prescription and only if you are married. In any case, Johnny says that his church will not permit it. So it's best to avoid sex altogether. *That can come when we're married*, I tell myself. What we're doing is safe. And it really isn't sex. That would be a sin. I have enough to feel guilty about.

"I love you, Johnny," I whisper.

"Me too, Beverly."

• • •

Johnny is home for Christmas and still hasn't asked me to go steady. I tell him I've turned down invitations for dates. I want to know where we stand. We decide that we should both date others and that he'll think seriously about our relationship. Most of my friends are engaged. Only last week, one of my girlfriends quit school to marry her naval officer– fiancé. I dream of marrying, of having stars in my eyes, of making a home of my own, far away from Momma. I wait for Johnny's letter.

When it arrives, I open the envelope to find three pages, filled front and back with his neat handwriting.

January 19, 1963
Dear Bev,
Being away at school has given me an excellent oppor-tunity to do some very conscientious thinking about our whole situation. This is not to say I haven't thought about it before but being so far away from everything has given me . . . well, you could probably call it a new perspective. I think about all the things that have

happened during the past year and a half, about our moments of closeness, and well, you know what I mean. Then, of course, this whole idea of love comes into the picture and I try to analyze it and relate it to you and me and us. I think about marriage and a family and a home. I ask myself what does one look for in a wife.

The really important subject of love has always been a source of anxiety for us. You know that the subject has been a big void in my mind. You meet all my requirements for a wife: understanding, kindness, sincerity, attractiveness, intelligence; you are the type of girl who would be a good mother for my children. There is nothing wrong with you, and there is nothing wrong with me. But when it comes to us, I have questions. If after a year and a half, I cannot honestly say that I'm in love . . . well, there just doesn't seem to be any sense in just dragging things out. You should know by now that I have a great amount of respect and feeling for you. This is the reason why I'm trying to be as frank as possible with you.

I fold the letter. This is it. The answer I've long feared. I've allowed Johnny to penetrate my heart. I'm in love with him. But he isn't in love with me. I'm devastated.

What could I have done differently? Is it too late to turn around our relationship? I've confused love with intimacy. I've been too eager to create a life of my own, to get out of my life with Momma—I've been too hungry for love. I've told Johnny too much, too many secrets. I've tried too hard to make him love me and I've failed. He doesn't want a girl from Passaic Street, a cute girl, a girl from a troubled home, after all. Why has he led me on so long?

I don't see any reason why we should have to break off our relationship completely. In fact, the idea of dating occasionally would make me very happy. There just doesn't seem to be any logic in going along at the same pace we have been. It's not fair to you to just wait for something that doesn't now look like it will ever materialize. This choice, however, will be completely up to you.

"Oh, my God. Are you crazy, Johnny?" I say out loud once I have the presence of mind to read the rest of the letter. I've gone out to a park near the school where I'm doing my student teaching. How dare he tell me he isn't in love with me but wants to keep spending time with me? Doing what? Going to his bedroom? Drinking Rob Roys in the fraternity house? I may be in love with him, but I know how to protect myself from further pain. Of course I will not date him. I can't believe he'd ask me to do that.

I'll never tell another man I love him. What a fool I've been. I should have known better. I have to protect myself, my feelings. I know how to do this. I let down my guard. I should have known all along it was too good to be true. After this, I'll never trust anyone with my heart. I'll not make this mistake again. I'll know better next time.

It wouldn't be fair to you to just let things go the way they've been. You have a bright future ahead of you and for me to shorten it by holding on is not right or fair. You said a short time ago that you would like to know what the score is and I suppose that you are now getting my answer. I hope that this letter has not given you too much hurt. As you can detect from its reading, this letter's preparation has had a lot of time put into it and still it was a very difficult thing for me

to do. Although love has not materialized on the one hand, my respect and admiration for you will never deteriorate on the other.
Take good care of yourself and be good.
Johnny

Lunch break is over. I have to face the afternoon with my fourth grade class. I walk to the school bathroom and replace the cotton in my teeth. But I don't have anything to stuff into the hole in my heart.

Chapter 23

TO WHOM IT MAY CONCERN

January 15, 1963

"To whom it may concern . . ."

That's what I finally settle on as the proper opening for the letter I'm writing to my father.

During my first five years, I called him "Dad."

But after the fight, after he disappeared and never came back to visit Sharon and me, I didn't know what to call him. He is still "Dad" in my memories and during the times I see him in a crowd, only to rush around people to find it's not him at all—simply a mirage.

It's been seventeen years since he turned and walked away from me in Yonkers. That was right before the start of my life as it was going to be: life with Ron Radzai as my stepfather and Momma as her post-Dad, post-Yonkers self.

Calling him "Dear Dad" just doesn't seem right.

"Dear Father" is too formal. I never called him "Father" before, so why should I start now?

"Dear Sir," meanwhile, is too cold. Too aloof. For years I tried to remember his face, his square chin, his big smile. Momma cut up all of his photos and the pictures in my mind faded. "Dear Sir" might work, after all.

But in the end, I decide to skip the "Dear Whomever" salutation altogether and go right to the heart of the matter:

> To *whom it may concern,*
>   *I think you are my father.*
>   *Just a month ago, someone knocked on our apartment door. From my bedroom I heard Momma shout, "How dare you show up here, you Guinea bastard." I knew immediately it was my father. The person left but later I found a package outside the door, with matching yellow sweaters for Sharon and me.*
>   *If you are that person, we want to thank you. They fit nicely and look good on us.*
>   *Where have you been all these years? I've waited so long for you to come for a visit. Now that you've found us, I want to know why you didn't persist. Why didn't you tell Momma that you have a right to see your girls? Of course, not paying child support for seventeen years may be part of the problem. Do you know how much grief that's caused me?*

This letter is going in the wrong direction. I can't send it. Too sarcastic. There's so much I want to say, so much anger and sadness, anticipation and regret. For years, I imagined he'd swoop down and save me, that he'd be the angel-father I remembered, the kind, gentle man who read stories and pushed me on the swings. But who is he now? Why didn't he try to find us before this? I can't believe he was right here, on Passaic Street. That he walked up the same eighteen marble steps I use every day. That he was outside our door. Even though I've written many letters to him in my mind all these years, now that I actually have his address, I can finally write a real letter.

But what should I say to a man I no longer know? A man I hope will save me, rescue me from my horrible life with Momma?

I try again:

> *Thank you for the matching yellow nylon sweaters. They fit Sharon and me well and look good with our dark hair.*
>
> *I'm a senior at Paterson State College, majoring in Elementary Education. I'll graduate in June. I'm sure I'll be able to line up a teaching job for the coming school year.*
>
> *Sharon's a senior at Garfield High School. She wants to be a nurse and has been accepted at Martland Medical Center in Newark.*
>
> *I'm sending this letter to the Indianapolis address you wrote on the package. I'm glad I saw it before Momma threw it away. If you get this letter and if you're really my father, I hope you'll write back. You can address your letter to me in care of Reverend Alfred Jones, First Methodist Church, 145 Paulison Avenue, Passaic, New Jersey.*
>
> *Beverly Radzai*

I don't tell him I miss him, that I've longed for a father, that I love him. I don't tell him anything about Momma, the Blond Man, or my brothers. I don't really know this man, my father. I'm not going to beg, complain, or get emotional. I'll just tell him the facts.

• • •

I sneak a five-cent stamp from Momma's writing box and put it on the envelope I've addressed to Mr. Anthony Armento, 1819 South High School Road, Indianapolis, Indiana. I don't write my address anywhere on the letter or the envelope. What if Dad's address is wrong and the letter comes back to me? What if Dad forgets about the Methodist Church and sends a letter to our apartment? Then Momma will see it, and I'll have hell to pay. She'll be furious I'm communicating with Dad. There would be plenty of rage over Tony Armento and my attempt to find him.

For all my daydreaming about what he looks like, what he sounds like; for all my wishing and praying that he'll show up and take me away; in spite of all that, my hand shakes as I put the letter in the mailbox at our street corner. I'm frightened to find him, to see him. I can't help but wonder if he still loves Sharon and me and if he regrets not seeing us grow up. I regret not having a father to protect me, encourage me. I tell myself that he's a wonderful man and that he didn't leave me on purpose, that he meant all along to come back. Sharon and I have long fantasized about him—how handsome he is, how good a man he is, how he will swoop us up and take us to a new life, a safe place. I pray our fantasies are true.

April 1963

A black car with darkened windows pulls up in front of the First Methodist Church. This is it. Here he is. My dreams, my hopes, my father. All inside this car. It's been a lifetime of wishing that he would return, take me to the park, snuggle with me, tell me stories, push me on the swings. But my memories are so old. My life since we last saw each other has been so different from the one we shared in Yonkers, and I'm sure his has been too. We are different people. Who is he now? Does he still love me? Here I am, a senior in college. A trembling, frightened adult about to meet my father, the man I hope will change my life.

Once upon a time I hoped Johnny O'Brien would be the man to save me, to love me, to change my life, to take me away from Momma. Dating new men from school has helped me put my sadness about Johnny in a box, store it away, and find love in new places—like in my father. He's supposed to love me. I'm his child, a part of him. This is his responsibility—to love me, to save me from danger. I'm counting on him to be a new part of my life. To care for me like a daughter. To fill that huge hole in my heart.

I open the back door and peer in, trying to see the man sitting inside. It's dark inside the car, even though it's eight thirty in the morning and sunny outside.

I slide onto the backseat and scoot close to him, leaving enough room for Sharon to slip in next to me. He puts his arm around me and pulls me into his chest. I'm overwhelmed by his Aqua Velva smell, the same aftershave Ron Radzai splashes on each day. My face is plastered onto his shiny, quarter-size silver Jesus necklace. A flood of memories washes over me. I touch Dad's medallion, press it to my cheek.

"You remember my Our Lady of Mount Carmel medal, don't you?" he asks.

"Oh, now I do," I say. "I'd forgotten." It all comes back to me. Dad never takes off his Our Lady medal, even when he showers. My heart pounds as I remember my life an eternity ago. "That's the church you attended when you were a child," I say softly.

"And that's where you were baptized," Dad says.

"Really? Was I really baptized?"

"Of course you were." Dad laughs. "You were only two months old, so I'm sure you don't remember it. Didn't your mother tell you?"

"Hmmmm," I mutter. Momma insisted I was already baptized when I begged to get dunked in the pool at my Miami Baptist church, but I don't remember hearing the details.

I snuggle my face into the black, curly hair that pokes out from his blue, open-collared, polished cotton shirt. His warm chest provides a soft manger for Jesus and for my face. I recall the many times he cuddled me against his chest, told me how much he loved me; the happy times when he'd swing me into the air and set me down on a big rock at the park; the tender times when he'd bend into me, his handsome face touching mine, his rough whiskers tickling my cheek. I smile as these long-lost images cascade over me.

Here he is. Finally. My dad.

I choke up. My body heaves in his embrace. After all these years of hoping and praying, he is finally here, right beside me, holding me. The weight of this long journey has finally lifted. I sob into his chest, into Jesus, into my father, my savior.

I look up at his face. Tears run down his dark, scruffy cheeks. His chin is square, just like I remember. His hair is black, slicked back. I feel the bristly stubble of his cheeks on my face. He's the same man, the father I love. It all comes back to me: The dollhouse, the tricycle, the walks in the park, the fight, the day Dad walked away from me. My baby sister, screaming in her crib. The good memories, the bad—they swirl together.

I scrunch close to him so Sharon can fit in beside me. My pink-and-white-flowered skirt poufs over his blue polyester slacks. Dad stretches his right arm over my shoulder and touches Sharon. Our loud sobbing fills the car. I'm not sure if I'm happy and relieved or scared and apprehensive about what lies ahead.

"I've missed you girls." Dad chokes out the words.

"I missed you too, Dad," I say.

"Me too," Sharon says, although she was only eleven months old when he left.

I've only just realized there's another person here; my eyes took a minute to adjust to the dark car.

"I'm Mimi." The woman in the driver's seat turns around and extends her arm toward me. Her pleasant-looking face is framed in short, curly brown hair. She's not nearly as pretty as Momma and looks older than Dad.

"I'm Beverly."

"I know," Mimi says. "I'm so happy to finally meet you. Your dad worried about you all these years. I'm your stepmother."

I worried about him too. All the time. Where was he? Was he looking for me? What was he doing?

"I'm Sharon."

"Little Sharon. This is wonderful. You're just as cute as I imagined." Mimi is full of smiles. Sharon and I gulp, trying to recover.

"Let's drive over to the D'Angelo home and then we can really get to know each other," Mimi says as she starts up the car.

Besides Reverend Jones, the only other person who knows we are meeting Dad today is Catherine. When I told her the good news, she immediately invited us to her home. "My folks would be honored to host you, and my mom will cook up a storm."

• • •

The sweet aromas of tomato and garlic fill the air when Catherine opens the door of the two-story, white wood–framed D'Angelo home. We greet each other with bear hugs and kisses. Mrs. D'Angelo motions us into the living room, filled with upholstered chairs and a soft, pillow-laden sofa. Framed photographs of Catherine, her brother, sister, and their parents cover the walls and grace the antique tables scattered around the room.

"I've got a few finishing touches in the kitchen," Mrs. D'Angelo says, excusing herself.

"I'll help you," Mimi offers. The two women and Catherine disappear into the kitchen while Dad and Mr. D'Angelo chatter like long-lost Italian relatives. I sit beside Sharon on the sofa and stare at my father, waiting for an opportunity to join the discussion.

Dad is short and stocky, not tall and thin as I'd imagined. But the essence of my childhood father as I remember him is here, in his face and his mannerisms. He's animated, waves his arms when he talks. His voice is throaty, breathy, like mine. This man is my father. I know him.

I am his daughter, and he loves me. This is all that matters.

• • •

I think back to how this day came about. Dad did respond to my initial letter, and he did remember to send the letter to my church. We corresponded for the last two months.

"I'm so happy we've found each other," he wrote. "I've remarried, a lovely lady named Mimi. She and I want to make another trip to New Jersey to see you girls. I'll send your letters to the Methodist Church, as you requested. I'm sorry to see you are not going to a Catholic Church. I also see that you no longer use the name Armento. That makes me very sad."

Apparently, I told him more than I intended in my initial letter.

I decided not to argue with Dad when I wrote back. I wanted to say, "Well, why didn't you show up for me, act like a father? If you had, I'm sure I'd still be using your name." But I decided not to show any of my anger, not to ask any of the questions that have been on my mind all these years or let on in any way how my life changed when he left.

At least Ron Radzai takes care of us. We don't have much, but he works hard and does the best he can. In any case, I've gotten used to my name. Everyone in high school and college knows me as Radz. My high school diploma says I'm Beverly Radzai. My degree from Paterson State will be awarded to a Radzai. My students call me "Miss Radzai." I even have a Social Security card and driver's license in my assumed name.

Before Dad brought it up, I'd almost forgotten I was really Beverly Armento.

•   •   •

"Dinner is ready," Catherine announces. Dad stands up, walks toward the sofa, and opens his arms wide. Sharon and I know exactly what to do. We find our places in his embrace, like he never left. He kisses each of us on our foreheads and we grin our way to the dining room, where large platters of food cover the buffet table: antipasto, vegetable casseroles, spaghetti, sausages, meatballs, lasagna, loaves of crusty bread. What a feast.

"Let's say grace," Mr. D'Angelo says.

The seven of us stand around the dinner table and hold hands.

"Dear Jesus, we are so thankful that Sharon and Beverly have been reunited with their father and their beautiful stepmother. Please protect and guide this family. We are thankful for this, Thy bounty, and for those hands who have prepared this meal. Have us use this food and our bodies to serve You. In the name of the Father, Son, and Holy Ghost, Amen."

Everyone makes the sign of the cross. Everyone, that is, except Sharon and me. Dad's eyes are on me. I look straight ahead and take my seat between Dad and Mimi. Yes, I know all about the promises Momma made to raise us Catholic. It just didn't happen.

"Your home smells just like mine when I was a kid," Dad says to Mrs. D'Angelo. "My parents were from San Mauro Forte in the Basilicata region of southern Italy, and my mom cooked all the traditional favorites. Our place always smelled like garlic and pork chops."

He laughs. Everyone joins in.

"Our families are from the south too, from the Naples area," Mrs. D'Angelo says.

"Mimi and I are getting ready to move back to Florida soon," Dad says, changing the subject. "We've bought a new home in Sarasota. We're going to open a restaurant, and Mimi will be the chef."

That's news to me. He hasn't mentioned that in any of his letters.

"Will it be an Italian restaurant?" Mrs. D'Angelo asks.

"Oh, yes, for sure. I have all my mother's recipes from the old country. We'll make pizza and a few other hot dishes—spaghetti with meatballs, lasagna, and ravioli, for starters," he says. "We'll go slowly and expand as we can. We'll have a bar too, so folks can get a beer or wine with their food."

"The success is all in the gravy," Mrs. D'Angelo says, laughing. We all nod our heads.

"Your gravy is the best," Dad says. "What's your secret?"

"Time," Mrs. D'Angelo says. "Lots of time for slow cooking. Everything must be fresh. Nothing from a can. Big, whole tomatoes, garlic, basil—all straight from the garden. Extra virgin olive oil. You've got to take your time. This gravy simmered all day yesterday. I make up a big batch about every ten days and freeze more than half of it to use as we need it."

"It's the best I've ever had," Dad says. "Maybe even better than my mother, Madeline, made. Of course, I barely remember her actually doing the cooking because she died when I was only seven. But it's her recipe that we use in our home, and it'll be the one we'll use in our new restaurant. You know, Beverly"—Dad turns to me—"I wanted to name you Madeline after my mother."

I've heard this story—at least, Momma's version. I want to ask Dad why Momma refused to name me after his mother, as was the tradition in all good Italian homes. How did that discussion with Momma go and how did he explain my name to his family? Was he mad about naming me Beverly? What other things did he and Momma fight about? *What went wrong, Dad? Why was Momma so mad at you? Why did you leave?*

"I hope my girls will come and live with us in Sarasota," Dad continues, smiling broadly. He winks at me, like we share a secret.

Sharon and I look at each other, not knowing what to make of this news. We both smile broadly too. I glance over at Mimi, who's beaming and nodding. It's clear they've discussed this invitation and have agreed it's time to invite Dad's girls into the family.

Maybe this is the message from Jesus I've been waiting for. Dad's going to make my life better. He'll whisk us away from Momma, take us to Sarasota, where we'll be safe. But we're both in school, have plans for the coming year. How will this happen? Is it possible? I'm cautiously hopeful.

"All we have to do is sell our Indianapolis home. Then we'll be ready to move. I'd say we'll definitely be in Sarasota by Thanksgiving. We're sinking all our savings into the restaurant," Dad says, looking directly at me. I wonder what message he's giving me.

"It sounds exciting," I say, though it's really too much for me to process. "Did you live in Sarasota before?" It's just dawned on me that Sarasota and Miami are a short peninsula-span apart.

"Oh, yes, I met Mimi there." Dad beams at Mimi.

She glows, a pink flush rising on her cheeks.

"We lived in Miami," I offer.

"Oh, yes," is all he says.

"When did you live in Sarasota?" I ask.

"These are the best meatballs I've ever tasted," Dad says to Mrs. D'Angelo, changing the subject again.

We start talking about how good the food is, and everyone compliments and thanks the D'Angelos for this fine dinner. Dad has ignored my question. Is it possible that he was in Sarasota all the time we lived in Miami? Did he know we were there? Did he look for us?

"Dad, I just noticed it's twelve fifteen," I whisper to him. Church is usually out by noon, and Momma thinks that's where we are. So we have to be home by twelve forty-five at the latest, the time it usually takes us to walk from Passaic to Garfield, or Momma will get suspicious and accuse us of doing something behind her back. She'd be very surprised to hear we had lunch with Dad.

"It has been so good of you to invite us over and to serve us such a magnificent meal," Mimi says to the D'Angelos. "I'm really glad to know you. Please come visit us in Sarasota. We'd be so happy if you would be our guests at our new restaurant."

"Thank you, thank you," Dad says. He pumps Mr. D'Angelo's hand and kisses Catherine and her mother. We all do the same. Pretty soon the four of us are back in the car.

This time, Sharon and I sit in the back. Dad is up front in the passenger seat.

"The D'Angelos said I can send letters to their home," Dad says as Mimi starts up the car. "Then Catherine will get the mail to you, Beverly."

"How nice of them to do this for us," Mimi says. "Delicious dinner."

Mimi parks the car a few blocks from our apartment. I open the back door.

Dad reaches across the front seat and grabs my hand. He presses a piece of paper into my palm and closes my fingers around it.

"This is for you and your sister," Dad says. "Now, keep writing to us. We want to hear from you. I'll let you know when we get to Sarasota. We love you girls."

We hug him and Mimi over the seat and get out of the car.

Sharon and I stand alone on the sidewalk. We stare at the black car as it turns the corner and disappears.

"What did he give you?" Sharon asks.

I open my clenched fingers and unwind the $20 bill from my clammy hand.

My eyes blur. The movie from that day so long ago, a lifetime ago, when Dad bent down and pressed two quarters into my palm plays in my mind.

"This is for you and your sister," he said.

• • •

This entire day has been bizarre. My full belly is witness to the fact that the day actually happened, but the last four hours were more like a movie than reality. My father and his wife spent the morning with the daughters he's not seen for seventeen years. We acted like nothing ever happened, like we were just a normal family out for a meal with friends. We picked up where we left off, back when I was five and Sharon not yet one.

Like my life with Momma, silence shrouded the important issues in our lives today. Dad didn't ask about our graduations, only weeks away—mine from college, Sharon's from high school. Not a word about my teaching future. Nor about Sharon's nursing school. Not a question about Momma. He suggested we move to Sarasota but offered no timeline, no details. False hope.

What are we to think? Dad talked about his life, not ours. He didn't ask about our dreams, how the last two decades had gone. He didn't ask if were happy. If we were safe. Had enough to eat. Didn't ask our forgiveness for abandoning us, for his financial neglect.

My daydreams of finding my father are over.

I've found him.

He's a mirage after all.

Chapter 24

A NEW CHALLENGE

January 1963

I'm starting my student teaching, the last hurdle before graduation, today. My supervising teacher is Mrs. Judy Wise, and I'll be in her fourth grade class in Paramus.

As soon as I enter the school, I'm swept into a whirlwind of uplifting images, sounds, and smells. Everything—from the children's art that fills the walls to the mobiles hanging from the ceiling, the ambient sounds of laughter, and the lingering lunchroom aromas—is positive, wholesome, welcoming. I'm optimistic. I smile. I walk into the school office at exactly one in the afternoon, the appointed time for this first day.

"Good afternoon," I say to the school secretary. "I'm Beverly Radzai from Paterson State College. I'll be working with Mrs. Judy Wise this semester."

"She's been looking forward to your arrival, and so have we," she says. "The principal, Mrs. James, is in a parent conference now. Be sure to stop in to meet her before you leave today. Here's a packet of information on the Paramus School

System. When you arrive each morning, please sign in on our visitors list and then sign out with the time you leave. Wear this name tag whenever you're in the building."

"Thank you," I say, pinning on my new identification badge.

"Mrs. Wise's class is down this hall and to your right. Room six." She points, indicating which way I should turn as I leave the office.

I make my way down the long corridor of the one-story elementary school. Children's voices flow into the hallway from behind the closed classroom doors—happy, eager voices. I envision my new class of fourth graders. I've long thought this would be the perfect age to teach—old enough to be thoughtful and young enough to be idealistic. I put a skip in my step and open the door to my professional future.

I don't spot the teacher at first. All the kids are seated on the floor in half-circles; desks are pushed out of the way, half up against the windows and the rest along the opposite wall of art-filled bulletin boards. Drums, tambourines, shakers, and triangles lie across the laps and in the hands of the children, and their attention is riveted on a red-headed, freckled elf sitting cross-legged at the front of the group.

The elf-teacher lifts her arms, the instruments rise into place, and the class bursts into "Matilda." They sway and beat their drums, jangle the bells, clap the wood blocks. This must be music class. I check the door number to be sure I'm in the right place. Mrs. Wise. Fourth grade. This is it. I take a seat in the back of the room and sing along. Harry Belafonte. One of my favorites. I know all the words.

Mrs. Wise gives me a little wave and a smile. "By the time we finish 'Yellow Bird,' let's be ready for social studies," she instructs the class.

"Yellow bird," the class sings softly.

At the end of the first verse, the kids in the outer semi-circle rise, continue singing, and sashay past me to the cubby holes that line the rear classroom wall. Everyone smiles at me as they pass. A few kids pause to shake my hand, then deposit their instruments and, like a slow-moving stream, flow to their desks. The entire room is in motion. There's not a sound except for singing and the gentle scrape of the one-piece metal-legged desks on the white linoleum floor. Like a choreographed modern dance, children, desks, instruments, and books swirl until the room is transformed into five small groupings of five desks each. Paper, pencil, and books are soon atop each rectangular wooden desktop. The ending strains of the song linger as the master conductor stands at the front of the room, commanding the attention of twenty-five nine- and ten-year-old children. She's taller than I thought, but youthful, with a smile that dominates her face and a personality that fills the room. I've never seen anything like this in my entire life. My head is spinning.

"Ladies and gentlemen, please welcome our student teacher, Miss Radzai," she says.

The kids clap and smile at me.

"She'll be with us until the beginning of June."

Welcome home.

"Come on up front, Miss Radzai. Let's co-teach this social studies lesson."

I'm in a trance, alive, lifted into a new realm, a special place—like my own fourth grade classroom back at Little River, only better. This time I'm about to learn what it means to be in my teachers' shoes. But at this instant, I'm petrified. I have no idea what the social studies lesson is about. I don't know the students' names. I'm not prepared to be a teaching partner.

I'm in way over my head.

• • •

In the weeks that follow, Judy Wise helps me see what good teaching looks like, why it's important—she reminds me why I chose this career path in the first place. I reflect on all my own teachers—the one who taught a crying first grader how to read, the blonde angel who escorted me to the spelling bee, the one who made sure I had a corsage for an important occasion, the high school English teacher who encouraged me to apply for a college scholarship. I remember the weight of a teacher's glance, the calm of a hand on the shoulder, the power of encouraging words—words that could be used to harm or as a healing balm. For many kids like me, the teacher is the surrogate parent, the social support system, the one who says, "Yes, you can do this. Let me show you how."

My teachers have made learning painless and fun for me. My classrooms have been safe and secure environments—places where I could try out my voice, create and nurture my personality. Each of my teachers was unique and challenged me in supportive and caring ways. I want to be like them. But I really, really want to be like Mrs. Wise. She's charismatic, magnetic, and talented. She uses music to create a mood, to unite the class, to build common experiences that define the particular group of kids who are lucky enough to share this year with her. By the time of my arrival, in January, she's established a caring culture in her classroom; it's a place where each child thrives, in large part because she makes sure of it. The kids not only spontaneously break out in song between subjects, they also speak out in discussions, unafraid to express their own points of view. They listen to and respect one another, own the classroom, take responsibility for tasks, exert their personalities, and are curious and energetic about their own learning. This is the atmosphere I want to have in my own classroom. But I can't sing, can't play a musical instrument. So I'll have to figure out my own classroom personality and learn how to adapt all that I'm soaking up from my new mentor to suit my own skill set.

Judy Wise is my role model both inside and out of the classroom. She invites me to her home, where we're Judy and Beverly. Once again, I get to practice using two forks at dinner time.

"Why don't you set the table while I finish mixing this salad?" Judy asks as we stand around in her kitchen the first evening I join her and her husband for dinner.

I grab the pile of silverware she's set out and walk into the dining room. Once there, I realize I can't recall my 4-H table-setting lessons.

"Ummm. Could you remind me how this goes?" I ask, sounding like a fourth grader.

"I can never get this right, myself," she says, laughing, as she sets one place as my model.

I watch Judy Wise like a hawk, studying her, listening intently as she discusses issues and interacts with friends and students. I see her play the devil's advocate with students, forcing them to take alternative positions and to substantiate their statements. I work alongside her as she structures lessons, discovering clever ways to seduce kids into learning something complex. I listen as she weaves students' comments together and encourages each one to participate, to learn, to question. I become a serious student of the art and technique of teaching, going beyond my methods classes and into the wondrous world of practice—but not just any practice. Here in Mrs. Wise's classroom, I'm witnessing polished, exquisite, meaningful teaching and learning. I'm learning from a master educator, and I'm fully aware of the honor.

"You have to know the content of instruction inside and out," Mrs. Wise says. "But in the end, it doesn't matter that *you* know it. It's not about you. It's about them—the students—and how you get them to process information and ideas. Your main job is to get them to want to know something, to be eager to dig into the topic, to be willing to remember related knowledge and create new ways of thinking. Be a detective: listen and watch the students carefully, and you'll come to understand how they're thinking, what their misconceptions are, what their patterns of reasoning are.

From there, you'll know the next best question to ask. Good questions are the keys to meaningful learning."

Even though I've heard something like this in my methods classes at Paterson State, hearing Mrs. Wise's philosophy and seeing it in action hits me square in the face. I get it. Observing children the moment they grasp a new idea is a thrill. The sparkle in their eyes, the confidence in their voices, the energy in their bodies—this is what teaching is all about. This is what makes me work harder to be the kind of teacher I have to be. There is only one option: I have to be an expert, like Mrs. Wise, or not be a teacher at all. I have to find creative ways to get kids to think, to wonder, to question, to want to learn.

"And the teacher needs to have fun too," Mrs. Wise says. "Otherwise, you won't want to teach for long."

I'm having the time of my life. I feel energized, creative, purposeful, happy deep in my soul, hopeful for my future, committed to my students and my career. I figure I could teach for the next fifty years.

Toward the end of the semester, I apply for a teaching position in Paramus. With Mrs. Wise's glowing recommendation, I'm offered a job for the coming school year. I'll have a fourth grade class also, at another elementary school.

No longer am I the kid who counts on my teachers to encourage and embolden me. Now I'm the one my students will look up to. I must push myself to rise to the task, to have the confidence to show all the teachers I've been helped by that I'm their faithful student and I can and will pass on the lessons they've taught me.

It's my turn to dig deep and to become an inspiring teacher like those I've been privileged to study under all these years.

Chapter 25

GRADUATION AND GOOD-BYE

July 1963

Ron Radzai checked out.

He was always home, religiously, a half hour after he clocked out of US Rubber, where he was a miscellaneous assembly line worker. For years, his life at home followed a predictable pattern. He went to bed about ten in the morning and slept until six. He got up, showered, ate dinner, and drank coffee. No wine, beer, or hard liquor were ever in the house. Certainly, no drugs. He sat at the kitchen table for his meal and stayed in the same chair for the many games of gin rummy he and Momma played until it was time for him to fix the snack he took to work. About eleven thirty, he headed out for work and his cycle of life started over. He'd be home by eight the next morning, have coffee, play a game or two of gin rummy, and go to bed, usually with Momma beside him.

In June, I graduated from Paterson State College, and a week later, Sharon graduated from Garfield High School. Three weeks later, Ron Radzai didn't come home. Not that day. Not the next. No letter. No phone calls. No announcement. Just an empty chair.

No one talked about it. We all knew what it meant.

That's it. He's not coming back.

I'm not exactly sure when he decided to leave. Perhaps it was when he realized that Momma had been cheating on him the same way she'd cheated on Dad so many years earlier. Now it was Ron Radzai's turn to be the lover scorned. Or maybe it was when he realized his life was little more than rituals and silence, punctuated by Momma's rage and violence. Then again, maybe it was the last time she stabbed him in his arm with the kitchen knife and blood splattered all over him and the floor. "Everything's okay," he said when the police showed up. That wasn't the first time he sent the police away empty-handed. But it would be the last.

That he had three sons with Momma and that he stayed for seventeen years was impressive to me as I looked back on our lives together. I'm not sure what he thought he was getting into when he and Momma had their tryst in Yonkers, or exactly when he knew he was in over his head.

I think back to his last evening at the apartment. Was there a clue I missed? The more I recalled that evening, the more I realized it was a night like all the others.

This is how I remember it:

All four of us kids and the dog, Smokey—the barely house-trained German Shepherd–Lab mix that Ronnie found and brought home—are sprawled across the pull-out sofa bed in the living room, each of us trying to claim a comfortable space. Momma and Ron Radzai sleep in the one bedroom in our new place, up one flight in an old apartment complex in Paterson. All of us kids and the dog sleep in the living room.

We moved a week after Sharon's graduation, finally leaving Garfield, our home for seven years. It dawns on me now that Ron Radzai had probably been planning his departure for some time and our move to Paterson was his effort to get us into a smaller and less expensive apartment. This new place is a real downsize move for us. One tiny bedroom, a small bathroom, the living room, and a nook of a kitchen. I'm not sure what happened to the rest of the furniture we had in Garfield, including another double bed and dressers. I guess Momma sold them.

Now this move to this tiny apartment starts to make sense to me. Ron Radzai figured Sharon would soon be off to nursing school, so once he left, our family of six would turn into a family of four: the two boys, Momma, and me. The four of us can easily fit into this compact apartment. However, it also means the boys will have to enroll in new schools and I'll have a longer trip to Paramus.

While we tussle about on the sofa, Momma and Ron Radzai are in the kitchen playing gin rummy. The apartment is so small, the kitchen table is only a few feet away from the living room sofa. The sounds of card-playing fill the air. Shuffling. Dealing. Snapping down cards. Showing the winning hand. Adding up the scores. Shuffling the next hand. Ron Radzai is an expert shuffler, fanning out the cards, melding one stack into the other, mixing them up in magical ways that Momma can't replicate. Momma divides up the pack, eases one half into the other, does that a few times, and deals out the cards: one-one; two-two . . . ten-ten. You can tell who won the last hand by who shuffles next and you can tell who's shuffling by listening.

This is just another iteration of the evening ritual that's played out for as long as I can remember. Lucky Strike exhales and coffee cups clunking on the Formica table are the only other sounds from the kitchen. There's no discussion. No talk about the weather or politics. Nothing about twelve-year-old Mikey's sore eyes, which often keep him home from school, or the fact that fifteen-year-old Ronnie's eyes are blurring again since the corneal transplants he had five years ago. Nothing about Momma's corneas fading again, even after two

232 SEEING EYE GIRL

sets of transplants. No talk about the car I'll need to get to my teaching job in a month or Sharon's imminent departure for Martland Medical Center. Nothing about the color TV Momma wants or the fact that we'll all need new clothes for the coming school year.

A little after eleven, the chairs scrape on the floor. Ron Radzai gets up, makes a sandwich, and puts it in a paper bag. He gives Momma a kiss. Then he steps into the living room, walks past the sofa. He doesn't say a word to any of us kids— no kiss for his boys, no pats on the back. No "It's been nice" or "Take care of yourselves" or anything. All he has in his hands is his paper lunch bag. No extra clothes. No toiletries. No deck of cards. He opens the door, walks through. Closes it.

For the last time.

I wonder what he was thinking. Was he relieved? Did he worry how we'd survive without him?

Ron Radzai has been a part of our lives for the last seventeen years. He paid the rent, bought the groceries, the furniture, our clothes; performed the roles he thought were his; and obeyed Momma's implicit rules. Like me, he knew he must be home on time or Momma would accuse him of having a girlfriend or conspiring behind her back. He never lingered over a beer or coffee with his buddies. He knew how to aggravate Momma and how to appease her and he always chose to keep the peace. He did whatever Momma wanted: took us on vacations to western New York for Robinson family reunions, reserved the cabin at Letchworth State Park where my dad worked during his CCC years, visited with Momma's side of the family, took photographs with all the cousins. He took us over to Yonkers to see his Radzai relatives, where we read our cousins' huge collections of comic books and ate Polish food. I never heard him complain or say he didn't want to do anything Momma desired.

The best time of all for us kids was when he was happy and decided to make a heap of potato pancakes. That was his specialty. It has been a long time since he stood over the cabinet counters, hand-grating a few pounds of potatoes into a big bowl, then a couple of onions. The rest of the recipe was a secret, he told us. We knew it had something to do with an egg or two and a pinch of flour, salt, and pepper. The most pleasing part, next to the feast we were about to enjoy, was when he fried the pancakes in bubbling vegetable oil in a deep skillet. The sweet aroma filled the apartment and made all of us smile. He heaped our plates with pancakes, sausage links, and a dollop of applesauce. The pancakes, thin and crispy, brown and crunchy, were everyone in the family's hands-down favorite meal, and we couldn't get enough. But those days were few and far between. And now they are ancient history.

Now that I have a teaching job and Sharon's ready for nursing school, I'm sure he thought, *What better time to leave than now? The kids are almost grown up.* And with that, he left the four of us to figure out the future for ourselves, without the man we've all counted on. Even though he seldom talked to any of us, we always knew he was here. There was food in the refrigerator. The rent was paid.

Silence and rage filled the home Momma and Ron Radzai created. There wasn't much in between, except for the continuously running television and radio. The four of us kids came and went, did our homework, watched TV, and maneuvered ourselves around one another until it was bedtime. During the Garfield years, the two of us girls lived our lives in our bedroom, the boys in the living room. We were treated as two pairs of kids, the dark Italian girls beaten for having a good-for-nothing father, the lighter Polish boys ignored and generally left to fend for themselves.

I had little occasion to see Ron Radzai when he was awake. I was never afraid of him and never saw him raise a hand to any of us kids. Our lives silently passed by one another, year after year. But I counted on him to be there, to keep the family secure and stable, and he did just that. I never imagined a day would come when he wouldn't be part of our lives.

I took Ron Radzai for granted.

Momma did too.

And now, he is gone.

Chapter 26

THE CAR

July 1963

I'm the breadwinner now. That's the way it is.

"How soon until you get your first paycheck?" Momma asks.

I won't have an income for two months. There are no savings. There's no money hidden under a mattress. We have only a few cans of soup in the kitchen. We're in a new city and don't know any neighbors who can lend us a cup of milk. There's not enough time to get a summer job. I've got a good job that will start soon but not soon enough. I need money now—to tide us over and for a down payment on a car.

I rack my brain to think of someone who can help. I can't ask any of my friends for a loan. How humiliating. For some reason, Dr. Yerzley, my physics professor, comes into focus in my mind. Just a few weeks ago, at Paterson State's graduation, he congratulated me and hung around with Momma, Sharon, and me at the reception.

"If I can help you in any way in the future, don't hesitate to call me," Dr. Yerzley said. He gave me a bear hug and pressed a card with his phone number into my hand. Catherine and I had a special relationship with him for the four years we spent on campus, but I've never thought of him as a person to call if I needed help before.

I quickly dismiss the idea. What could be more embarrassing than to ask one of your favorite college professors for a loan?

Over the next few days, I find myself staring at his phone number and thinking of his kind eyes and all the times he tutored me after class, all the times he asked how I was doing, as though he really cared. Finally, I break down and dial.

"Beverly, I am so glad you called," Dr. Yerzley says. "I was about to call you. I'm driving to the Jersey Shore tomorrow with my son to spend the weekend. I'd like you and your mother and sister to go along with us. My treat. I want to ask Catherine also. What do you think?"

"Ooh, what a nice surprise." I'm stunned by this idea. This was the last thing I imagined Dr. Yerzley saying. "I'll ask my mother. When would we leave?"

"We could pick you up early in the morning, say seven. We'll return late on Sunday. If you can go, I'll call Catherine."

• • •

So it comes to pass that Momma, Sharon, Ronnie, Mikey, and I drive with Dr. Yerzley and his college-age son to the Jersey Shore. We meet up with Catherine and Lou, as well as Catherine's mom, who owns a second home there. We sun ourselves, eat like we're food-deprived—which we are—gather shells, build sand castles, and take lots of photographs. Momma assumes her best *being out in public personality* and dons her pink sequined bathing suit with its ribbed bodice that shows off her stunning figure.

This is the first time since we lived in Miami that all four of us kids have been to the beach. We laugh and act like we don't have a care in the world. I wear my zebra-striped one-piece bathing suit and Dr. Yerzley poses with Catherine and me for a photo like we're old friends.

"Do you know what I like about the two of you?" he asks as Catherine and I walk beside him along the crowded beach.

"You couldn't like how unprepared we were in science," Catherine says.

"Well, that's part of it. In spite of your weak science background, you fought hard to understand difficult concepts. You weren't willing to take low grades. You both had high expectations for yourselves and you worked hard to learn."

"With a lot of extra help from you," I say.

"I could see that our after-hours study sessions paid off. Life will bring many challenges your way. Physics was just one. I want both of you to promise me you'll never give up when you're faced with a challenge."

"I promise," Catherine says.

"I promise too," I say, beaming.

• • •

I never did ask Dr. Yerzley for a loan.

It's Monday now, and I'm back where I started. No money. No car. No ideas.

I finally think about my father. Perhaps he can help. I've secretly corresponded with him a few times since our meeting in April. Once I start teaching, he can send letters to my school, but for now they're still going to Catherine's.

Since the matter of money has never come up, I'm apprehensive about asking. But I can't think of an alternative, so I swallow my pride and write:

Dear Dad,

I hope you and Mimi are doing well as you get ready for your big move to Sarasota. Sharon leaves for nursing school in a few weeks, and I start my new teaching

job in Paramus in late August. I'm excited about work-
ing with another fourth-grade class.

Dad, I really need a car, and I hope you can help
me with a small loan. I promise to pay it all back as
soon as I start teaching. Right now, though, I have no
savings and no credit so I think it will be hard to get the
bank to give me a car loan. All my college loans have
been used up helping to support the family, and all the
money I've made babysitting and from my job at Two
Guys from Harrison is gone too. Momma expected me
to go to work to help with the family's expenses, so all
the money I ever made was spent on groceries, rent,
and clothes for all of us.

I'm not complaining. Just want to explain this
to you. I think if I could scrape together a deposit,
I'd have a better chance to get a loan from the bank.
I don't want to go to Benten Finance Corporation
because they'll charge me a fortune and I already have
my college debt to repay.

Please, Dad. I hope you can help me out with this
request. I don't think I need much. Perhaps a few hun-
dred dollars. I promise to pay you back right away as
soon as I start teaching.

Could you write back soon, please? I have to hurry
and get this done because we don't have any transpor-
tation for the family now.
Love,
Beverly

"I've just received a letter for you from your dad," Catherine says when she calls me a week later.

"Great. Can you open it and read it to me?" I ask.

"Sure."

Dear Bev,
Received your letter and was glad to hear from you
but not glad to hear of all your troubles. I noticed this
was the first time in our correspondence that you have
called me "Dad." That made me very happy.

"That's sweet," Catherine says.
"It is," I agree.

Mimi and I are leaving for Sarasota in two weeks.
All our money is tied up in our new home and the
restaurant we're buying. I really can't help you now.
I don't know why you didn't plan for this. You are a
smart girl.

Catherine's voice gets soft. She pauses.
"It's okay, Catherine. It's sort of what I expected." I regret
writing to Dad; wish I could take it back. What was I thinking?
"What else did he say?"

I'll help you but not until you can prove to me that
you will get out of that mess and until you start using
your legal name, Armento, again.

"I didn't know that," Catherine says. "Your legal name
isn't Radzai?"
"Someday I'll tell you that story." I laugh. "Did he say
anything else?"

I don't like what I see, Beverly. You have a double
personality, and it shows. I don't owe your mother one
thing and I believe she is behind your request for money.
Do write soon.
Love, Dad

I'm devastated by my father's response. He doesn't trust me. He thinks I have a double personality and that I'm being manipulated by Momma to extort money from him. Amazing! I'm furious. He's as suspicious of Momma as she is of him. He's suspicious of *me*.

It's clear that Dad has no remorse, no guilt, for abandoning us girls or for his lack of financial support all these years. He wants me to get out of "that mess." I wonder what, exactly, he thinks "that mess" is. He's never asked me about Momma or about my life since he left. I'm not sure he wants to know. He feels entitled to tell me what name I should be using, but no obligation to help me. I'm disappointed—and angry. Angry with myself for assuming Dad would help me. Humiliated that I groveled, begged him for a loan. I will not make that mistake again.

I'm still empty-handed.

• • •

"What have you bought so far on credit?" the Benten Finance Corporation loan officer asks, his hands locked behind his head, his body rocking back in his black leather swivel chair, his desk covered with stacks of paper, and his brown trousers shiny from one too many ironings.

"Nothing," I say. I've taken the bus to the closest BFC office, determined to solve my problem by myself. My Paterson State College diploma, driver's license, and contract with Paramus City Schools are in a manila folder on my lap. I've worn my best white blouse and straight black skirt to strike a professional look. Thank goodness I learned how to drive back in high school and have a valid license. I'm hopeful my diploma and teaching contract for $4,600 for the school year will convince these folks they should invest in me.

"How much do you have for a deposit?"

"I don't have a deposit, Mr. Stolski," I say from my overstuffed leather chair, looking over his oversize brown desk at him. The desk sports a fishing trophy and a hand-carved name plate that reads CHUCK STOLSKI. My feet dangle in the air. I don't care. I'm a grown-up and I'm determined to walk away from this meeting with a car.

"Do you have a man who can vouch for you and cosign a loan?"

"No."

"Your father?"

"I don't have a father."

"Your husband?"

"I don't have a husband."

"If you don't have a deposit and have no one to cosign, it's going to be hard for me to give you a loan," he says, swaying back farther in his chair, comfortable with himself and with the statement he has probably used thousands of times before. "Where did you say you were going to be teaching?" he asks, his voice rising like he suddenly got the solution to an algebraic problem.

"Paramus. Here's my contract and my salary." I stand up, push the paper toward him, and point to the line I want him to read. "I start in a month. Sir, I have no way to get to Paramus. I need a car. I'm a responsible person. I'll make all my payments on time. You can count on me."

Mr. Stolski picks up my contract and stares at the salary line. He abruptly sits up straight, swivels around, stands up, and pulls a folder out of the top drawer of the four-drawer metal file cabinet behind his desk. I study his shiny trousers and imagine the wife who presses them steadfastly each week. I wonder what kind of car she drives.

He reads something, closes the file drawer and plops back in his chair. "Do you have car insurance?"

"No. I need to borrow enough money so I can purchase insurance."

"Do you have a car in mind?"

"No, I haven't looked for a car yet." This isn't going well. I imagine riding the three buses I'll have to take to get from Paterson to my school in Paramus. I have no trouble riding the bus. The problem is being at school by seven thirty each morning, carrying heavy textbooks through rain and snow and waiting for a bus that's apt to run behind schedule.

Above all, I hate to be late.

"I'll tell you what," he says. "You're a nice kid. I'd like to help you. Here's the name of a used car lot where we do business. Go see a guy named Sal. Pick a car."

I can't believe he's saying this to me. I jump to my feet and stand at attention in front of Mr. Stolski's desk. I want to break out in song, but I restrain myself and plunge out my hand to shake his.

"Come back with all the information, and I'll draw up the loan for you," he says, smiling at me.

I smile back, exhaling like a pierced helium balloon.

"I want you to know this is a high-risk loan," he continues. "That means you're going to pay a substantial interest rate on the amount you borrow. You don't meet the requirements for a low-interest-rate loan. You haven't even started work yet. Once you start teaching, you must make your payments on time every month. If you miss a month, even one payment, we repossess the car. Period. Do you understand?"

• • •

The next day Momma and I take the bus to meet Sal at his sprawling car lot in Paterson. Sal's a fast-talking, fast-eating, big-bellied, sloppy Italian guy. He's full of personality and good deals. He talks me into a beige 1963 Plymouth Belvedere. Four doors. Automatic. Faux-leather bench seats front and back. The whole family can fit in the car.

"Best bargain in the lot," he proclaims. "Hardly any mileage. No scratches. No dents. Really like a new car. You won't regret this decision." He asks Momma, his arm around her shoulder and now on her waist as he pulls her closer, "Cutie, are you going to be driving this baby too?"

"Oh, no," Momma demurs. "I can't see very well." She gives Sal a big smile, all happy for the attention.

"Let me slip my card into your hand, beautiful," he says. "You call me anytime you get lonely, you hear?"

We're getting more than a car deal here.

Chapter 27

CATCH AND RELEASE

August 1963

Sharon's round face is aglow, the magic of fireflies twinkling in her eyes, her long, straight black hair shimmering as it falls to her waist. She's a princess. For a moment, I think she's seven again and she, Ronnie, and I are out in our side yard in Miami at twilight playing the game she invented, "Catch and Release."

By day, we played hopscotch, jumped rope, shot marbles, and organized games of kickball, hide-and-seek, and tag with the neighbor kids. Come early evening, the three of us got our empty peanut butter jars and prepared for the dazzling light show that was about to begin. Thousands of lightning bugs came to frolic, enticing us with their blinking lamps until one of us was close enough to grab it before it flew into the dark, tall grasses or honeysuckle vines. Once we had the critter in our hands, we opened the lid quickly—just a sliver—to get the bug into the jar before it escaped our clammy hands. Then we pivoted and headed for another. Before long, each of us had trapped dozens of prisoners. The breathing holes weren't large enough to let the bugs escape, so our collections grew and our jars flickered brighter and brighter as the evening sky darkened.

Finally, Sharon said, "I think it's time."

The three of us tiptoed to the darkest spot in the yard.

"On the count of three," Sharon whispered. "One. Two. Three."

Each of us unscrewed our jar's lid and released our captives. Hundreds of little bugs turned the black night air into a magical fireworks show, bringing the heavens and all the stars to us, lighting up our railroad tracks, our backyard, our faces. The creatures encircled us, joyous at their sudden freedom, thankful to reunite with their mates, grateful for the evening's adventure. They danced just for us and we twirled, threw our arms up into the air, and turned our faces to the sky. Our bodies were lit up by the pleasure of this star-studded display, and we became lost in this simple, pure moment.

This game brought great joy to Sharon. Her little-girl face stretched into its broadest smile, and her high cheeks glowed in the insect light, her happiness boundless.

That's how she looks today.

It's the day Sharon's been waiting for. It's the day I've dreaded. Today, I have to release her—my pal, my co-conspirator, my confidant, my little sister. She's going off to nursing school. As she should. As I want her to. The recipient of a full scholarship—tuition, room, and board, awarded in part due to financial need and in part due to her "Why I want to be a nurse" essay. How proud I am of her. But now that the time has arrived, I'm in shock, as though I've only this moment learned that she's going to be a nurse. That she's going to Newark. That she's going to leave me. Now there will be no one to share the beatings, the rage, the delusions, the accusations—all of which have intensified since Ron Radzai left me to be the de facto financial head of the household and since fat Sal, the car salesman, starting coming around at night to visit Momma.

Even though Sharon and I look alike, we are actually very different. She's the bubbly, outgoing, gregarious, slaphappy, cute one who went to the prom. I'm the reserved, serious, bookworm, worrywart one who stayed home. Together, we're a balanced, whole person. Separate—well, we are about to find out. We've been together for the last eighteen years and for most of those have eaten our meals, done homework, and slept alongside each other, whispering secrets and trying to make sense of things, like how sex works and what's wrong with Momma. In spite of our "you're on my side of the bed" fights, our shared experiences and knowledge of "what really happened" bind us together like the individual threads in a piece of twine.

"Can you take me?" Sharon asks.

• • •

It has already been a miserable day. Mikey wailed over yet another sore eye and Momma sat in her big leather chair, smoking one Lucky Strike after another. Just another Saturday like most others. Except now my stepfather is not sleeping in the bedroom and the refrigerator is empty. In two weeks, I'll have earned enough to pay the rent, buy groceries, and make the car payment. I'll drive to Paramus every day for preschool planning, and the boys will enroll in new schools in Paterson. Momma will be home alone.

If things had worked out with her art career, she'd be standing at her easel each day while we kids were gone at work and school, making a living as a commercial artist, as some of the top artists predicted she would only a decade ago.

But now there's no easel, no pastels, no drawing paper. Momma listens to the radio day and night, her eyes clouding over again as her disease reinfects her corneas. She can't read the newspaper, but she can follow the news about Martin Luther King and how he might be a communist. Even though the Red Scare has long been over for most people, that's not the case for Momma. Her delusions and violence are fueled by thoughts that "the communists" are after us—our family—and that teachers, including me, are communists.

It's at night, after Ron Radzai used to go to work, that Momma's raging mind explodes, with Sharon and me the likely targets. After my stepfather left, she gave the bedroom to the boys. Now the three of us girls sleep in the living room on the pull-out sofa bed. After Sharon leaves, it will be just Momma and me.

This thought brings me to the edge of insanity. My fear of living alone with Momma hits me square in the face. But I'm her seeing eye girl; my job is to guide her, keep her safe. It's my job to protect her, not to be afraid of her. My responsibility to Momma is deeply embedded, and even her beatings over years have not shaken my loyalty. Now, at twenty-two, ready to take on my life as an educator, I realize how strong and dysfunctional the chains that bind us are. I am trapped in Ron Radzai's role as the breadwinner, the caretaker of the family. Today I'm confronted with the reality of my dilemma. I do not have the knowledge, skill, or willingness to take care of Momma, yet I believe it's my task, my ethical obligation. My future.

I won't really be alone with Momma, but it seems that way. Ronnie and Mikey will still be here, but the boys live in physical and psychological spaces that are different from those us girls inhabit. It's been that way for so long we're accustomed to not communicating, not interacting, not getting in each other's business. Ronnie is distant, withdrawn, silent, angry. Mikey has the innocent, energetic, sweet, caring personality of my students. I'm drawn to him, and I try to mentor and encourage him. But like Sharon, he can't save me from Momma's blows, stinging words, or sudden wrath.

• • •

"Of course I'm going to take you," I snap. "How else do you think you're going to get there?"

Deep down, I'm happy for Sharon. But I'm not happy right now. I don't want to be rational. And I certainly don't feel like being nice.

• • •

Just get on the 46 and head south. In a half hour or so, you're there. It's a straight shot past Clifton, Nutley, Bloomfield, East Orange, then Newark—a big, dirty city full of racial tension, unemployment, poverty, and twelve-story housing projects, notorious for their crime and drugs. I've lived in public housing for much of my life, but Mulford Gardens and Victory Homes never looked like the squalor I see in Newark. This is the kind of poverty Michael Harrington talks about in *The Other America*. I read his book during my last year at Paterson State, before I'd seen many urban slums. This is a new kind of poverty for me. Windows are broken out of the apartments. There's no grass outside the dingy buildings, only dirt. And litter. Buildings are run down, shabby. Many white people have fled the inner city, but they still hold most of the power. They are the teachers, the principals, the business owners, the politicians. Black people are the students, the customers, the unemployed, the citizens. They are the humans living in the high-rise slums.

This is the stuff of the civil rights movement that is sweeping the country. President Kennedy says that poverty and civil rights are moral issues. This resonates with me. He gives words to ideas I have but can't articulate. I believe schools should be integrated. Housing too. Brown vs. Board of Education is almost a decade old, but schools are still segregated. Black people are not allowed in many restaurants and hotels. They're discriminated against in hiring, in voting. Next week, Martin Luther King will lead a huge march on Washington to highlight demands for equal justice and to support the civil rights legislation Kennedy has sent to Congress. All summer, there's been racial unrest in many cities. Newark has all the ingredients for more violence.

This is where Sharon is going to be for the next two years: at Martland Medical Center, affiliated with Newark City Hospital—in the heartbeat of the city's center. She's on the backseat of my new Plymouth, surrounded by five large paper bags stuffed with her clothes, books, new notebooks, two sets of towels, a set of sheets, a pillow, and a blanket. Momma is in the front seat with me, lighting each new Lucky Strike from the one she then throws out the window. She looks straight ahead, silent.

But she talked plenty before we left the house.

"You have no business going off to school," Momma screamed at Sharon. "You need to get a job and start paying me back for all the money I've spent on you over all these years."

Sharon didn't say a word. She learned a long time ago that there's nothing to be said. She has never bought into the guilt Momma tried to instill in both of us. I have. I believe it's my responsibility to take care of the family. But Sharon just kept her mouth shut, packed her bags, and loaded them into the car. Momma and I followed.

And here we are. Almost there.

"How do I get to Bergen Street?" I ask, turning my head toward the backseat, where Sharon has the map on her lap.

"What street are we on now?" she asks.

"Forget it," I say. The least she can do is read the damn map.

"Here's the hospital," I say, spotting a sign on the street corner, making an effort to change my tone. *I have no reason to be upset*, I tell myself. But Sharon's the last cog holding together the wobbling wheel of my world.

"Okay, this is Bergen." An ambulance passes us, its siren blaring. I follow it as it makes a left at the next intersection, where a large group of teenagers hangs around outside a liquor store.

Here we are, right outside the emergency room. I see the sign for the nursing school and we park. All three of us get out of the car. Momma hugs Sharon and says, "Study hard and come home soon."

Really? I say to myself. *Come home soon—are you serious? Why would she come home?* I have an aching feeling in the pit of my stomach that she'll never be back.

"Okay," Sharon says to Momma, as if she means it. She and I grab the bags, scrunch them up in our arms and head for the building. Another siren-blaring ambulance screeches to a halt at the hospital.

"We have to take the steps," Sharon says when we enter the building. Her dorm room is on the second floor. We trudge up a steep, dark flight of stairs and locate her room. It's small, with a twin bed pushed up against each of the long walls and a tiny desk at the foot of each bed. Group bathrooms are out in the hall. Her roommate has not arrived and the dorm room is quiet, ready for my sister and her new life.

This is where we part. This is where I lose it. Sharon's a part of me. We wear the same clothes, finish each other's sentences, doctor each other's wounds. How am I going to live without her?

Sharon's deep brown eyes sparkle. I hug her. She's where she wants to be, ready to twirl into the unknown. She can dance amongst the fireflies. She'll be free. Finally able to breathe.

I feel the catch in my throat. My tears come hot and fast. I hold her tight. Then turn to go. She wails.

I turn back. We cling to each other, sobbing into each other's necks.

I need to leave her.

Fly, little one, fly.

Chapter 28

ONE DAY IN NOVEMBER

Friday, November 22, 1963

A wad of yellow hair peeks out from the tiny blue bundle on the far side of the sofa bed. Once the alarm clock rang forty minutes ago and I hopped off, Momma tucked the loose blanket around her body. We've been bed-partners for five months now. It's no fun being this close to a mother who pinches and bites. Nor to one who has a night visitor. The boys close their bedroom door to escape, but there are few places in our tiny apartment for me to hide when Sal drops in to frolic a few times a week.

I gather my things, knock on the boys' door and tell them it's six forty-five. Turn off the living room lamp. Tiptoe to the apartment door. Once I'm out in the hallway, I pause to collect myself. Make sure I have all my books. My peanut butter sandwich. My lesson plans for the day. I take a deep breath, then skip down the steps and outside to the parking lot. The dark early-morning air is clear and crisp on this last day of the school week. Next week, we'll have just two days of school before

Thanksgiving break. Today, my twenty-five fourth graders will finish their "I'm thankful for . . ." poems and stories. We'll read them out loud before I post them on the bulletin board.

Fourth graders—they *are* the perfect age. I confirmed that they were who I wanted to work with during my time with Judy Wise. They want the world to be at peace, want everyone to get along. No war, no strife. No poverty. No evil. They don't understand why Governor Wallace of Alabama proclaims, "Segregation now, segregation tomorrow, segregation forever," or why Negro students are blocked from entering a school or a restaurant. Even though our suburban school has only white students, they—and I—think the world would be a better place if it were integrated. Peacefully. But that's not the way it's happening in 1963.

Once settled on the front seat of the Plymouth, I start the car and let it warm up for a few minutes. I snap on the radio and grin at myself in the rear-view mirror. Inspect my front teeth. I'll stuff the cavities with cotton once I get to school. The newscaster says President Kennedy, his wife, and the vice president are in Dallas today to kick off the president's campaign for his second term with a motorcade. I snap off the radio.

Okay, let's go. I exhale. I'm ready to leave my life with Momma here in the parking lot and prepare for the day ahead. This is my transition time, the quiet moment when I block out one part of my life and let the other emerge. The journey to school is when the happy, confident, creative me comes alive. I anticipate the day ahead, envision the people I'll see and the tasks I'll perform. I smile as I prepare to enter the world where I'm competent and free. This ritual sustained me during my years as a student. Now I'm the teacher. I concentrate on presenting myself as a committed educator, one who only thinks about my students and is not distracted by personal matters. During this special travel time, I have a conversation with God, like I do every day. He knows I have to drive while we're talking, so I can't bow my head. Nevertheless, reverence prevails as I talk to Him out loud, the beige leather seats my witness.

"Dear God, I'm so thankful for all the blessings You've given me—my good health, my wonderful students, Sharon, Ronnie, and Mikey. Thank You for all my friends who encourage me and for all the teachers who inspire me. Please bless Momma and help her, if You can. Please help me make good choices in my classroom today. I want to say and do those things that help my students learn and feel proud of themselves. I want to be a strong and capable teacher and a good person. Oh, Lord, I'm so weak sometimes, and I have bad thoughts. Some days I don't have the strength to go on and I fear I'll go mad, that I'll be like Momma. Please help me, God. I don't want to think this way, but I am despondent much of the time lately and each day I fear I shall crumble. Please help me to be brave and to think clearly. By the way, there's been a brilliant sunrise this morning during our conversation. It's all thanks to You. I ask this in Thy name, Amen."

I exhale. My depression has deepened this year as Momma's verbal and physical abuse has become more intense. I fear that all the emotions I've long suppressed will bubble over soon and I'll lose control, fall into a state of chaos, madness. I see no way to make the situation better and worry that I'll lose my own sanity in a desperate search for a resolution for my life. I don't know where to turn for help. I can't see a way out of my despondency, out of my life as I know it. I'm filled with guilt. I feel responsible for everyone and know I'm losing myself in the struggle. Kill myself or stay and bear it—those are my choices. Sharon and my friends urge me to "just leave." Somehow that makes no sense to me. I don't have the courage to walk away. It's easier to end it all. I've lost hope that Momma will change, that my life will improve. The Yonkers Momma is gone forever. No one is going to save me, bring an end to my misery. Strong Beverly has to face this alone.

My life at school is my salvation; it's the place where Strong Beverly still lives, the place where she has hope, has a purpose. Making every day wonderful in the classroom is a goal I can achieve. It's a goal I get excited about, that I can "get up for." One day at a time. I work hard to keep Weak Beverly locked outside of school and my classroom. There is no place for her there. I owe that to my students.

Almost there. Oh, I've got to remember to get Brenda's interview with the first grade teacher on how she likes the New Math program. I also need to put our class newspaper, *The Valley News*, to bed today so it'll be ready for distribution next week to the fourth, fifth, and sixth graders. That reminds me: Brian's puzzle and Debra's poem are still outstanding. And the class mother is joining us for lunch today.

My favorite parking space is open.

It'll be a great day. I'm ready.

• • •

I sign in at the front office, say hello to the principal. Get my mail. Good. There's a letter from Dad and one from Sharon. I'll read these after school. Too many things to do before my class arrives. Anyway, I've switched to my school personality. I can't afford to mess up my mind with news of my other life. I've managed to effectively compartmentalize my two lives, my two personalities, all these years, but my increasing sadness this year means I work harder to maintain the walls between my home and school lives, to keep Weak Beverly from bleeding over into Strong Beverly.

Kathy Mulcahey, my team partner and new confidant, bursts into the office, her vivacious personality preceding her actual freckled, blond, solid-body self.

"Hey, you rascal, you beat me in today," Kathy says, grabbing me in an embrace. We were acquaintances at Paterson State but now that we're each teaching fourth grade, our classrooms across the hall from one another, we've become close friends. We plan social studies and science units together, cover each other's classes when one of us has to use the bathroom, and create bulletin boards for our end of the hallway. She's got the best sense of humor of anyone I know. We laugh and cut up at faculty meetings, to the point that the principal often gives us *the look*. We cackle all the time, even when we share the serious issues in our personal lives. She's planning to marry her longtime boyfriend once school is out for summer, so we're constantly talking over all the wedding details. And after she commented on my bruises one day early in the school year, I told her about the beatings, the chaos at home, and Momma's delusions. She knows that my sister, dad, and a few friends correspond with me at school. But she doesn't know about my visits to the Passaic River. There are some things I just can't talk about. To anyone.

Kathy and I walk arm in arm out of the office and down the hallway toward our classrooms. We check in with each other every school day to confirm how we're *really* doing. If one of us is having a bad day, the other one pays particular attention, trying out various antics to change the mood. Kathy knows how to cross her eyes and make crazy faces. She pops into my class at unexpected times to make me laugh. I don't have as many tricks as she, but I try to mimic her techniques.

"I'm good today," I say.

"I'm good today too," Kathy says with a wink. "I love you, Beverly."

"I love you, too, dear friend," I say as we part midway down the corridor. "I don't know what I'd do without you."

"I'll see you during your first tooth break," Kathy says, laughing.

I giggle too.

We joke about the condition of my teeth and the state of my life. Might as well laugh about it. Now that Sharon's off to nursing school, I need a confidant—a person I see daily just to confirm that I'm alive and will survive another day.

I arrive at my classroom, drop my books and lunch on my desk, put the letters inside the middle drawer, and look out the bank of windows that line one side of my classroom. The sunrise's reds and pinks reflect off the blacktop playground, where some of my students are playing hopscotch or talking in small groups. I smile and wave to them and walk across the classroom to tack up Robin's and Billy's essays on the OUR WRITING bulletin board. I've set up my classroom like Judy Wise's—small groups of five kids each. I wheel the overhead projector to the back corner and head to the front blackboard to write the Daily Schedule under the American flag that hangs at a diagonal above my desk:

8:15–8:30	Opening Exercises.
8:30–9:00	Current Events.
9:00–10:30	Language Arts: Directed Reading, Skills, and Activity.
	Today, we'll rotate groups every half hour.

Mrs. Wise taught me how to organize my reading instruction so that I get maximum time with small groups of students and they each get a range of challenging, appropriate activities during the hour and a half devoted to Language Arts. I modeled this process the first month of school, and the class now operates independently with just a few guiding words from me. I lead the directed reading lessons, keeping close tabs on how each child is processing what they read, probing each one for deeper meaning and applications of the material. Groups rotate through skill instruction at learning centers I've created and then a creative application activity. Today they'll finish up their work for the latest edition of our class newspaper. By the end of the hour and a half, each student will have made progress on comprehension and use of language, worked on a range of skills, and teamed up with different students in each activity.

10:30–10:45 Break and Calypso Band.

I couldn't resist. The class made their own instruments, and I used recordings of folk and calypso music to teach them lyrics early this semester. Before long, my classroom was ringing out with music: during breaks, and whenever someone felt like spontaneously singing (usually when something really good happened). I go beyond using music solely as art lessons by having my students analyze the lyrics for social issues and points of view.

10:45–11:45	New Math. Large group. Multiplying fractions. Follow-up practice with a partner.
11:45–12:30	Lunch. Our class mother, Mrs. Cenicola, will be our guest. I hear she's bringing a special treat.
12:30–12:45	Recess. Should be a good day to be outside.
12:45–1:30	Science. Science Fair Project work session.
1:30–2:15	Social Studies. Complete our "Overview of Europe" unit.
2:15–2:30	Clean-up.
2:30	Dismissal. See you on Monday. Have a terrific weekend.

At eight in the morning, I position myself at the classroom door to greet the students individually as they bubble in.

"Good morning, Miss Radzai," Jessica sings out, giving me a hug.

"How are you, Jessica, and how is that little brother?" I ask, returning the hug and smile. To another student, I say, "Look at you, Tommy—what a good-looking haircut." I frame his round face with my hands and beam at him and his new buzz cut.

"Thank you, Miss Radzai. I really like it this short." He turns around slowly so I can admire the fullness of his new look.

It's important to start off the day with a personal comment to each child—to say each student's name and acknowledge them individually, as so many of my teachers did for me. This is one way I *check in* with each child, as Kathy and I do for each other, every morning: "How *are you* today?"

It's almost three months into the school year, and all the classroom routines run smoothly and the students get along well. I've hit my stride. Many parents visit during language arts to listen to individual kids read out loud or construct their own stories as the others take dictation. The parents sing along with us when one of the kids hums or chants the first line of a song. I love the community feel of my classroom, the ways the children care for one another, and the joy I feel each day working with them.

"President Kennedy pardoned a turkey this week," John tells the class during current events. He shows the photo from the local newspaper. "He also said we'd beat the Soviets to the Moon."

I make sure the class knows what's going on in the country and the world. We spend a lot of time on current events, even though they're not included in the formal curriculum plan. My students witness racial strife on television and hear adults talk about the tension in American cities, among other contemporary issues. My job is to raise questions, play devil's advocate, and urge them to investigate, to find the facts, and to construct an opinion based on evidence.

"Why do you think the president wants the United States to be the first on the Moon?" I ask, sparking an animated and thoughtful discussion. I've taught them how to look at and listen to each other, to build off each other's comments, and to extend and dispute ideas with information. Students hurry to our classroom library shelves, where our set of well-worn encyclopedias is stored, to read more about a topic and to check on the facts.

We work our way through our daily schedule and before I know it, the day is over. After a rousing rendition of "Matilda," I stand at the door and say personal good-byes to each child.

By two forty, the classroom is quiet. I sit at my desk and pull Sharon's and Dad's letters from my middle drawer. I position myself so I'll have a clear view of the playground and the neighborhood beyond where many of my students live in tidy two-story clapboard homes, each with a spacious backyard; the swing sets are visible from my perch. Small groups of my students walk across the playground and onto the grassy field that separates the blacktop from their homes. I look down at Sharon's letter.

"I won't be coming home for Thanksgiving."

I knew it. Last time I saw her was in September, when she got a ride to Paterson, donned her new, crisp, white nurse's uniform, and posed with Momma outside our apartment for photos.

"Carmella's mother invited me over for the holiday," she writes. "We'll take the bus to Connecticut."

Oh well. Let's see what Dad has to say.

"Mimi and I have fixed up our guest bedroom so that you and Sharon can share it," he writes. "I hope you'll consider moving here."

I wish he'd stop thinking I was going to leave home and live with him. How in the world would I do that?

"There are good schools here in Sarasota," he continues. "I'm sure you could get a teaching job. You need to leave the mess you're in and start over."

Dad's never asked me one direct question about the quality of my life. I believe he'd rather not know. I'm still aggravated with him over his mean car-loan letter. Why does he think it's so easy for me to just walk away from Momma? He has never said he's sorry for leaving us girls. Why would I want to live with him?

I lay both letters on my desk. Sigh. I glance out the windows. Several high school kids run toward the elementary students. They talk intently and wave their arms in the air. Like a bolt of lightning, the cluster of fourth graders explodes. Kids run in all directions, most back toward the school. I stand up, go closer to the windows. The kids are screaming something, crying. What are they saying? I hurry outside.

"What's wrong?" I holler into the chilly air.

"President Kennedy's been shot," JoAnn cries, flinging her body into mine. I wrap my arms around her.

"He's dead, he's dead," Susan screams.

I grab her and pull her close to me. More kids crowd onto this pillar of grief.

I'm bewildered. Shocked. Tears cloud my eyes. When? How? Why? Is this real? President Kennedy is my hero. I think back to June and the rousing speech he gave about the need for civil rights legislation. That same night, Medgar Evers was killed in the driveway of his home. I wonder if Kennedy was shot because of his civil rights beliefs. Who could have done this? Why? I have so many questions—but all I can do at this moment is console my students, hold them, and assure them the world will not end. They are safe.

I'm not sure about anything I'm saying, but I need to be the strong one, the teacher. I need to get them home safely and into the loving arms of their parents. And that is what I do. I walk them across the blacktop, across the grass. I deliver each one to their parents. There is nothing to say. Nothing to do. Just a lot of wailing kids. More sadness than most nine-year-old children and their teacher can sustain.

I run back to the school. The teachers are gathered around the radio in the school office. Everyone is crying.

"Oh, my God," we say, over and over, to no one in particular. We hug, sob, our eyes wide and bloodshot, our mascara-streaked faces twisted into strange, grotesque masks.

"President Kennedy was declared dead at one this afternoon, Central Standard Time," the broadcaster says.

Kathy pulls me close to her. We cling to one another. There are no words left to say.

It's well after four by the time I get to my car and snap on the radio.

"At two thirty-eight this afternoon, Central Standard Time, Lyndon Johnson was administered the oath of office aboard Air Force One, flanked on his right by Lady Bird Johnson and on his left by Jacqueline Kennedy, the widow of the late President John Fitzgerald Kennedy. Mrs. Kennedy wore her pink suit, now stained with her husband's blood. The coffin holding the late President Kennedy has been taken aboard the plane for the flight back to Andrews Air Force Base."

"Oh, God. How did this happen?" I ask out loud.

"President Lyndon B. Johnson will fill out the rest of President Kennedy's term, one year and fifty-nine days," the broadcaster says.

I snap off the radio and turn the car toward home. Who could have known this morning that by the end of the day I'd have a new president?

I have to stop. I can't go directly home, can't face Momma. I'm not strong enough.

Like a magnet, the Passaic River draws me to my spot, the place I've chosen. I park where I can see the fast-moving river. It's ready for me, awaiting the day. The day I'll drive in. When my car will disappear. Sink. Fast. My baptismal waters. The place of my salvation. I will be cleansed, free. This is where it will all end. Soon. As soon as the school year's over. But I'm so low now. Kennedy's death makes me even more sad. Am I strong enough to make it to the end of the school year?

I've come here often over this last month, contemplating my future. My coping strategies are crumbling. For years, I've stashed my emotions away and have just *gone on* to the next challenge. I'm good at switching personalities, suppressing the pain, putting on a happy face, turning into my competent self at school. But now my emotional swings are extreme. When I leave home to go to school, it's more difficult to shake myself out of my sadness. Somehow, I show up each day as a smiling, happy-go-lucky-teacher. At the end of each day, I have to gear up for what I'll face at home. I'm running out of energy. Out of hope.

There's no way out for me, no way to change my life. All my choices are bad. I don't like any of the consequences. The Passaic River is the choice I'll have to make. I see no other way. I'll die by Momma's hands or my own. My soul is dying. Some days my despair swallows me. Even on days when the president has not died, I'm forlorn on my journey home.

"Oh, God. Why did President Kennedy die? This is so difficult to believe. You know I'm already depleted. Please give me strength, dear God. I'm empty. I can't go on much longer. It's getting too hard for me to bear each day. You know how weak I've become. Please, please give me a sign that You hear me, that You have an idea for me. Because You know the idea I have. I know You don't like my choice. But it's the only way out, unless You can come up with something better. Please help me. Please help me, God."

I sit for a long time. Numb. Stare at the rushing, dirty waters. I pray for a sign. I've really made up my mind. There's only one decision I've not made.

Will anyone be in the car with me?

Chapter 29

WRESTLING WITH GOD

Wednesday, February 26, 1964

"You stopped to see him, didn't you?" Momma takes a drag from her Lucky Strike and rises from her black leather recliner.

Him is Sal. Her fat-slob-of-a-used-car-salesman boyfriend. He's over here several times each week. She accuses me of *fooling around* with Sal. Nothing I say convinces her otherwise. I have neither the time nor the energy to think about finding a boyfriend. Ever since Johnny and I ended our relationship, my life has been one emotional crisis after another. I no longer think about him; I've compartmentalized that sadness and pain along with all the Momma-generated grief I hold. It's one more loss I can do nothing about. I have to pick up, go on, face each day, and survive. I have more important things on my mind.

"You communist slut." She pinches my arm, smacks me across my face.

I have to pee. I turn—and the broom comes at me. *Smack.* Over the years, Momma's beaten me with just about anything she can grab, from the broom to the telephone receiver to

Mikey's wooden bat. What she prefers, though, are her own hands and mouth—for the pinch, the hair pull, the bite that brands me for days. It's her verbal harangue, though, the accusations, that crush my soul, scar my heart, deplete my energy.

"I'll kill you, you son of a bitch."

And she just about does.

Like the ebb and flow of the tide that full moon night,
Momma's rage waxes and wanes
Over the many hours of the evening.
Just when I think she's exhausted,
Her volatile power erupts once more.
Then drains away.
Her force, driven by deep and unknown currents,
Erodes my sand fortress,
The mound that is me.

Finally, Momma is quiet.
It's midnight.
Sal is here.
What's left of me is on the kitchen floor,
Arms clasped around raised knees,
Huddled under the table.
I'm spent.
Defeated. Hopeless.

Weak Beverly—the frightened, vulnerable, powerless me trapped in Momma's maddening snare of anger, insanity, and rage—is going to win. I cling to the sliver of hope that I can keep Strong Beverly alive long enough to survive the school year. Then I know I must make a conscious choice. I must do something to break out of this desperate cycle—this prison of fear, guilt, and obligation that has held me hostage for years. Do I have the will to sever the chains that bind me to Momma?

I have this moment, this temporary respite from Momma's violence, to struggle with God one more time, to beg for mercy, to plead for a sign. Is my life worth saving? How can I reconcile the competing forces that allow me only to consider committing suicide or staying here in my role as Momma's protector?

Those are the only two choices that are clear in my mind: Take the easy way out and end it all. Go to the river.

Or, stay here. Support the family. Live with Momma's abuse. Work harder to maintain my sanity.

I think about this all the time now. I don't like either of my choices. I don't want to kill myself, and I don't want to live the rest of my life as Momma's captive. On days like this, when I'm most distressed, driving into the Passaic River feels like the right way out, my only viable choice, the end of my misery. I won't have to see Momma ever again, and I won't be around to face the consequences.

Creak. Creak. Creak.
The rhythmic rise and fall of the sofa bed,
Of bodies intertwined,
Lost in the gravitational pull of the earth's forces.
Sal and Momma.
Adrift on the sea of life,
In search of some unattainable shore.
The waves crash.
All is still.

Tick. Tick. Tick. An hour passes. In five hours, I'll turn off the alarm and dress for my other life—my life as a teacher, the life that keeps me going, that gives me purpose. My life as Strong Beverly.

• • •

I think of my meeting three weeks ago with Reverend and Mrs. Jones.

After school that day, I drove to Passaic and parked outside my Methodist church. The fact that I've been a faithful parishioner since 1956 didn't make this meeting any easier. I'd called Reverend Jones and said I had to see him. It was urgent.

After knocking, I entered the minister's cozy office, with its dark paneling, upholstered chairs, and area rugs. Framed photographs of the magnificent Gothic church that burned to the ground in 1954—stained glass windows, rare organ, and all—covered the walls, alongside photos of our new, modern church and its historic bell, the only thing saved from the massive fire.

"Please have a seat, Beverly," Mrs. Jones said, her arm around my shoulder.

"Reverend Jones, Mrs. Jones," I said. "I need your advice. I need help. My mother's sick. Mentally sick. She's getting worse. My stepfather tried to take her to a doctor—on several occasions—but she refused. She refuses to take any medication. I tried to get her to go again, just last week. She beat me for suggesting that."

I'd never let on to my minister before that there were problems at home. I'd always hidden the evidence, but now I was hopeless. I wanted to shout, *Haven't you seen my bruises all these years!?* I didn't know what to do, where to turn for help. I'd sought advice from various social workers before, but they were convinced Momma was indeed the Housewife of the Year and acted like I was the hysterical child who imagined her mother beating her and taking her children on midnight walks. I'd given up trying. But my minister? Surely, he would help.

"She beats you?" Mrs. Jones asked, a look of shock and disbelief on her face.

"Well, yes, ma'am. This is not new. She's beaten me since I was seven. But it's her delusions. They're getting worse. She thinks I'm a communist."

Ever since JFK's assassination, Momma has been hooked on the conspiracy theory that communists killed him. She believes all teachers are communists. So that means I'm one and, by definition, involved in the plot to kill the president.

"A communist?" Reverend Jones repeated, his voice high and puzzled. He, like everyone, was afraid of communists.

"Sir, I'm going to commit suicide," I blurted out. Might as well get to the point. This was the first time I'd said this word out loud. I was shocked at its sound, its harsh reality, its finality, its sinfulness. But it was too late to take it back.

"Oh, dear, why would you want to do that?" Mrs. Jones asked. She placed her hand on my leg. They looked at each other. Reverend Jones got up from his chair and walked behind his desk, like a timid soldier hiding behind his tank.

Afraid of God's wrath, I dared not say more about how I planned to end my desperation. But I knew Reverend Jones wouldn't look favorably on the suicide idea, so I waited for him to talk me out of it.

He didn't. Perhaps he was more concerned that I might be a communist.

"Have you prayed about this?" he asked.

"For years," I said. I knew where this conversation was going. "Look, I need help. Who can I call? Can I force her to get help?" *Help me!* I wanted to scream.

"You can't commit her or force her to go to a doctor against her will—unless she threatens to hurt herself or someone else," Reverend Jones said, getting back on the topic.

"Well . . ." I said, my head down.

"Have you ever been admitted to a hospital for injuries caused by your mother?" he asked.

"Hospital?" I repeated. "Well, no. I've never been to a hospital." Since when was that the criteria for abuse? After the many bat, broom, and belt beatings we'd suffered over the years, though, I was amazed neither Sharon nor I had had a broken bone or a concussion. Then again, maybe we *had* had concussions. Who knew? No one I knew went to doctors. Certainly not to the hospital. However badly we'd been beaten, we just bucked up. Put ice on our wounds. A bandage. Moved on.

Reverend Jones walked around his desk, sat in the upholstered chair next to me, took my hand in his. Mrs. Jones held my other hand.

"Let us pray," he said.

We bowed our heads.

"Heavenly Father, please guide Beverly in the days ahead. Help her to be strong and to keep her faith in you. In Jesus's name. Amen."

You must be kidding. Was this all he could say?

Reverend Jones stood up. Meeting over.

"We will continue to pray for you, Beverly," he said, leading me out of the office.

"Thank you," I said to my spiritual leader. "Thank you."

Clearly, I had unrealistic expectations.

I had no new options. No one who knew how to help me.

I had no church.

I had no hope.

• • •

My shadow and I crouch on the floor in the tiny kitchen. It's four in the morning. Sal and Momma are asleep on the sofa bed. I'm only steps away. Aside from their rhythmic breathing and the tick, tick of the clock, all is quiet.

My body doesn't feel the pain anymore—my shadow captures the blows, holds the torment for me, hides it deep within. But I can't hide the suffering from my damaged soul. My soul draws me to the river. *Oh, God, I know You are listening. Please help me. Take me to the river. The river can make all this end. I know suicide is not the honorable way out of my horrible life, but it's easy, fast, final. I know You will forgive me, dear God, for being so weak.*

A wrong turn into the river. "A tragic accident," people will say. I can leave with a semblance of respectability. People won't have to confront the truth—that I was too depleted to go on, to face an uncertain future. Who will miss me, anyway? Certainly not Momma. She gave up caring for me long ago. I want my life as I know it to end. Soon. Perhaps tomorrow.

Sal stirs. His bulk, illuminated by the moonlight streaming through the window, dominates the bed.

"I have to go," he says, his hand on Momma's arm, gently rocking her awake.

The light exposes his profile, his nakedness.

Sal bends over. His odor of sweat and grit fills the room. His flabby gut bursts out under his shirt, hangs loose over his belt.

Please stay, Sal, I pray. *If you do, Momma will ignore me for the rest of the night.*

No such luck. Sal kisses Momma on her forehead and leaves. The door clicks behind him.

Momma gets up, pulls her nightgown over her head. Goes to the bathroom. Returns to the kitchen. To me. To what remains of the sand fortress.

• • •

Even though Momma's had two sets of corneal transplants—one in 1950, another in 1956—she is once again blind. Her disease continues to cloud over her eyes, making her life difficult. But she knows her way around the apartment, and she can always find the silhouette that is me.

Why don't I hit her back? Why don't I block her, use my body against hers, smash her, throw her down, pummel her, punch her in the face, and smack her on her back like I did so many years ago in my Yonkers bedroom?

I'm strong. I could overpower her. I'm twenty-three years old—a grown-up, for God's sake. I'm not that little Beverly hiding behind her doll house. I'm a competent teacher, a good person. A strong fortress about to fall.

But I can't hit her. I won't. She's my mother. She's blind. She's sick. And if I try to hit her, she *will* kill me. She'll fly into a rage, and that bat will connect with my head.

I deserve it. All this is my fault. I'm guilty. It's my father who never supported me and made us scrape. I took food out of everyone's mouth. I'm the bad girl. And now I'm responsible for taking care of the family, to make up for all those years when Ron Radzai took care of me. Sharon, Ronnie, Mikey, Momma— they're all my responsibility. Guilty. I'm guilty. What would they do without me? How would they survive? I have to stay here with Momma. But how will I make it? I'm sure I'll not survive another year. Is staying here the price I'll pay to assuage my guilt?

In my mind, I go back to the river. Drive in. Quiet. Smooth. Hardly a ripple. The cold river water fills the car. Fills my lungs. It's fast. Easy. I'm not afraid to die. Living only brings me closer to the edge—the place where sanity and chaos meet. I'm close to that now. I'm dying. Unable to hang on. Each day I search deeper for the energy to survive. Suicide is the only way to end this torment. Death will save me from madness. My final immersion in water. My baptismal pool. A purification from my sins. A rebirth into a new life. Nothing matters but one thing: I can't go mad. I refuse. I will not become Momma.

But how can I do this to those who care about me?

What would my students think?

"Why isn't Miss Radzai here today?"

"Oh, didn't you hear? She had an accident."

They'll get over it. No, they won't. They can't get over JFK. For my fourth graders, losing him has been like losing a family member. I'm part of their families. I can't do this to them. I know the sorrow I'd create.

My friends. Kathy, Judy, Catherine. My sister. How could I drive into the river knowing the grief I'd cause them? They love me. I love them. And how can I leave Mikey? He's only thirteen— just a kid. What would it do to him if I drove into the Passaic River? But I'm a coward. I'm going to take the easy way out.

I'm going mad. I don't know what to do. *Please, God, can you hear me?*

I can't commit suicide. I'd chicken out at the last minute. Or I'd seriously injure myself but not die. Something could go wrong. I don't really want to kill myself, anyway. I'd hurt too many people.

That solves it—my only choice is to stay here. Toughen up. Take care of Momma and the boys. Teach another year in Paramus. I can do it. I need to be stronger. I have to tolerate my life. I can't leave Momma. What would she do without me? This family is my responsibility. I have to stay here. But can I hold up, can I live through another night of beatings, of humiliation?

Dear God, when will I break? Will you give me the strength to pick up the pieces?

• • •

It's quiet. It's five now. Momma's gone to bed. The sea is calm.

I sit on the cold linoleum floor. Head buried in my knees. I breathe. Slowly. In. Out. Ebb. Flow.

The cold river washes over me. Rises. Fills my mouth. Swallows me. Yes, this is my choice. I'll be frantic. For a moment. Then it will be over. The agony will be over. No more beatings. I'll be free. Everyone will move on. They'll be okay. The boys have a father. He'll take care of them. They'll be fine. Sharon's in school. She's an adult. She has a father. She doesn't need me. Momma will survive without me. She has a mother and seven siblings. Her government disability payments will keep her in shelter and food.

I have no good choices. Only bad consequences. I have to pick the least bad of the bad. All I know is, I can't survive another night like this one. *Oh, God. I know you hear me, God. I'm weak. So weak. Show me the way.*

My arms fall to my side. The moonlight warms my hands. My heart pounds against my knees. The only sound in the room. *Lub-dub. Lub-dub. Lub-dub. Save me. Save me. Save me.*

Listen. Be still. Turn off your racing mind. Listen to your heart. To your breathing. To your soul. Listen for God's voice.

"I'll be fearless. I'll be strong." I remember my promise to my blonde angel-teacher, my spelling bee heroine.

I hear Dr. Yerzley's voice: "Promise me you'll never give up."

"I promise."

How can I disappoint my teachers?

Oh, God, what should I do? What is the right thing to do? God, please help me. I have no hope. No reason to live. I can't bear my life as it is. Weak Beverly is going to win.

No. I am not going to let her win. I do have a purpose. My students are my purpose. My purpose is to teach. This year, next year. That's my identity. My reason to live. To empower children as my own teachers empowered me.

The moon's light surrounds my broken body. The heat fills me.

Just leave. Leave. Walk away. Do what your friends have advised. Leave. That's what I can do. But how? I can't leave now, in the middle of the school year.

Wait, then. Wait for school to be over. Then, leave. Live. Save yourself.

My students. I have to live for them. Strong Beverly has a purpose. A reason to live.

God, did you send me this message? Is this the right answer?

Live. *Lub-dub. Lub-dub. Lub-dub.*

Lub-dub. Lub-dub. Save me. Save me.

Tick-tick-tick. Lub-dub.

I am still. My breathing slows. The battle is over.

Thank You, God.

• • •

The moon's light brightens the kitchen. I remember being a child in Yonkers—when I thought my life was a fairy tale, when Momma and Dad loved me, doted on me. All these years I've longed for my Yonkers Momma to return, to love me as her daughter, her eldest, her seeing eye girl. But I've lost her. She's not coming back. My dream, my fantasy, is over. I'm a grown-up now. I have to claim my own life. I have to separate from Momma, break the bonds. Strong Beverly is alive. She has goals. She has a purpose. She has hope.

My vision clears. I have only one choice—the choice I have long refused to embrace. This is the only thing I can do. It's the only right decision. To save my soul. To save my sanity. To save my life. To reclaim hope—hope to live another day; hope to teach another year. This is my choice. My final choice. I must leave Momma. I must walk away from this life, make a new path for myself. I'll leave the last day of school. Yes. That's the plan. This is right.

God, I hope this is the way You see it, too. This is the only way forward.

A veil of peace settles over me.

• • •

It's six o'clock. Momma's asleep on the sofa bed.

I'm wide awake. I dress for school. I'm cleansed. Renewed. I gather my books and lesson plans. I open the closet door. My college textbooks are stacked on the floor. I find it right away— big, blue cover. My favorite. *American Poetry and Prose.*

I put it on top of my stack of books. It's part of my plan: take an item precious to me each day, to remind me of my intent, to strengthen my resolve, to keep me focused on my goal. These few beloved possessions will be my link to freedom.

I walk out of the apartment. Close the door. The latch snaps into place. I stand there. Breathe. Take stock.

I have my lesson plans. My peanut butter sandwich. The book I'll take into my new life.

I exhale. Walk slowly down the steps.

Tomorrow I'll take my *Anthology of World Literature.*

EPILOGUE

August 9, 1983

"You can put your mother there," Dr. Len Maholick says, pointing to the coffee table, as I walk into his comfortable living room.

Soft upholstered chairs, a sofa, end tables with countless boxes of tissues, lamps, and his favorite oil paintings complete the homey feel of Dr. Maholick's office. From any spot in the room you can see the traffic on Peachtree and Piedmont, one of the busiest intersections in Atlanta. I hold the boot-size white box straight out in front of me in both hands, like an offering.

It has been nearly twenty years since I last saw Momma. We're meeting now to take care of unfinished business.

• • •

It was the middle of June when Mikey, my little brother, tracked me down at my Grant Park home. When I answered the phone and heard a voice say, "I'm looking for Beverly Radzai," I knew my running days were over.

At my father's urging, I changed my name back to Armento as soon as I arrived in Sarasota. Since my name had not been legally altered, Dad's attorney simply drew up an affidavit stating that *Beverly Jeanne Armento is one and the same person as Beverly Jeanne Radzai.* Hearing myself referred to now as Beverly Radzai brought back the memories I'd tried to forget.

Since leaving home on June 20, 1964, I'd been running away from my early life, my life with Momma. Running from the nightmares, the terror, the beatings, the fear that Momma would find me, kill me. Running from the guilt—of being my father's daughter, of leaving Momma and the boys. Running away, too, from a thirteen-state missing person alert—Momma called the state police to report her daughter had gone missing, had never come home after her last day of school as a first-year teacher.

And now, running away from the guilt of living a comfortable, middle-class life as a tenured associate professor at Georgia State University. I ran from one life only to run through my new one, living on the surface, racing to prove myself to everyone, especially myself. This is the private me, the Weak Beverly, the tormented me.

The public me is a confident, capable, happy young professor busy restoring a 1917 bungalow in an in-town neighborhood. A teacher of teachers, an inspiring educator, active in the community, a writer and researcher, and a bubbly, outgoing person: Strong Beverly. Hidden is the wounded me.

Dr. Maholick's diagnosis is depression, bulimia nervosa, and obsessive-compulsive personality disorder. My compulsive personality has served me well: I've earned a master's and doctoral degree and I'm successful professionally. The bulimia has served me well also. It's my way of extending Momma's battering by inflicting my own punishment on my body from the inside out. I use my overeating/purging behavior as an excuse to avoid social engagements and intimate relationships. I have too many secrets, too many deadlines, too much intestine growling to cultivate the one thing I crave: a healthy social life.

I'm empty, insecure, and racked by guilt and fear—full of shame, sadness, and remorse. I've always known a crisis of some sort would force me to confront my demons, but my workaholic self could only see as far as the next invitation to write a chapter in a prestigious publication, to create a research proposal, to develop a new curriculum project. Even singer Karen Carpenter's death from eating disorder complications a few months ago and the subsequent attention that has been paid to anorexia and bulimia hasn't scared me enough to seek help. Nor have the occasional nightmares that awaken me and leave my body wet with sweat. Nor has the fear Momma will show up at the door at any moment.

But Mikey's call brought my double life to a screeching halt.

I last saw him early that Saturday morning—the last day of school for teachers, the day we posted our grades and made sure our classrooms were ready for summer break. My students and their parents knew I was going to Florida to live with my dad, and they showed up at the school to bid me tearful good-byes. But I never told Mikey I was leaving. He was two months shy of thirteen.

Now Michael (as he prefers to be called) is a manager at a Sears store in New Jersey. Ronnie is homeless—somewhere on the streets of Pennsylvania, having dropped out of Rutgers, where he had a full scholarship. Drugs took the upper hand in his life, and he wasn't able to overcome the addiction. Sharon and I have remained close over the years. She stayed in Newark until she completed her nursing degree, then moved to Columbus, Ohio. She's now the mother of a three-year-old son—the first grandson Momma never knew. Dad disowned both Sharon and me when he received a photograph of the bride and groom cutting their wedding cake. Sharon had neglected to tell him she was marrying an African American man.

• • •

"Momma's dead—hardening of the arteries. Ronnie and I tried to have her committed to a mental institution years ago. In three days, she came home. She'd talked the doctors into believing there was nothing wrong with her. I'm married now. When I came in for my weekly visit, she was dead." Michael blurted this out all in one breath.

I was calm until our phone call ended. Then, I wailed. The uncontrolled cry I'd been afraid of releasing all these years, the one that would take me over the edge and into the abyss, where I feared I'd be forever lost—it finally burst out of me.

It was only then that I sought help.

• • •

"Where are your mother's remains now?" Dr. Maholick asked during our first session after I gave him the summary of the story.

"They're in New Jersey, at the crematorium," I said. "Unclaimed."

"I think you need to bury her. Along with little Beverly."

It was the right thing to do.

• • •

Leaving Michael was one of the hardest things I've ever done in my life. After I arrived in Sarasota, I wrote to Ron Radzai at the US Rubber plant and told him I'd had no choice but to leave, to save myself. I asked him to take his boys out of the home, to provide them with a stable life. He wrote back saying that he'd never known just what to do, that he'd tried to get Momma to a doctor on several occasions, and that she'd refused to take any medications or return to the doctor. He said he'd cared for her very much and that he "tried to treat all of you alike, as if you were my own."

"I've never tried to take the boys away from her, and I really don't know if I would," he wrote. "They will realize by themselves just like you have."

I urged him to be there for his boys. He shouldn't wait until they figured out something was wrong. I was sure they already had that idea. But he never did take the boys away from Momma.

In many ways, Ron Radzai's struggle was mine. We both loved Momma, were providers for the household, and were victims of her untreated mental illness. Neither of us had the emotional or physical resources to change the situation. Neither of us knew how to talk about our lives. We never thought to confide in each other, to work together to get help for Momma. We each left as our own final acts of self-preservation. We both walked away but carried for many years the guilt and shame of our inability to address the problem. And in the end, neither of us returned. The toll of living with mental illness and abuse was heavy—for all of us. Each of our family members paid a price. There were no heroes, no villains, no easy answers, no clear choices, no good outcomes. No winners. Only heartache.

• • •

I place the sturdy box containing Momma's cremains on Dr. Maholick's coffee table. He has set two chairs on opposite sides of the table. One chair is for me. The other is for Momma.

Dr. Maholick, the highly respected psychiatrist I first contacted after Michael's call, eases his tall, lean body onto the upholstered sofa. His gentle eyes survey the tableau he's created.

I open the large manila envelope I've brought and spread photographs out on the table, around the white box—anything to give me a little more time, to delay the conversation. There are pictures of Momma and Dad with Sharon and me back in Yonkers. Ron Radzai and all of us kids at the beach in Miami. Momma in one of her gauzy gowns at a Robinson family reunion. Ronnie, Michael, Sharon, and me, wrapped in scarves and hats, laughing in the snow during our brief life in Clifton.

I take the chair Dr. Maholick indicates is for me. I stare at the box.

"I think you have a few things to say to her. What are you feeling?" Dr. Maholick prompts.

Feeling? What am I feeling? For years I've survived by hiding my feelings, pushing emotions deeper and deeper into the dormant volcano that was my body. I'm a different person now, in 1983, than I was twenty years ago. I see the past with new eyes. Yet I'm having trouble sorting out my own emotions. Essentially, at my core, I'm the same person, the same two personalities who drove away from New Jersey: my professional, competent teacher-self and my battered, struggling guilty-self. I'm still coping with life by submerging my emotions, glossing over my true feelings, shoving it all down, increasingly frightened of the eruption that will surely happen one day. Is this that day?

Now I have to face it all: the anger, the sadness, the fear, the guilt, the regret. Now is the time to forgive her. To forgive myself. To integrate little Beverly into the adult self I've become.

I think back to the day I last saw Momma. She was asleep on the sofa, wrapped in the blue blanket, that Saturday morning when I clutched the last of my beloved college textbooks to my chest and whispered, "Good-bye, Momma." She was still sleeping when I closed the door behind me.

· · ·

A week after I left her there, the police showed up at Dad's home in Sarasota. It was late. Probably close to midnight.

"I'm looking for Beverly Radzai. Can you tell me if she's here?"

I heard a man's loud voice ask this from my new bedroom—the one Dad had prepared for his girls, the one with twin beds and flowery bedspreads, the one with a window through which I peered at the pulsing red lights of the police car.

"No," Mimi said to the police officer. "Beverly Armento is here. She's also known as Beverly Radzai. She's twenty-three years old and left home of her own free will. She's asleep now, but I'll get her if you need to see her. She's in good health. She's safe here with her father and me."

"No, ma'am," he said, "I don't need to see her. Her mother is worried about her. I'll report that she's safe."

• • •

Free will. I like those words. Yes, I chose freely to leave home. It was that or drive the car into the Passaic River. The idea that I seriously contemplated suicide, even planned it, is inexplicable now. It's difficult to imagine being so emotionally empty, so frightened of my mother, so fearful of becoming her, so close to the edge of hopelessness that death was a viable choice for me. For me, breaking the chains that bound us together was the difference between death and survival.

I recall the last time I heard her voice.

Two weeks after the police officer arrived at Dad's home, the telephone rang. I was home alone. I stared at the phone for a long time. Then picked it up.

"Is Beverly Radzai there? This is her mother." Momma's voice was clear, strong, like it was in Yonkers. But she wasn't my Yonkers Momma. That mother no longer existed. Our lives together were over. My search for the mother I'd once loved was over.

I stood. Frozen. For the longest time. Then I placed the receiver in the cradle without a sound.

"No," I said softly. "Beverly Radzai's not here."

I was too afraid to talk with her then, but I have to talk with her now. I have to step back into my life and go back to 1964. I have to face the silent culture where no one knew how to talk about mental illness and the tragedy it brought to an entire family; where the rage was absorbed and hidden; where each person figured out their own survival strategies; where the issues were never discussed, the separate realities not spoken.

Whatever Momma's diagnosis may have been, her illness and anger filled our lives and tragically affected each of us. Perhaps Momma herself was affected most of all. The promise of a successful artistic career was dashed as her mind filled with frightening delusions and rage that left little room for the creative drawings she'd once done so well.

Dr. Maholick looks at me and smiles. I have to do this. I have to face Momma, talk with her, imagine what she might say to me. I'm not very good at this. I'm a teacher. That's what I'm good at. That's my mission, the arena where I give back to all those teachers who encouraged me, who saved me. I think back to my sixth grade class at McIntosh Middle School that first year in Sarasota, to those eager faces in my classroom on the first day of school.

"Good morning," I had said to them. "I'm Miss Armento, your teacher this year. I'm here for you, and together, we're going to fly. We'll learn together, think together. We'll grow and mature as we live together this year. I promise that you are the center of my attention."

Little did they know that I was alive *because* of them. They were the hope that saved me—the promise of yet another year of teaching, of being able to influence young people, of empowering them to be anything they wanted to be, to dream of their best selves, to be free to make mistakes, to be happy. I'd love them, believe in them, and think that each one was brilliant, just like my own angel-teachers had believed in me.

At Georgia State, I preach to prospective educators that teaching is a moral enterprise. Your every word, your actions, the choices you make every day—these will either harm or nurture a child. If you are not up for this, choose another profession. Your work as an educator is important—to every child you encounter.

I know.

From personal experience.

•   •   •

"Momma, I'm sorry," I sob. "I had to leave. There was nothing else I could do." I sit and stare at the box, imagining my mother at the end. Blind. Staring into space. I try to envision the mother I loved, the sweet, gentle mother of my first five years—the mother who mushed finger paints onto my easel, who laughed and helped me dress my dolls, and told me stories of her childhood. That's the mother I have to remember. The one I want to remember.

I move to the empty chair Dr. Maholick has designated as Momma's. How am I to imagine what she would say to me? Surely, she's angry with me. But what about the loving mother, the one I always hoped would re-emerge? What about her?

"I'm sorry, too, Beverly. My life didn't turn out like I'd hoped. Something went horribly wrong. I never meant to hurt you." I say the words I hope are Momma's.

•   •   •

We buried Momma at the end of August in the family plot in Warsaw, New York—where she grew up, where she met Dad, where she was married by a justice of the peace. One of Momma's favorite brothers facilitated the arrangements and from that time onward became my emotional rock, perhaps as a silent acknowledgement of the family's failure to respond to my pleas for help in 1964.

The minister spoke well of Momma—of the good person she was, of the challenges that plagued her throughout her life. After the final prayer, our aunts and uncles stepped back.

Michael stepped forward. He placed his long-stemmed red rose on top of the cremains now sitting only a foot beneath the ground, a small mound of dirt heaped to the side. He stepped aside.

Sharon stooped down, silent. She gave her rose to Momma. She stepped back.

It was now my turn. It was just Momma and me.

I gave my rose to Momma and tossed a shovel full of dirt onto the grave site.

"Good-bye, Momma."

I scooped more dirt. Let it fall.

"Good-bye, little Beverly."

Thus I began the long conversation that continues today—the search for peace, for forgiveness, for meaning, for consciousness.

ACKNOWLEDGMENTS

It's not an exaggeration to say that my teachers saved my life. To each and every one—many long deceased but alive in my memory—a sincere thank-you from a grateful student.

To my own students, who, over my fifty-year career, have challenged me and enriched my life—I love you more than you'll ever know.

My sister, Sharon, has always been there for me and has urged me for years to tell "our story." You are my rock, Sharon. To my brother, Michael, who stood strong and invented his own coping strategies, and to Ronnie, now deceased—I remember your sweetness as a child. I love each of you and thank you for your bravery and fortitude. I appreciate you, my siblings, for your interest in reliving our childhoods, in refreshing my memory, and in confirming our strength and our bonds.

To the many outstanding authors and writing teachers with whom I've had the honor of working, my gratitude for your insight and thoughtful feedback on this memoir, especially: Suzanne Van Atten, Jessica Handler, Christal Trivett-Presley, Hollis Gillespie, Linda Joy Myers, Brooke Warner, and Kathleen Craft Boehmig. To my writer-critique friends, always ready to read and offer sound advice—Tiffany Courtney-Graham, Rebecca Myers, Jean Tomlinson, Anissa Wells-Gray, Gayle O'Shaughnesey, Pamela Wright, Alison Auerbach, Louis Cahill, Laurie Eynon-Wells, Angela Stalcup, Melissa Bauer, Jennifer

Little, Kathleen Gizzi, Stacy Nathan, Terry Stuermer, Dara Mathis, Theresa Mamah, Brett Belcastro, Helen Perry, Anne Marie Lacy, and all my friends at the Atlanta Writers Club, the Writers' Circle, the Decatur Writers' Co-op, and my Write Your Memoir in Six Months Class—I am forever thankful.

Sincere thanks to the beta readers who gave generously of their time and expertise: Skip Atkinson, Lou D'Amelio, Carole Hahn, Dara Mathis, Beth Roberts, and Matthew Willoughby.

A special thank-you to Ally Machate and Don Weise at the Writer's Ally for thoughtful developmental editing and for urging me to dig deeper.

To all my dear friends dating back to my seeing eye girl days, especially Carolyn, Janet, Judy, Kathy, and Lou—you have been with me through turmoil and joy, and I'm so grateful for our lasting friendship and love.

A sincere thank-you to Henry R. Hensel, for helping me locate so many of my Paramus students, and to Cathy Aschliman-Hollar, for keeping me in touch with our Sarasota classmates.

To the entire She Writes Press family, thank you for believing in *Seeing Eye Girl* and for bringing this book to the public. My special thanks to Brooke Warner, Publisher, She Writes Press, whose support and encouragement guided me through the process; to Samantha Strom, my Editorial Project Manager, who kept me on track, always with a smile; to Julie Metz, for a stunning cover design; to Krissa Lagos, for editorial insight; and to all the other behind-the- scenes folks who played important roles in the publishing process.

To the entire team at Books Forward, my sincere appreciation for a creative and personalized publicity and marketing plan to bring visibility to *Seeing Eye Girl*.

To Rebecca, my confidant: I'll never be able to thank you enough for your uncompromising belief in me and this book, your depth of creative insight, and your positive affirmations over the many years it took to construct *Seeing Eye Girl*.

ABOUT THE AUTHOR

Inspired by the many teachers who mentored her, Beverly J. Armento became an educator and enjoyed a fifty-year career working with middle-school children as well as prospective teachers. Retired now, she is Professor Emerita at Georgia State University and holds degrees from The William Paterson University, Purdue University, and Indiana University. She currently lives in Atlanta, Georgia. *Seeing Eye Girl* is her first book for the general public.

Author photo © Erin Brauer Photography

SELECTED TITLES FROM SHE WRITES PRESS

She Writes Press is an independent publishing company founded to serve women writers everywhere. Visit us at www.shewritespress.com.

Don't Call Me Mother: A Daughter's Journey from Abandonment to Forgiveness by Linda Joy Myers. $16.95, 978-1-938314-02-5. Linda Joy Myers's story of how she transcended the prisons of her childhood by seeking—and offering—forgiveness for her family's sins.

Don't Leave Yet: How My Mother's Alzheimer's Opened My Heart by Constance Hanstedt. $16.95, 978-1-63152-952-8. The chronicle of Hanstedt's journey toward independence, self-assurance, and connectedness as she cares for her mother, who is rapidly losing her own identity to the early stage of Alzheimer's.

Scattering Ashes: A Memoir of Letting Go by Joan Rough. $16.95, 978-1-63152-095-2. A daughter's chronicle of what happens when she invites her alcoholic and emotionally abusive mother to move in with her in hopes of helping her through the final stages of life—and her dream of mending their tattered relationship fails miserably.

The S Word by Paolina Milana. $16.95, 978-1-63152-927-6. An insider's account of growing up with a schizophrenic mother, and the disastrous toll the illness—and her Sicilian Catholic family's code of secrecy—takes upon her young life.

The Shelf Life of Ashes: A Memoir by Hollis Giammatteo. $16.95, 978-1-63152-047-1. Confronted by an importuning mother 3,000 miles away who thinks her end is nigh—and feeling ambushed by her impending middle age—Giammatteo determines to find The Map of Aging Well, a decision that leads her on an often-comic journey.

Fourteen: A Daughter's Memoir of Adventure, Sailing, and Survival by Leslie Johansen Nack. $16.95, 978-1-63152-941-2. A coming-of-age adventure story about a young girl who comes into her own power, fights back against abuse, becomes an accomplished sailor, and falls in love with the ocean and the natural world